JUSTICE DENIED

THE NG CASE,
THE MOST INFAMOUS AND
EXPENSIVE MURDER CASE
IN HISTORY

JUSTICE DENIED

THE NG CASE, THE MOST INFAMOUS AND EXPENSIVE MURDER CASE IN HISTORY

JOSEPH HARRINGTON
AND
ROBERT BURGER

PLENUM TRADE · NEW YORK AND LONDON

Library of Congress Cataloging in Publication Data

Harrington, Joseph.
   Justice denied: the Ng case, the most infamous and expensive murder case in history /
Joseph Harrington and Robert Burger.
      p.   cm.
   Includes bibliographical references and index.
   ISBN 0-306-46013-0
   1. Ng, Charles Chitat. 2. Serial murders—California—Case studies. 3. Homicide—Califor-
nia—Case studies. 4. Murder—California—Case studies. I. Burger, Robert. II. Title.
HV6533.C2H372   1999   99-18575
364.15′ 23′ 0979444—dc21   CIP

ISBN 0-306-46013-0

© 1999 Joseph Harrington and Robert Burger
Plenum Trade is a Division of Plenum Publishing Corporation
233 Spring Street, New York, N.Y. 10013

10 9 8 7 6 5 4 3 2 1

A C.I.P. record for this book is available from the Library of Congress

Printed in the United States of America

To the victims' relatives of the
Charles Chitat Ng murder trial case

No pictures of victims are included in this work

Justice delayed, is justice denied.
—William Ewart Gladstone

Plate sin with gold,
And the strong lance of justice hurtless breaks;
Arm it in rags, a pigmy's straw does pierce it.
—Shakespeare, *King Lear, vi 170*

Contents

PART III   JUSTICE

Preface

In July 1998, the Judiciary Committee of the United States Senate passed a proposed amendment to the Constitution to establish a national standard of victims' rights. The sponsors of the amendment were Diane Feinstein (California) and Jon Kyl (Arizona).

Thirteen years earlier, an event occurred that is part of this story. The mayor of San Francisco stood on the steps of City Hall and announced a reward of $50,000 for information leading to the arrest of the person or persons responsible for a series of mysterious disappearances in the Bay Area. Within months, the case began to unravel. Within days, a task force was on its way to a remote mountain hideaway, where it was discovered that at least eighteen men, women, and children had been lured and slaughtered.

But this was a case that would not be concluded even as the Victims' Rights Amendment was launched. Ironically, the mayor who posted that reward in 1985 was Diane Feinstein.

Those 1985 serial killings have become the most expensive murder–prosecution case in the history of the United States. Every year as the trial has drawn nearer, California taxpayers have spent some $2.3 million each year for court-appointed attorneys to sift through the case files. When it is all done, perhaps in 1999, some $20 million will have been poured into this sinkhole, at the same time as the state recycles 1970s textbooks for the children of the public school system for want of funds.

San Francisco attorney Joe Cotchett, who knows something about money from the $3.5 million judgment he won in the Charles Keating

Savings & Loan scandal, concludes, "We spend millions of dollars allowing [accused mass killer] Charles Ng to avoid trial and spend nothing on after-school programs."

But money isn't the real scandal. The ultimate disgrace is how the justice system has been brought to its knees—not by "dream team" attorneys or craven politicians, but by an archaic legal system that has simply collapsed of its own weight. Who suffers from this collapse? First, the relatives of those who were massacred: they have not had closure to their grief. Second, the hundreds of law enforcement people who did their jobs to bring the perpetrator to justice: they cannot be satisfied that their "law" will ever lead to "order." Third, the public in general: how can we ever again place our trust in the swift execution of justice?

This case is not at all an usual example of justice gone wrong. It is rather an extreme demonstration of the absurdities of our present justice system in capital cases, and it is exposed in detail in this book because of that fact. It is an embarrassment to judges and attorneys, a scandal to taxpayers, and an affront to the victims of crime. And it will get worse unless more than Band-aids are applied to the wounds.

Basic reform of the justice system occurred in France several generations ago. The charade of "rehabilitation" no longer obscures the reality of what penology is: punishment. Convicts do "hard time," without parole; yet sentences are more realistic and evenly meted to everyone. Many would argue that U.S. penology is, by contrast, more dangerous to the criminal and society alike because our prisons have become schools for crime. Jim Bergland, director of Patmos, which helps some fifteen thousand relatives visit prisoners each weekend, estimates that more than half of all prisoners are behind bars in this country because they are physically sick rather than socially in need of "rehabilitation."

There is no reason why serious reform cannot be considered now in this country for the justice system as it has been for a dozen other aspects of our society. We used to pollute our rivers and bays. We used to think drunk driving was funny. Even in such relatively minor things as seat belts and motorcycle helmets, we have taken serious steps as a society.

This book is an attempt to find, in the bitter lessons of this case, avenues of measured but basic reform for justice.

There would be no reason for outrage if there were any signs from the legal or judicial profession that this charade would not continue. But lawyers and judges, themselves victims of a protocol that rewards delay and punishes change, cannot be expected to reform it. Worse, the delay of justice here is only one obvious manifestation of the distortions that the death penalty is causing: great differences among states in legal representation; great disparities among races in sentencing; virtual ignorance of mental capacity as an ameliorating condition; and wide variations in standards of legal ethics. As William Sharon, former lead prosecutor for Alameda County (California), has told the authors, "The recommendations in this book are only a first step, but that step should have been taken fifty years ago when our criminal justice system was not so distorted by the fears of citizens and the spinelessness of judges and other politicians."

In the California example that is the test case of this book, his public defender blithely ignored a gag rule by the trial judge and supplied videotapes to national television that showed his client to be a "dupe" of his partner. Thus were 200,000 pages of testimony submitted in the preliminary hearing summarily dismissed on commercial television.

We can learn from disasters such as these, and apply this knowledge both to justice for criminals and rights for victims. The chapters that make up Part I, "Law," recount the facts of the case that were meticulously brought out in police reports and the preliminary hearing that resulted in indictments on twelve counts of murder. The chapters in Part II, "Order," tell the story of the legal battle from 1985 to 1998. And those in Part III, "Justice," offer several recommendations to begin a process of reform.

Although these issues are debated in these pages by jurists, legislators, and attorneys who have been involved with death penalty cases much of their lives, this debate is not about capital punishment. Rather, the authors intend this discussion to bring wider issues into focus—especially the issue of judicial delay—and the seriousness of all victims' rights into public consciousness.

Acknowledgments

The authors gratefully thank the following people for their wisdom and help on the ramifications of this project:

Law

All the members of the thin blue line who performed with professional distinction in Ng's bizarre case—with a personal appreciative nod to:

Irene Brunn, Policewoman, San Francisco Police Department
Tom Eisenmann, Sergeant, San Francisco Police Department
Diarmund Philpott, former Deputy Police Chief, San Francisco
Cornelius Murphy, former Police Chief of San Francisco
Joe Long, San Francisco District Attorney investigator
James Connolly, Captain, San Francisco Police Department

Order

Francis Xavier Belotti, former Lieutenant Governor and Attorney General of Massachusetts
Terrence Hallinan, District Attorney of San Francisco
Paul Cummins, Assistant District Attorney, San Francisco
Katherine Lapp, Advisor to Governor George Pataki on Criminal Justice, New York State
Ephraim Margolin, former president of the Trial Lawyers' Association of America

Ed Koch, former Mayor of New York City
William Sharon, former Assistant District Attorney, Alameda County, California

Justice

Professor James W. Bergland, President, Patmos Foundation
Judge Robert G.M. Keating, New York City
John Ellement, reporter, *The Boston Globe*
John Coons, Professor of Law, University of California, Berkeley
James Q. Wilson, author

Part I

Law

In my opinion, anyone who thinks he is happy now would have done what I did, if he had the money and the time.

—JOHN FOWLES, *The Collector*

Chapter 1

A Madman's Soliloquy

Date: Unknown (except videotaped prior to January, 1985)

The video camera was angled in a fixed position, filming a large, middle-aged man sitting in a chair. He said, "What I want is an off the shelf sex partner. I want to be able to use a woman whenever and however I want. And when I'm tired or bored or satiated or not interested I simply want to put her away."

The man glanced at the ceiling, his brow furrowed, then continued in a modulated voice, "Put her away. Lock her up in a little room. Get her out of my sight, out of my life."

Against the room's faded turquoise walls, the man sat in a maroon chair. The room was stark: a window, no drapes, a nondescript picture, and a metal filing cabinet. His fingers drummed a noiseless tune on his thighs that resonated in time to his words. "Dirty old man . . . pervert. I'm attracted to young women. Sometimes even as young as twelve. Although, to be fair, certainly eighteen to twenty-two is a pretty much ideal range as far as I'm concerned."

The man was bearded, but bald, with a circle of hair surrounding a shiny pate, like a medieval monk's tonsure. "I like very slim women, pretty . . . of course . . . petite."

The bearded man was more than six feet tall and weighed more than two hundred and forty pounds. His chest was massive. He spoke softly, "Small breasted, long-haired. Such a woman, totally enslaved, would be used for the mundane chores."

3

Leonard Lake

The man's hands moved to emphasize certain words. "Chores that I have to do, but not particularly interested in doing . . . cleaning house, washing dishes."

A thick hand rubbed the shiny dome of his head. "Slave. There's no way around it."

Both hands now waved, as if to punctuate the word "slave." The chair's leg rest was up. The man's feet wiggled. "Whether I can do this or not will remain to be seen. Obviously, I've never done such a thing before and it may not work. However, I want to try."

The man tilted his head back, and closed his eyes. Then his head bent forward. He stared into the lens of the camera and repeated, "I want to try."

The man folded his hands as if in prayer. "Life as I'm living it is boring. The challenge of this project, the thrill if it succeeds, even the exciting experience if it fails . . . as long as I don't get caught, is very attractive."

The man's breathing was a low whistle of air through clenched teeth. "It's something that I fantasize."

July 24, 1984, 9:00 a.m., Greenwich Street, San Francisco

Irene Brunn was a grandmother, but hardly looked it. She had close-cropped, dark brunette hair, an athletic figure, and unwrinkled clear Latino skin. Depending on the situation, she alternated between the cold, analytical approach required of an investigative police officer and hot-blooded intensity.

She drove up to San Francisco's Missing Persons building on Greenwich Street. A red sports car was parked in the spot labeled "Irene Brunn." Irene parked behind the car blocking it in.

Irene entered the police facility and went to her desk. A brunette woman in her early twenties was waiting for her.

Irene said, "You own a red sports car?"

"Yes."

"You owe the city forty bucks."

"I . . . I . . ."

"And if you don't hurry and move the vehicle you're going to owe the tow truck company another two hundred and eighty."

The young woman rushed out the door, then returned. "You're blocking me in."

"Yep." Irene tossed over her car keys. "Move mine, move yours, and put mine where it belongs."

A few minutes later the young woman returned. "I'm a reporter. I want to do an article on the San Francisco Police Department's Missing Persons Unit."

"Like I can afford the time."

"Captain Philpott told me to report to you. This article—"

"I need a quid pro quo. You know the drill."

"I'll make sure that a photo of a missing person accompanies the article."

Irene pulled over a stack of files.

The reporter said, "The captain said you were to explain what your job was like."

"My job's like a brain surgeon's. Most of my cases end in sadness. Or tragedy."

"How many a day?"

"How many *what* a day? Missing persons? Bouts of sadness? Tragedies? Cups of coffee?"

"Missing person cases a day?"

Irene pointed at the manila files. "Give or take one or two, there are forty new cases in that pile. From just the past twenty-four hours. I've a staff of two. It's impossible to work them all."

"How do you choose which ones to concentrate on?"

Irene flipped open a file. "Case number 19576-A. Man, forty-two, married eleven years, two kids, left yesterday morning. Never came home last night."

"Something's happened to him."

"Yep. He's cooped up in a motel with his secretary or some waitress. He'll show tonight, or next week."

"How do you know?"

"Odds. I might be wrong, but I'll be right ninety-nine percent of the time." Irene opened another case file. "Case number 19576-B. Sixteen-year-old female. Police officer taking reports from parents wrote, 'Had fight with mother.'" She tossed the file aside. "Runaway."

"Which cases do you investigate?"

"Cases that don't fit the mold. People in jeopardy. Come back tomorrow. After I've had a chance to sift through what comes in. Maybe I'll have an example."

July 24, 1984, 6:00 p.m., Yukon Street, San Francisco

The street was a dead-end, but looked nothing like the image that word usually conjures up. Trees lined the sidewalk. Rows of Victorian flats, each arrayed in multicolors of pastels ran up one side and down the other. In the middle of the block a man climbed the one flight to the upstairs unit and opened the door.

He embraced his wife, then lifted a small infant from the crib.

The wife said, "Someone called about the equipment."

"Great."

"Coming over in a few minutes."

The man placed the child back in the crib. He went to the hall closet and removed a Hybrid 8 duplicating machine. He placed the duplicator on the coffee table. Next he removed a Sony cassette player from the closet and put it next to the Hybrid 8.

"Hope whoever it is buys this stuff."

Carefully, using one of his wife's nail polish brushes, the man placed an orange identification star on the Hybrid 8 duplicator.

The doorbell rang.
"I got it, honey."
The husband opened the door.

July 25, 1984, 3:00 p.m., Greenwich Street, San Francisco

The young reporter entered Irene Brunn's office. Turning on a tape recorder she said, "Find anything unusual?"

Irene pointed to a file. "First one I opened this morning. This is a case I *will* investigate. The Dubs family."

"Family?"

"Yes. Father, mother, infant. Reported missing last night. I have to investigate this case."

"Can I tag along?"

"Nope. Come back tomorrow, I'll fill you in."

July 25, 1984, 3:30 p.m., Marin County

Tom Eisenmann was a tall, well-built man, with thinning black hair. At forty-seven he was in trim shape. He ran five miles three times a week, watched his diet, and drank only infrequently.

He thought about a book he'd just finished reading, *Violence against Children* by David G. Gil. There were five signals of an abusive parent: misplaced conflicts, aimless life, mental illness, harsh discipline, and unspecified disturbance leading to battering.

Tom had bought the used 1970 book because it contained statistics of abuse during the sixties. He wanted to compare them with those of the nineties.

The statistics now were depressingly worse, he thought as he drove through the Marin Tunnel. The Golden Gate Bridge came into view, then the vast bay of San Francisco appeared. White triangles of sail boats dotted the blue water.

Eisenmann loved the water. His military service had been in the Navy.

He drove across the bridge, meandered through Cow Hollow, and pulled into his parking place behind the Missing Persons building.

Eisenmann was not with the Missing Persons Unit, but his work often involved missing persons. He kept an office in the same building and investigated sex crimes involving children.

Irene spied Eisenmann and said, "Got a strange one. Want to tag along?"

"Why?"

"Baby involved."

"Sure."

They left the building and climbed into Irene's car.

They arrived on Yukon, a shady dead-end street in the center of San Francisco. The Dubses' house was a two-story walk-up flat. Irene and Tom walked up the steps. There was a key in the door. She rang the doorbell. No answer.

"I'd sure like to open this," Irene said.

"Probable cause?"

"Three people missing."

"Call for a warrant."

"Always the cautious one."

"I'm as impetuous as the next guy, when I'm off work."

"I'll call for a warrant."

Irene rang the downstairs apartment's doorbell. A woman answered and identified herself as Barbara Spolter.

Checking her notes, Irene said, "A Karen Tuck called and reported—"

"That's Deborah's best friend."

"That's what she said in the police report. She stated that she spoke to Deborah Dubs yesterday evening. Then called back and no one was home."

Barbara said, "She called me to check. I saw the key in the door, rang the bell, then called Deborah back. I guess she called you guys."

Eisenmann asked, "Did you see anything last night?"

"I know that Harvey, Deborah's husband, was selling some sort of fancy video recorder. He ran an ad in the paper. I heard noises last evening, after six. I peeked out of my window and saw a small man helping another larger man tote out a duffel bag."

The two police officers continued to question the tenant. Satisfied that they had learned all the woman had to offer, Irene and Tom canvassed the block. An elderly neighbor across the street, Katherine McAuliffe, told them that she also had seen two men lug something down the stairs. Mrs. Murphy finished with, "And last night, no lights, the house was dark. That's very unusual for the nice couple. Their baby, Sean, what a darling."

The two police officers got back into the car. Tom asked, "What now?"

"Harvey's employer. Then a warrant. I want to find out what's in that house."

Harvey Dubs worked as a photographer, specializing in children's birthday parties. His boss's name was Stan Pedrov. They went to see him.

Stan said, "Someone called last night. Said Harvey was taking his family up to Washington. Strange, real strange."

"Why?"

"Never heard him say anything about relatives up north. And he had two weeks' pay coming." Stan held up a check. "Today."

A warrant was issued. The apartment was searched. No blood. No signs of a struggle.

Tom Eisenmann said, "Going to take a huge break to find out what happened here."

"A whole family?" Irene said. "I have a good imagination, but how do you make three people vanish? Without a sign of violence? Without any blood being spilled. We're both parents. You going to let someone highjack your family without putting up a struggle?"

"Of course not."

There was an ad in *The San Francisco Chronicle* listing the Dubses' phone number and offering a Hybrid 8 video duplicator and a Sony cassette player. Neither piece of equipment was in the apartment.

Irene found a receipt for the equipment. It was marked with an orange star. "Where are these people disappearing to?"

November 14, 1984, 7:30 p.m., Filbert Street, San Francisco

Paul Cosner finished having supper with his girlfriend. He was in his middle thirties, gray-haired, slender build, with a friendly smile. He held up a newspaper. "Finally got a response on the Honda."

"Great, honey."

"Meeting the guy in a few minutes."

"Here?"

"No, outside." Paul left the apartment.

December 14, 1984, 3:00 p.m., Parker Street, Milpitas

Milpitas is a small town just north of San Jose, in Santa Clara County. Kathy Allen, in her early twenties, worked at the Safeway Supermarket there. She got off work and met her boyfriend, Michael Carroll, outside. Kathy was very attractive. Michael was very handsome.

A Honda Accord drove up and a large, bearded man got out. Then a small Asian man followed him.

The bearded man said, "Mike, Kathy, been looking for you."

"Nice car."

"Just got it."

"We need a new car," Kathy said.

"Tough to pull off," Mike said, "with our budget."

"Some cars come cheap," the Asian man said.

"I'm having a party," the bearded man said, "up at my place in the mountains. Want to come?"

"Maybe later."

December 17, 1984, 3:00 p.m., Greenwich Street, San Francisco

Irene gave a file to Tom Eisenmann, then looked up and saw the reporter.

The young woman pushed back a lock of hair that had tumbled in front of her eyes.

Irene said, "I see you've let your hair grow out."

"Yes. Kind of a pain."

"That's why I keep mine short. What do you want?"

"Writing another article. I need to know more on how you investigate."

"Before I date I demand to see a medical history."

"I meant for your job."

"When I was seventeen, I read a Sam Spade novel. I knew I had to be—"

"I meant, how do you search for missing persons?"

Eisenmann said, "She hollers olley, olley, oxen-free."

"This is serious. What's your success rate?"

"Depends on whose cases."

"Your cases."

"I solve more of San Diego's missing persons cases than my own."

"You're kidding."

Irene opened a file. "And San Diego solves more of mine than I do. Remember the first two cases I showed you? The missing man and the teenage girl. The man was arrested in Seattle, DUI. After ten minutes he broke into tears and confessed he had abandoned his wife."

"The teenage girl?"

"Picked up for prostitution in L.A. Both cases closed, ending in sadness: for the man's wife, the girl's family."

"I thought cases usually end in sadness or *tragedy*."

"Some involve homicide."

"But then there's a body."

"Not every one," Eisenmann said, "shoves a butcher knife into his spouse and waits for the morgue to clean up the mess. Don't forget, S.F.'s neighbor is a big ocean."

"Anything else?"

"Most murders involve a domestic quarrel. A few involve random murder, like the Zodiac killings."

"Serial killers?"

Irene said, "And anyone's a potential victim."

January 5, 1985, 9:00 a.m., Fillmore Street, San Francisco

A Honda Accord was parked in front of a dilapidated hotel in the heart of San Francisco. A bearded man got out and approached three people, two men and a woman. He said, "I need to hire some casual laborers. To build an outbuilding up in the Mother Lode."

They agreed on a price. All four got in the car. They drove to Calaveras County. A few miles from the tiny hamlet of West Point, on Blue Mountain Road, they took a turn off and drove up a driveway to a single-family residence.

The bearded man said, "Home, folks, for the next few weeks."

A few days later, the bearded man ran an ad in the local paper asking for more day laborers. Scott Mosher, a fifteen-year-old, applied.

The building was half finished, a concrete block structure. Scott said, "That looks like a bomb shelter."

The bearded man said, "Looks can be deceiving."

Scott pointed at a pile of materials. A box was marked "Two-Way Mirror." He said, "I thought they only used those things in police stations."

"You thought wrong."

April 15, 1985, 3:00 p.m., Blue Mountain Road, Calaveras County

The concrete bunker was finished. It was gray, bleak, foreboding.

The bearded man stood in front of the ominous structure drinking a beer. He walked around the building, inspecting it carefully.

Up the hill, a few hundred yards away, was another house with a balcony. A young woman stood on the porch holding an infant.

The bearded man walked up the hill. He called out, "Brenda, is Lonnie home?"

"Be back in a few minutes."

"I want you guys to come over for dinner. Just finished the interior of my project. Let's celebrate."

"I'll ask Lonnie."

April 15, 1985, 4:00 p.m., San Andreas, Calaveras County

Claud Ballard was a substantial man, big in body, big in spirit, big in heart.

He was sheriff of Calaveras County.

Calaveras County is about one hundred and twenty miles, as the crow flies, due east of the San Francisco Bay Area. It is one of those intermediate places that catches some of the tourists headed south for Yosemite National Park, or east to the ski slopes of State Highway 88.

The foothills here are a no-man's-land between the stately Sierra and the lush San Joaquin Valley. Just north of San Andreas, at Sutter Creek, the cry of "Gold!" went out in 1848.

Here the river beds are worn smooth from centuries of runoff of the snow crags above. Every canyon is cut with a network of rivulets, searching for a common path to the flatlands. At times the crystal liquid plunges into motionless pools, at times it washes over sandstone or cuts into mineral-laden banks. Each rock field is a sluice that sucks heavier metals into its web of silica and quartz, working and reworking the heaviest metal into flecks, sometimes globules.

Sheriff Ballard was three years into his second term. His area of responsibility ranged from the Mother Lode foothills to the high country of the Sierra Nevada.

There is not one stop light in the county. There is not one town with a police force. The highway patrol takes care of the main arteries. State Highway 49, the road that follows the route of the gold miners, snakes through canyons that once rang with pickaxes and shovels. Highway 88 is the main route from the valley to the high country. Everything and everywhere else, from a drunken brawl in one of the bars to an amphetamine lab camouflaged in the forest, was Sheriff Ballard's responsibility.

The county seat, where his office and jail were, is in San Andreas, of Calaveras County. San Andreas is Spanish for Saint Andrew. Calaveras translates to "skeleton."

Ballard liked to attend his information officer's lectures.

Tourists who visited the Gold Country would occasionally stop by the sheriff's office to learn about the history of crime in the county.

Ballard leaned against the back wall of the auditorium and listened to the information officer speak to a small group of tourists.

The deputy sheriff said, "The countryside here is beautiful—a peaceful land of cattle ranchers and dairymen and grape growers.

"The words 'San Andreas' resonate throughout California. For reasons of geography it is the name of an earthquake fault that runs almost the length of the state. It is the name of the county seat of Calaveras, the home of the 'Big Trees' that startled the world in the late nineteenth century as the oldest living things on our planet. Mark Twain celebrated the giant leaping frogs of Calaveras, an innocence unmarred by riotous exploits of harlotry, drunkenness, and mayhem that were the divine right of the forty-niners. In 1885, the gentleman bandit Black Bart held up his last stage coach, and was tried and convicted at the San Andreas Court House."

Ballard thought, Black Bart was a dapper scoundrel. Crime wasn't so elegant anymore. Now just drunks, people driving Highway 49 like it was a freeway, domestic disputes, and drug-related killings.

This sylvan piece of God's country was not L.A., not S.F., not Sacramento. Nothing spectacular had happened here in the hundred years since Black Bart ripped off Wells Fargo.

May 4, 1985, 10:30 a.m., Blue Mountain Road, Calaveras County

The Pacific Gas and Electric Company's meter reader parked his truck by the Honda Accord. He had just been transferred to this rural area. He glanced at the concrete bunker and walked around it. Nothing in back except a large incinerator. No meter.

He walked around the house. Large shrubbery made it impossible to find the meter.

He walked up the front steps and knocked on the door.

No answer. He knocked louder.

The door opened. A bearded man, wearing an apron, stood in the doorway. His shirt was off. His arms were covered in blood. His chest hair was matted with blood. The apron was soaked in blood.

The meter reader stammered, "Are you all right?"

"Fine. Just butchering a hog."

Chapter 2

A Shoplifting Goes Awry

Sunday, June 2, 1985, Noon, South San Francisco

The clerk at the counter of the South San Francisco Lumber Yard studied an Asian customer, wearing a parka, in the fisheye mirror at the rear of the store.

The parka-wearer pondered bench vises. Suddenly a vise disappeared into the folds of the parka.

The clerk told a fellow employee, a stock boy, to call the police, then followed the Asian man out of the store.

The man tossed the vise into a car trunk, then slammed the lid. He stared over the top of the car, directly at the clerk, then walked away.

The stock boy appeared and said, "Cop's on the way. Where's the vise?"

"In the trunk."

A bearded man left the store and asked the clerk, "What's going on?"

"Shoplifting. Asian guy."

"He's a pal from work. What did he take?"

The key was still in the trunk's lock. The clerk opened the lid and said, "That vise."

"I'll pay for it."

* * *

Officer Daniel Wright worked for the South San Francisco Police Department.

Over his radio came the message, "Crime in progress at South City Lumber; shoplifting. Asian, wearing a parka."

The police car's blue and red lights went on as he pulled into the lot. Wright parked his car in front of the 1980 Honda. A man wearing an Ace Hardware apron and a bearded man waited by the car.

The clerk pointed, "There's the stolen vise."

In the trunk was the vise, a bag with "Ace Hardware" printed on it, plus two green tote bags.

Wright asked, "Who opened the trunk?"

"I did," the clerk said.

Wright could see the outline of a gun in one of the tote bags. Using his radio, he read the car's license plate numbers to headquarters, "838WFQ."

The bearded man said, "Here's the receipt. I paid for the vise my friend took. There's no need for the police."

Officer Wright feigned interest in the receipt while waiting for the car's license plate report. He asked, "Who's the car belong to?"

"Lonnie Bond."

"Where's Bond at?"

"Up north."

The squad car radio blared out, "The car's license plate is issued to a Buick, not a Honda. The Buick's license plate is registered to a Lonnie Bond."

The bearded man said, "I was just trying to help out a friend. The vise is paid for, what's the big deal?"

"The switch in the car's license plate. That's a crime," the police officer said, then asked, "What's in the tote bags?"

"Beats me. This is not my car."

"What are you afraid I might find?"

"Nothing."

"Then you don't mind if I have a look?"

"It's not mine."

Officer Wright pointed at the outline of the weapon pressing against the tote bag. "I love weapons. I know that's a gun. I just want to look at it."

The bearded man opened the bag. Inside was a light green-gray, zippered pistol case. Inside was a Ruger .22 pistol.

Officer Wright jotted down the serial number: 1270329. In the tote bag he saw a metal tube, six inches long. One end was threaded. A silencer.

Wright thought, *a silencer?*

The policeman smiled. "Nice weapon, I have one at home."

The bearded man returned the smile.

Wright said, "I don't hunt, just shoot beer cans."

"I love hunting."

"Do you use this weapon?"

"Yes."

Wright asked, "May I see some identification?"

The bearded man held out a California driver's license. The name on it was Robin S. Stapley. The birthdate made him twenty-six.

Twenty-six? Wright thought. This guy looks over forty. Returning to his squad car, he called in the serial number on the .22. It was registered to Robin Scott Stapley.

Officer Wright pushed the bearded man against the car. "Hands on top of the roof. You're under arrest."

"For what?"

"Owning an illegally altered weapon."

"I don't own that weapon."

"Your ID says you're Stapley. The gun's registered to Stapley."

Wright read the bearded man his rights, applied handcuffs, and put him in the back seat of the squad car.

He called in an all-points bulletin to the station: Asian male, slight build, about twenty-five, last seen wearing a parka.

Wright called the station and requested that the Honda be towed to the South City impound yard.

He pulled the squad car into the station and led the man to an interrogation room. He had the bearded man empty his pockets.

He took out a number of keys and a receipt from Golden Crest Travel made out to Charles Gunnar.

Charles Gunnar? Wright thought. Who's he? He said, "We can end this now, if you'll tell me what's going on."

Another officer signaled to him from the door. "The Vehicle Identification Number on the engine block of the Honda is SNF, 2023947."

"Registered to Lonnie Bond? Robin Stapley? Charles Gunnar?"

"No. Paul Cosner, of 1918 Filbert Street, San Francisco. I called S.F. He's been missing since last November."

"Did you report this to S.F.'s Missing Persons Unit?"

"The desk sergeant's contacting them now."

"Do they want me to continue interrogating?"

"Didn't say."

Wright sat across the table from the suspect. "The car's identification number doesn't match the phony plate. The car is registered to Paul Cosner, missing since last November."

The bearded man's body suddenly went limp. Defiance left his eyes.

"Are you really Robin Stapley?"

The suspect whispered, "I need a pen, paper, and a glass of water."

"A confession?"

"A note to my wife."

Wright filled a Styrofoam cup with cold water. He tore a sheet of paper from his notebook and placed it and his pen by the cup of water.

The man held up the handcuffs and said, "I can't write with these on."

Officer Wright removed the cuffs.

The bearded man scribbled something on the paper and put the note into his shirt pocket.

Wright offered, "I can have that delivered for you."

The bearded man said, "Who would have thought that a lousy work bench vise would bring me to this?"

"I beg your pardon?"

"My partner's name is Charlie Chitat Ng. Chitat, pronounced cheetah, and Ng, pronounced Ing."

Officer Wright wrote this information in his notebook.

The bearded man said, "You want to know who I really am?"

"Yes."

"I'm Leonard Lake, fugitive from the Feds." He grabbed something from the lapel of his shirt and sucked it into his mouth. He gulped the water and repeated hoarsely, "Lake."

His chest convulsed; his pupils rolled back.

Wright shouted for a medic. He took the man's pulse. Feeble, but still there. He thought, you don't kill yourself over a stolen car.

He called Kaiser Permanente Emergency and asked for an ambulance.

Wright's sergeant said, "I reached S.F.'s Missing Persons Unit. They're contacting the officers involved in Paul Cosner's case."

"Who's handling it?"

"Irene Brunn and Tom Eisenmann."

"Eisenmann? I've heard of him, but he's not in Missing Persons."

"What's he in?"

"Child abuse and kiddie porn."

Sunday, June 2, 1985, 2:00 p.m., Marin County

Eisenmann parked behind the Missing Persons building and entered it. The dispatcher called, "We got a lead on Cosner."

"Finally."

Once a month Tom Eisenmann pulled weekend duty in Missing Persons. The Cosner case had come up on his watch.

Eisenmann knew that when a man is gone without a trace for months, the odds aren't good of ever seeing him again. There are only a few reasons people disappear: homicide, suicide, simulated suicide, amnesia, psychoses, abandonment.

The dispatcher handed him a Teletype. A cop in the parking lot of the South City Lumber and Supply Company had picked up Cosner's 1980 Honda.

Irene Brunn was in her apartment when Eisenmann called. He said, "Cosner's car is in South City."

They met at the South City police station. Officer Daniel Wright said, "The suspect I took into custody, Leonard Lake, tried to kill himself."

"Where is he?"

"Kaiser Permanente Hospital. He's in a coma. He had two cyanide pills taped to the underside of his lapel."

Irene said, "I've never come across a suspect with cyanide on him."

"That's World War Two spy stuff," Eisenmann said.

"But why? Not over a stolen car."

"This guy had to be doing something far more serious," Eisenmann said.

Wright handed them a note. "Lake wrote this just before he popped the pills."

The note read: My darling, I'm sorry. I love you. I forgive you. Please forgive me.

Irene said, "Love you? Forgive you? For what?"

"Don't know."

"Who's his wife?"

"Don't know."

"You sound like most of my suspects," Irene said. "Where's the Honda?"

"We had it towed," Wright answered. "It's here, behind the station. Except for the slides, the gun, and Robin Stapley's driver's license and various cards, it's exactly like I found it."

"Where's that evidence?" Irene asked.

"Evidence locker room."

"I'd like to have Cosner's car moved up to the impound yard in San Francisco."

"I don't see any problem. A missing person means more than shoplifting. Besides, once you look in the car, I think you'll agree this is a lot more serious than even a missing person."

Irene Brunn said, "What else? Lake didn't swallow death because of car theft. This is homicide."

* * *

In the South City Police Station's evidence room Irene studied the driver's license: Robin Stapley, San Diego. She called the San Diego police. She found that Robin Stapley was one of the founders of the Guardian Angels in San Diego. The Guardians, a national organization, started in New York City to "assist" the police in urban areas and protect citizens from criminals.

Robin Stapley had been missing since April.

Monday, June 3, 1985, 9:00 a.m., San Francisco's Police Impound Yard

Irene Brunn and Tom Eisenmann searched the trunk of Paul Cosner's Honda. They found a couple of black-and-white slides: an image of a man and a woman on one and a child on the other.

On the rear seat were some clothing, a cardboard box, and a wrench set. On the passenger's seat was a work jacket.

Under the front seat they found a First Interstate Bank card in the name of Randy Jacobson and an assortment of cards from AAA, National Enterprises Medical, California First Bank, Saks Fifth Avenue, and GEMCO Department Stores and Supermarkets—all in the name of R. Scott Stapley, 4755 Felton, Apartment 4, San Diego.

There was a dark maroon stain on the front passenger's seat. There was a bullet hole where the passenger's sun visor should be.

In the glove compartment were repair bills, all in the name of Cosner. Scraps of paper and receipts littered the passenger side of the car. There were two spent shell casings under the front seat and a Pacific Gas & Electric bill.

The bill was made out to Claralyn Balazs, with a post office box address in Wilseyville, California.

They continued the search, but the PG&E bill was the only item leading them somewhere.

"Who's Balazs?" Irene said.

Eisenmann said, "Maybe another missing person?"

"There can't be too many women with a name like Balazs in the whole state."

"Where's Wilseyville?"

"Mother Lode, I think."

"What's the address of the property? A P.O. box doesn't help."

They called the business office of the Pacific Gas and Electric Company and ran a quick computer check on Balazs. Within minutes her name came up on older PG&E bills in Philo, California. The older bills showed another name on the account as jointly responsible. The name was Leonard Lake.

They called telephone information and learned that a Balazs was no longer listed in Philo. Another check was run—this time with the Department of Motor Vehicles in Sacramento. Claralyn Balazs showed a San Bruno address, on Cabrillo Street, just a few miles from a lumber yard.

Irene contacted Claralyn and made an appointment. The two police officers arrived at the Balazs residence one hour later. Waiting for them were Claralyn Balazs; and, as it turned out, Gloria Eberling, Lake's mother; and two of Lake's sisters.

Irene explained the events of the previous day, then asked Balazs, "You are married to Leonard Lake?"

Claralyn answered, "Was married to Lake. We broke up over two years ago."

"He wrote you a note," Eisenmann said. "What's he forgiving you for?"

"I don't know."

"Why's your name on a PG&E bill in a car he was driving? A car registered to a missing person?"

"We were married when we lived in Philo."

"The bill has an address in Wilseyville."

"It's off Route 88, above San Andreas, in Calaveras County. There's a cabin there my father owns."

Irene asked, "When did you see Leonard last?"

"I haven't seen Leonard in months. I don't see what this has to do—"

"We have a link between Paul Cosner, who has been missing for months, and your ex. That link leads to you."

"I can't—"

"The front seat of Cosner's car is covered with blood. Two shell casings were found in the car. This could be a murder case. We want to see this cabin. What's the address?"

"It's impossible to find."

"Then take us there."

"No one's staying there. No one can get in."

"We're getting in," Irene said.

"You'll never find the place. Those mountains are really remote."

"No mail boxes?" Irene asked.

"The cabin's address is a P.O. box number on Star Route, Blue Mountain Road."

Tom said, "That doesn't sound too hard to—"

"You'll never find the place."

Eisenmann motioned to Brunn and they went outside. He said, "Let's compromise and get her to agree to meet first thing in the morning. Besides, we have to get clearance from the Calaveras Sheriff's Department. It's their jurisdiction. That'll take time."

They rejoined the four women and suggested the compromise. Claralyn agreed to meet the following day. "Ten o'clock," she said. "There's a grocery store just outside of West Point, at the intersection of Highway 88 and Blue Mountain Road. Can't miss it."

* * *

Claud Ballard had been the sheriff of Calaveras County for seven years.

He agreed to let San Francisco law enforcement agents enter his jurisdiction, adding that he wanted two of his officers present.

The sheriff said, "I have a roster of only thirty-two full-time personnel. I can't afford more than two on only a suspected situation."

Tuesday, June 4, 1985, 9:00 a.m., San Andreas

Tom Eisenmann and Irene Brunn arrived at the Calaveras County Sheriff's office. They met the two deputy sheriffs assigned by Ballard to go with them: Detective Norman Varain and Detective Steve Mathews.

Detective Mathews, a narcotics officer, was a well-built man with a lantern jaw and a trimmed mustache. Sheriff Ballard had sent him because Eisenmann had found a file on Lake involving drugs in another county: suspicion of growing marijuana in Humboldt County on the Northern California coast.

The four officers drove to the grocery store.

Claralyn entered a few minutes after ten. With her was Lake's mother, Gloria Eberling.

Irene said, pointing at her watch, "I thought you said ten."

"Sorry."

"I was raised so that when I told someone I'd be somewhere at ten, I was there at ten."

"We went to the cabin first. There were things—"

Eisenmann said to Gloria, "I want you to step outside."

Detective Mathews said, "I'll accompany her."

Eisenmann tried to control his anger as he eyed Claralyn. "You came up before us?"

"Leonard was a slob," Claralyn said. "Gloria wanted to clean up a bit. Why do you want her outside?"

"Standard procedure," Eisenmann said.

Irene added, "Separate everyone when you think something's going on."

Eisenmann said, "I think something's going on."

"So do I," Irene said. "What did you do at the cabin?"

"There were things there that are personal. Nothing to do with this."

"I warn you," Irene said, "you may have obstructed justice."

"If I told you what I took," Claralyn said, "you'd just laugh."

"Make us laugh," Irene said.

"Leonard liked to take pictures."

"Pictures?"

"They weren't really pictures, they were videos. Of me nude. I'd be embarrassed if you saw them."

Eisenmann asked, "Did you find the videos?"

"No."

Irene asked, "What else did you take out of the cabin?"

"What else? I told you I didn't take any videos."

"Right. What else did you take?"

"Nothing."

"Did you *burn* anything else?"

"I don't have to put up with—"

"Yes," Irene said, "I'm afraid you do. Let's find out what's *still* in the cabin."

* * *

The police cars followed Claralyn's vehicle to the cabin. They turned left off Blue Mountain Road, then down a road for some fifty yards. They made a hard left and went up a driveway. A cinder block structure was on their right. The house was straight ahead. There were pines and foothill oak around the property.

The ranch-style cabin was built on a platform that kept it above the occasional runoffs from heavy winters. The attached carport was vacant. Parked nearby were an old Plymouth sedan and an even older, gray Chevrolet pickup truck with personalized license plates that read: AHOYMTY. There was obvious damage on the driver's side of the truck.

Irene said to Claralyn, "This is remote, but not that remote."

"Right," Eisenmann said. "Given proper directions, we could have found this place."

Irene said, "Of course, then we might have found those embarrassing videotapes."

Claralyn opened the front door of the house and stepped back.

Detective Varain suggested, "Irene and I can search inside the house. Steve, why don't you stay here—with Gloria and Claralyn?"

Eisenmann said, "I'll check the grounds."

Irene glanced at her watch: 10:20. She made a note of the time as she and Varain entered the front room.

Irene was in her element. A search. She thought to herself, be methodical—meticulous.

It was a two-bedroom, one-bath cabin. There were dried spots of a dark maroon color on the sheetrocked living room ceiling. An Olympia typewriter sat on a desk in the corner. Next to it was a turntable. By the desk was a guitar.

One wall was covered with a painting of a forest going through the colorful changes of autumn.

Be methodical, Irene thought as she studied the bullet hole in the center of the scene.

The kitchen was ordinary, except for wallpaper displaying a full-sized depiction of Buffalo Bill.

Be meticulous, Irene thought as she studied a bullet hole in the linoleum floor.

The spare bedroom was painted purple. The bed was covered with a multicolored bedspread. Two oak-framed mirrors hung on the wall.

The master bedroom was painted light green, the carpet and drapes dark green. An empty gun rack decorated a wall. Tied to each of the corners of the four-poster bed were frayed electric cords. Fastened to the wall behind the bed was an outdoor light, 250 watts. Eyebolts were anchored into the floor, one at each corner of the bed.

Irene opened the top dresser drawer. It was filled with women's lingerie in a variety of sizes, some torn, and some with dark maroon stains on them.

She went back into the front room. Deputy Sheriff Varain was writing down the identification numbers on the twenty-five-inch television set.

Irene went back into the master bedroom. The bed had a colorful quilt on top. She grabbed one end and lifted it. Underneath was a mattress covered with a dark, maroon stain.

With evidence like this, Irene thought, you don't have to be methodical or meticulous. Clues are everywhere.

She returned to the front room. She spotted two pieces of video equipment on a bookshelf. She went over, put her reading glasses on, and studied the Sony cassette player and a Hybrid 8 generator—a professional-quality piece of equipment for mixing tapes. An orange star stood out against the black metal.

A Hybrid 8 generator? she thought, bells going off in her mind. *The Dubs case.*

During the course of the initial investigation a list of property stolen from the Dubses' residence had been compiled. Among the items missing were a Sony cassette player and a Hybrid 8 generator—marked with an orange star.

Irene copied the serial number of the cassette player. The serial number on the Hybrid 8 generator had been filed off.

Using the radio in her car, she called the Calaveras Sheriff's Department and was forwarded to the San Francisco Missing Persons Unit. She got Inspector Glen Pamoloff, her regular partner, on the line, and read the serial number of the Sony to him.

Pamoloff pulled the Dubs file, thumbed through it, and quickly came back. "Verified. The serial number is the same."

Irene disconnected. Verified, she thought. Two pieces of video equipment missing from the Dubs' residence on Yukon Street in San Francisco have found their way to a bookshelf in a remote cabin in Calaveras County.

The Dubs family is dead.

* * *

The property was secured. Eisenmann and Mathews stayed with Claralyn and Gloria Eberling. Brunn and Varain drove back to San Andreas and went to the District Attorney's office. They spoke with Assistant DA John Martin, laying out the evidence they had discovered so far.

He agreed that there was enough to request a search warrant for the entire property. They found Judge Douglas Mewhinney in his chambers. They presented the evidence unearthed so far. Mewhinney signed a search warrant for the house on Blue Mountain Road.

Varain and Brunn returned to the property.

"I want to talk to Claralyn," Irene said. She saw Lake's ex-wife sitting on the front porch and went straight to her. She asked, "You said you came here to get videos?"

"Of me and Leonard."

"Mrs. Eberling, is that correct?"

Gloria Eberling sat, chin on chest, and twisted the strap to her purse into a tight knot.

"Mrs. Eberling?" Irene repeated.

Still no response.

"Mrs. Eberling," Irene continued, "ever hear the term *obstructing justice?*"

Claralyn said, "Leave her alone."

Irene asked, "All right, I'll leave *her* alone. Claralyn, when did you buy this house?"

"Never," Claralyn answered, "my parents did."

"Your parents?"

"They bought it from the fat guy."

"The fat guy?"

"I haven't seen the fat guy in ages."

"What fat guy?"

"The fat guy."

Irene thought, I'm blowing it. I'm not conducting a logical interview. I'm emotionally upset by what I suspect. Cosner's car, the Dubses' video equipment. Two families, totally unrelated, linked to this house.

This place smells of death.

She knew the hot-tempered side of her nature was overrunning the professional side. I need to calm down, she said to herself.

"Stay put," she told the two women and walked up the driveway and approached Eisenmann.

"Look at this." He pointed at a bumper sticker on the rear of a beat-up Plymouth. It read: "If you love something, set it free. If it doesn't come back, hunt it down and kill it."

Irene said, "Chilling, unless it's a joke."

"What I'll show you next is really unfunny."

Eisenmann led her to an incinerator. It was squat, with a blackened pipe rising from the top.

Using a branch, Eisenmann flipped the latch and opened the metal door. He pointed inside with the stick.

"What?" Irene asked.

"This thing's a kiln." He tapped the inside wall with his stick. "That's high-end fire brick. Capable of withstanding immense heat."

She reached toward white powder covering the hearth.

"Hold it!" Eisenmann ordered.

"Why?"

"We can't touch this until the lab looks at it. Look at the fire walls inside this—you don't need this thing to burn trash. This thing is built like—"

"A crematorium."

Chapter 3

Task Force and a Bunker

Tuesday, June 4, 1985, 11:00 a.m., Blue Mountain Road,
Calaveras County

"Our search warrant doesn't cover that structure." Tom Eisenmann pointed
at the concrete-block, windowless bunker. For an outbuilding, it was large,
over five hundred square feet. The rear of the building butted up to an em-
bankment. He said, "That's too big to be a wine cellar."

Irene said, "It's not underground, so it's not a bomb shelter. And if it
were a workshop, it would have windows."

The foreboding building was surrounded by dried spring grass lying
in brown, dead clumps. There was evidence of garbage and burn pits.

Eisenmann said, "We need a search warrant."

They walked back to the porch, where Balazs and Mrs. Eberling sat on
a bench. He took out a note pad and said, "Ms. Balazs, I need your help."

"What else have I been doing?"

"I mean real cooperation, not lip service. I'd like you to sign a waiver
and consent form so we can search that concrete bunker."

"I don't own this property."

"You pay the utility bills."

"I still don't *own* it."

"You have a key to the house."

"Yes."

"Do you have a key to the bunker?"

"Leonard called it his fallout shelter."

"Do you have a key to the fallout shelter?"

"No."

"Who has?"

"Leonard."

"Not on him. I saw the personal effects taken after his arrest: wallet, cash, coins, some keys, but no key to a padlock."

"I don't have a key."

"We don't need a key," Eisenmann said, "just permission to enter."

"Why are you harassing me?"

"I didn't think I was."

"Why harass me? Why aren't you after Ng?"

"What about him? Who is he? Why haven't you mentioned him before."

"You never asked."

"Tom, have you heard of him before?" Irene asked.

"No. But the South City cop, Wright, he said an Asian man fled the scene."

Claralyn said, "He was a friend of Leonard's. Charlie Chitat Ng."

"Cheetah?"

"Like the predator."

"When did you see him last?"

"He was at my home yesterday."

"What! Why?"

"He had called his landlady and asked if his paycheck, from the Dennis Moving Company where he worked part time, had arrived. She told him it had."

"Then what?"

"He asked me to drive him to his apartment. I did. It's on Lennox Street."

"I know that street," Irene said. "It's in the West Portal District of San Francisco."

Claralyn said, "Charlie went into his basement apartment and got his other Ruger .22 and some shells."

"Armed and dangerous," Eisenmann said.

"Yes. He packed some clothes in a suitcase and dumped them in my car. He picked up a California driver's license and a Social Security card. But they weren't in his name, I noticed. The name was Mike Kimoto. He grabbed an envelope with lots of cash."

Irene felt her cheeks flush. "Why didn't you tell us this earlier?"

"No one asked."

"Still," Irene said, "this is obstruction of justice."

Eisenmann said, "Calm down, Irene. Claralyn, do you know a Mike Kimoto?"

"No."

"Where did the money in the envelope come from?"

"I don't know."

"What happened next?"

"I drove Charlie to the San Francisco International Airport and dropped him off at the United Airlines curb."

"Where was he going?"

"I don't know."

* * *

Irene took several deep breaths. Calm down, she told herself. Anger doesn't solve anything. But, my God, this woman must have known that we would need this information.

What do I know? We have a missing person, Paul Cosner, and his stolen car containing possible bloodstains and two empty .22 shells. We have a .22 with a silencer, and a man using a driver's license issued to the Guardian Angel, Robin Stapley, of San Diego. We have a suspect trying to kill himself with cyanide, and a woman who dashes up here with her ex-mother-in-law to look for nude videos of herself. We have a Sony and a Hybrid 8 generator known to belong to three missing persons: the Dubses. We have a house with a blood-soaked mattress, two bullet holes in the kitchen floor, a bullet hole in the front room wall, and a master bedroom with enough light to be a film studio.

Snuff flicks?

Irene took two more deep breaths, then said, "It must have been difficult being married to Lake. Why don't you start at the beginning?"

"I met Leonard at the Renaissance Fair in Marin County. He was a good-looking man, clean shaven except for his mustache. I remember he had one of those serf hats that peasants wore in the Dark Ages. I had on a white dress, with a garland of flowers in my hair. He worked a booth where he charged people to have their pictures taken with his pet goat."

"Pet goat?"

"Leonard had rigged the goat up to look like a miniature unicorn."

"A unicorn?"

"Named Sir Lancelot. The goat had a phony horn in the center of its forehead. It was done surgically. Lennie asked for a date. We courted for a while, then he asked me to marry him."

"Marry him?"

Eisenmann grinned. Irene was using the interrogation technique of repeating the last few words the witness said. It propelled to the next statement without having to probe into unknown territory.

Claralyn said, "We found a small church in South San Francisco. That's when Lake introduced me to a roly-poly buddy, his best man."

"What about the roly-poly buddy?"

"The fat man, I call him, paid for the champagne and food at the wedding. He was five foot eight and weighed three-fifty to four hundred pounds."

"What's his name?"

"Charlie Gunnar."

"Where is he?"

"I haven't seen him in years."

"Where did he use to live?"

"Morgan Hill."

"After you married, what happened?"

"We moved to Philo, in Mendocino. Leonard managed a motel there. I was a teacher's aide at Anderson Valley Elementary School."

"What happened next?"

"Our neighbors were organic farmers and dairy ranchers. The whole thing seemed like a honeymoon that could go on forever."

"Then you started having problems?"

"The break came not quite a year after our wedding. That's when Charlie Ng arrived at the ranch and moved in with us. Leonard told me that Charlie, like him, had been a Marine. We got along pretty good for five months. Then Charlie left for a few days. He returned in a pickup one night."

"What happened?"

"Leonard and Ng did some sort of ritualistic dance under the moonlight. Then they put crates in the woodshed. At dawn I saw an Army truck pull up. A SWAT team of FBI men got out. Leonard and Charlie were taken to jail."

"What charge?"

"Stealing weapons from a Marine base in Hawaii. The army found guns in our woodshed. Bail was set at $30,000 each. My husband phoned Gunnar and he raised it. Leonard was released. His trial was set for early August, '82. Charlie couldn't raise bail."

Eisenmann asked, "Is that when you split with Leonard?"

"Yes. Leonard told me he couldn't stand the thought of prison. He wanted me to go on the run with him. He was going to hide here in the mountains. I wouldn't do it."

"Then?"

"He moved in here anyway. We saw each other once in a while, here and at my parent's home."

Her hands fluffed her hair, played with her earrings, fiddled with the strap of her purse.

"Why," Eisenmann asked, "was your name on the PG&E bills?"

Irene added, "You were harboring a fugitive."

"Harboring him? By letting him use my name on a gas bill?"

"Where's Ng?"

"How should I know?"

"When did you last see him?"

"I want an attorney."

Damn, thought Irene. "Will you give us permission to enter that concrete building?"

"No," she snapped.

"If you have nothing to hide, then why—"

"No!" Claralyn Balazs picked up her purse and yelled to Mrs. Eberling, "We're leaving."

The Pinto bounced down the gravel road toward Route 88.

Irene called in the information on Ng, United flight from SFO, false ID of Mike Kimoto, to Captain Philpott.

She turned to Eisenmann and said, "We have to prepare papers for the Calaveras District Attorney's office to allow us to get an additional search warrant for the bunker."

Eisenmann said, "I want to put in a call to the hospital. Once connected to the doctor, he asked, "How's Lake doing?"

"Still in a coma."

"Ah."

"You sound disappointed."

"I'm disappointed he isn't conscious. I'm aching to interrogate him."

He told Irene what he had learned.

She said, "We need to hit this place with everything we've got. We need a task force."

Tuesday, June 4, 1985, 1:00 p.m., San Francisco

Their request went immediately to the top. Police Chief Cornelius Murphy put together a twelve-man task force of San Francisco police headed by Joseph Lordan, Deputy Chief of Inspectors.

Chief Murphy then called Sheriff Claud Ballard. He also formed a special unit. It was agreed that Joe Lordon would lead the San Francisco team and Calaveras Sheriff's Lieutenant Bob Bunning would head the sheriff's unit.

Sheriff Claud Ballard would supervise both, when possible; otherwise Bunning would be in charge, with Detectives Steve Mathews and Larry Copland directly under him.

* * *

Inspector Richard D. Adkins picked up Katherine McAuliffe from her home on the end of Yukon Street.

The inspector said, "I need to take you downtown so that you can look at some pictures."

She pointed at a house. "My neighbors have been missing for almost a year. This has to do with them, right?"

The investigator drove her to the Hall of Justice on Seventh and Bryant. There Mrs. Murphy was shown six photographs of Asian males.

She picked out the photo marked "Number Four."

Inspector Adkins drove her home and picked up Mrs. Murphy's neighbor, Barbara Speaker. She was a tenant who lived below the Dubs family. The procedure was repeated at the Hall of Justice.

Barbara Speaker also picked out the photo marked "Number Four."

Tuesday, June 4, 1985, 2:30 p.m., Blue Mountain Road, Calaveras County

The police officers finished cordoning off the Blue Mountain Road driveway and cabin with yellow tape. A space was cleared in front of the cabin, under a large pine tree. Already a county truck had disgorged an array of furniture: two desks, a few dozen folding chairs, some garbage cans and two large tables—one for the lab and one for the pathologist.

The sheriff had ordered a locksmith to be brought to the scene to open the concrete bunker.

Irene reported to the sheriff on the preliminary inspection she and Eisenmann had done. "Next to the concrete bunker, the ground's been disturbed in a circle approximately ten feet in diameter. Also, there's a substance that strongly resembles lye."

"You suggesting a grave site?"

"Who knows? There's also clothing visible in the trench that runs from here to the base of the hill."

"Start on that first," Ballard said. "Label it Site One."

Next, the sheriff said to a dozen officers, "I want you men to begin a quadrant search of that trench, starting at the base of the road. I want each quadrant to be a five by five square, that's feet, not yards."

Tuesday, June 4, 1985, 3:30 p.m. Blue Mountain Road, Calaveras County

Irene Brunn stood at one of the large tables under the cluster of oak trees. At the next table, the Calaveras coroner, Terry Parker, was setting up his equipment.

Deputy Sheriff Mathews was in charge of cataloging the items brought in from the quadrant search. The men working the telephone trench would place any items found in a neat row a few feet away from their work area. Periodically, Deputy Sheriff Larry Copland made the rounds carrying a garbage bag.

The sandy-haired and tanned Copland was a meticulous peace officer.

Copland would note the location of each item found, date and sign the article, and place it in the bag. Then he would carry the bag back to Mathews.

Irene placed what she had found on the table.

Mathews entered the latest delivery into a log book.

Quadrant twelve: sixteen empty Budweiser cans, an empty pack of matches from the Gold Rush Cafe, a rusted Phillips screwdriver, and three sixteen-penny galvanized nails.

Irene watched the process and said, "Why aren't we digging?"

The coroner said, "Don't worry, we'll find bodies."

"You're sure?"

"I saw maggots, and in more than one location. They're not the kind that like garbage. These maggots are carrion eaters."

* * *

Sheriff Ballard called a meeting of all personnel.

Fifty-one-year-old Deputy Chief Bunning had arrived with five more officers from the Calaveras sheriff's department. They joined the San Francisco contingent, which had grown to twelve with the arrival of the extra personnel sent by Chief Murphy. The combined San Francisco and Calaveras force interrupted their tasks and assembled at the foot of the driveway. It had been a typically scorching summer day, approaching a hundred degrees, and had not cooled much with the approach of evening. But even with the aggravation of the heat, there was no friction between the two forces. Everyone suspected that this would be a monumental case.

The sheriff said, "I want to make one point crystal clear: mistakes made in the gathering and protection of evidence at a crime scene can never be rectified."

The twenty officers shuffled nervously.

Ballard asked Deputy Chief Lordan, "Do you want to add anything?"

Lordan said, "I don't want any of you scribbling your notes on scraps of paper. I know all about that habit and the flights of fiction that follow at the office when you're trying to decipher your own notes. It always comes out at trial and taints your testimony. Use notebooks, make your entries when you discover something, make them legible, note the time, be precise."

Ballard said, "I want a lid on this, no comments in town, no asides to your spouses or bartenders. The longer we have to work in peace without the world press trampling over the evidence, the happier I'll be."

Lordan added, "This isn't the big city where you can block access with a few squad cars at various intersections." He waved an arm at the surrounding Ponderosa pine and Douglas fir. "We're in the wide open spaces. It will use up a lot of manpower to keep people out of here, once they get wind of this."

The Sheriff said, "I want this driveway barricaded."

He glanced at his watch. "Where's that locksmith?"

Irene said, "I contacted one in San Andreas. He can't get here until tomorrow, mid-morning."

Ballard asked Irene to begin drawing a detailed sketch of the property, the cabin, the bunker, and the approximate location of the various trees. He finished with, "Include the next door neighbor's house, the one up there on the hill."

* * *

The S.F. crew now consisted of three detectives from headquarters, the two officers from Missing Persons, a three-man team of dog handlers, a forensic specialist, two patrolmen, and Deputy Chief of Inspectors Lordan. Even for a major case, this was a large number of personnel a hundred and fifty miles from home. And there were eight deputies on duty from Calaveras County.

A ninth deputy drove up and gave Sheriff Ballard a manila envelope. It was from San Francisco Police Chief Cornelius Murphy. It was a file on Leonard Lake.

Ballard read: Lake joined the Marines on January 27, 1964. He served seven years, two tours of duty in Vietnam, the first at Da Nang, the second for only one month.

Lake was returned to El Toro Marine Base in Orange County. Reason: unspecified medical problems.

Lake received the Vietnam Service Medal, two Good Conduct Medals, and a Vietnam Campaign Medal. After getting a medical discharge, he lived in San Jose, California, for five years. He married Claralyn Balazs, nicknamed Cricket. In 1981, they moved to Philo.

Irene came back from the neighboring house. "I called the owner of the property." She flipped open her notebook. "His name is Bo Carter. He lives in Burlingame. Mr. Carter told me that his tenants, a man named Lonnie Bond; his common-law wife, Brenda O'Connor; and their infant, Lonnie Bond Jr., didn't pay their rent when it was due on the fourteenth, last month. He called his real estate agent, who drove here."

"And?"

"And a man from this cabin came over and ID'd himself to the real estate agent as Charlie Gunnar."

"Gunnar?" The sheriff opened a file. "I thought so. That's the same man we identified from a Golden Crest Travel receipt in Lake's pocket. It was made out to Charles Gunnar." He flipped through the file. "And Lake's ex, Claralyn, said Gunnar was Lake's best man at their wedding. Eisenmann ran a check on him. The Morgan Hill police said Gunnar's been missing for two years."

Irene said, "The man IDing himself next door as Gunnar said the tenants had been gone ten days, that they'd skipped out on the rent."

"Three more people missing? And one an infant?"

"There's more. The real estate agent said that another man was living here with the young couple. His name was Robin Stapley. Stapley was the name on the driver's license Lake gave Officer Wright."

"Another missing person?" Ballard said in disbelief.

"There's more," Irene went on relentlessly. "The real estate agent said he noticed that freshly turned soil has been layered on an eroded bank where his property meets this property."

"Fresh dirt," Ballard said. "I'll get someone on it immediately."

Irene said, "Bo Carter, the neighboring landlord, drove up here last Friday to check out his property. A man showed up, said he was Charles Gunnar, and followed him around while he inspected the house. Carter said he found some items were missing, bedding and appliances. When he mentioned it, the man became agitated and kept saying that he didn't know anything about where the things went."

"Did Carter get a description?"

"Better. Carter told me that he recognized the man, who called himself Gunnar, on the San Francisco Channel Four news. After Lake took cyanide, they ran a local interest spot about crime and punishment on Sunday night showing his photo. The reporter, obviously, only speculated on why Lake killed himself. None of what's happening here has been made public yet. I didn't fill Bo Carter in on why I was calling. But that's how Carter learned the man's name was really Leonard Lake."

"Was anything found next door that suggested foul play?"

"In his rental, Carter found two suitcases filled with female and infant clothes."

"So?"

"Nobody skips out and leaves clothes behind."

* * *

The second day of the investigation of the Wilseyville crime scene began under another sweltering sun. The locksmith arrived. Sheriff Ballard made sure the additional search warrant, covering the bunker, had arrived from the DA's office. He ordered the locksmith to go ahead. The man knelt by the steel door to the bunker for a few minutes, then the door creaked open.

Eisenmann looked inside the bunker. Pitch black. The light outside shone for only a few feet. He turned on his flashlight.

The beams of light flickered eerily over dim shapes.

Irene stood behind Ballard and Eisenmann in the doorway of the bunker. Jim Stenquist, the Calaveras County information officer, had joined them.

Irene could smell an unidentifiable odor, faint, yet still pungent. The inside of the bunker was warm and dry.

"Don't touch anything," Ballard ordered.

The room was about twelve by twenty feet. It was obviously a work-shop. On one wall various tools hung from nails on a four by eight sheet of plywood. There was a hacksaw, pliers, heavy-duty chain cutters, a hand saw, a drill, and two circular saw blades. There was a workbench. The handle on the workbench vise was broken.

"There's something wrong with the dimensions of this room," Irene said. She went outside and paced, then returned. "Outside is twenty by twenty, inside twenty by twelve."

They searched. They found a latch on the edge of the four by eight sheet of plywood. The tool rack swung open, revealing an interior room.

Inside was a double bed, with a wooden end table covered with books and a reading lamp. Irene snapped on the light and turned off her flashlight. Military equipment was scattered about: boots, fatigues, canteens, bayonets, gun belts, and a Coleman lantern.

There was also an array of armament: rifles, shotguns, assault weapons, machine guns.

There were two surgical gloves, a hairbrush, two cases of Coca-Cola, and mouthwash.

There was a crude wooden plaque on the wall. Written in red ink above it was *"Operation Miranda."*

Words were chiseled into a plaque: *"The Warrior's Code—For those who thrive on the challenge of competition, whose being is intensified by impossible tasks and insurmountable odds, who even at the risk of defeat, will enter the arena in quest for victory."*

Ballard said, "I want everything itemized and analyzed."

Irene started writing.

Eisenmann found a shirt on the floor. Above the pocket were the words "Dennis Moving Service." A baseball hat, bearing the same company's name, was picked up in a corner of the room.

Envelopes, with the return address to the Philo Motel, were found on a desk.

The rear wall contained a bookcase. On the shelves were a first aid kit, a book on explosives, another on chemicals, and magazines on guns. There were manacles, handcuffs, and three knives, all long, all sharp.

A small window centered in the bookcase was sandwiched between the novel *The Collector* and the book *Principles of War*.

The window's dimensions were one foot by eighteen inches, and nothing could be seen beyond it.

Irene thought, no windows on the outside of the structure. *Why a window inside?*

On a shelf was a Starlight Scope on a tripod. The military sniper scope amplified moonlight or starlight reflecting off an object, magnifying the light fifty thousand times. At that degree of enhancement, a votive candle a half-mile away looked like the sun.

Thumbtacked to the left-hand wall were twenty-one photographs of women, all in stages of undress. They were all young, mostly teenagers.

Irene thought, these are candids of women in the act of undressing.

But they weren't actually women, just *girls*. Where were these taken? No telling. Not enough clues.

The background in nineteen of the photos was outdoors. The remaining two had an unusual background: wallpaper depicting scenes from nursery tales—Little Bo Peep, Jack and Jill, Billy Goat Gruff.

Irene said to Eisenmann, "I think I know where those were taken."

"Call it in to S.F. and have someone check it out."

Irene said, "Would you do it for me, Tom? I want to check something else out."

She felt a stab in her stomach. Possibly twenty-one more.

She again paced the outside of the bunker. Then she paced the inside.

Eisenmann returned and said, "I called your idea in to Missing Persons."

Irene interrupted him. "There's still something's wrong with the size of this bunker. I paced the outside dimensions. There's still about three by eight feet missing."

The missing space was behind the area of the interior window. But Eisenmann and Brunn could see nothing in the pitch black of the window. Their flashlights reflected an eerie glare off the pane.

"Look at the window caulking," Irene said, "I know that stuff, it's soundproofing." She tapped the window pane. "Hear that? That's not single-paned glass, and I don't think it's double paned either. At least triple-paned. If you were on the other side of this window, you couldn't hear a five-K generator roaring in here."

Irene went outside. The lab crew from San Francisco was unpacking their equipment from a van. She asked permission to find a way into the hidden room in the bunker.

Sheriff Ballard decided, "This mystery will have to wait until the lab does their stuff on all the property. That won't be until tomorrow."

Sheriff Ballard introduced the San Francisco lab crew, which was made up of two men and a woman, to his own staff. He said, "I want an impeccable chain of custody on anything discovered. I want intense protection of evidence, no alterations. There will be no negligence or accidents on this crime scene. One of you will take full responsibility for transporting what's found from here to my desk. You all know what we suspect happened here. Fingerprints could be vital in establishing identifications."

The lab crew went to work on the bunker.

The crime scene technician put on plastic gloves. He found a fingerprint on the window. Using a brush, he dusted the surface lightly and stepped back.

Irene photographed the print. She took out the photo, signed the back, dated it, marked the location of where the shot was made, and put it in a manila envelope.

She took it to Ballard.

Ballard sat at his outdoor desk and peered through a microscope at the first print taken. "Looks like an adult's," he said. "The ridges are too far apart to be a child's. I'd guess, left hand, forefinger."

Lt. Bunning said, "I'll call the Marines at El Toro and have them send a copy of both Lake's and Ng's fingerprints."

"Have them send Ng's military file."

"Will do. Is that print any good?"

"This is a full, clear print."

Another fingerprint was found in the bunker. The lab technician used cellulose tape to remove this one. The tape went through the same procedure: photographed, dated, signed, then sent to Ballard's desk.

Other prints were found on the window glass. Their patterns indicated two hands had leaned up against the window. Even palm prints were visible.

These samples made their way to Ballard's desk. He ordered Irene to get fingerprints from as many of the suspected missing persons files as she could. "And get another table set up. Every law enforcement agency in the state will be sending us their missing persons files."

Wednesday, June 5, 1985, 2:00 p.m., Federal Building, San Francisco

San Francisco Detective Ed Erdelatz entered the FBI offices on the seventh floor.

He rubbed a hand over his two-day stubble of beard. His was a well-known name in the city, and his own career in high-profile cases had brought him to the feds many times before.

The conference room of the FBI soon began bustling with agents.

Erdelatz spread his papers on the lectern. Special Agent Karen Alexander joined him.

Erdelatz said, "We have a fugitive from a capital case."

Karen added, "His name is Charles Chitat Ng. We've already notified Interpol, but we think we have him confined to the States. He boarded a flight from SFO to Chicago."

Erdelatz went to a chalk board. He drew six small circles on it in a horizontal row, labeling them "Hong Kong," "Hawaii," "Yorkshire," "Calgary," "Toronto," and "Chicago."

He tapped the chalk on the board. "Ng's father lives in Hong Kong. He's a wealthy businessman. Ng has ex-Marine friends in Hawaii. He has an uncle in Yorkshire. He has sisters in Calgary and Toronto. Yet he ran to Chicago. We've kept a good lid on this. So far, the papers aren't on to it. Ng may think we're doing nothing."

"When was Ng in England?"

"Ng went to prep school there in the seventies. One of you will have to touch base with Scotland Yard. I'll provide any information we have. Ng's father trades with all the Commonwealth countries. This is going to be a worldwide search."

Wednesday, June 5, 1985, 2:00 p.m., Blue Mountain Road, Calaveras County

The midday heat was oppressing. Evidence continued to mount on the examination tables.

Next to the driveway, what appeared to be two bones were found. They were taken to Coroner Terry Parker. He said, "I think one is a vertebra and the other comes from a leg, but I can't be entirely sure."

"What do you need?" Ballard asked.

"I don't have the equipment here to make a positive identification. Get someone to run these down to the Department of Justice crime lab in Stockton."

* * *

The second day of the investigation at the cabin was winding down. The results on the two bones that had been discovered were inconclusive. The Department of Justice in Stockton had not been able to confirm that they were human.

Lordan suggested using Doctor Boyd Stephens, the San Francisco chief medical examiner and coroner. He was called and said he would come the next day. He would make arrangements for any bones found to be transported back to the Bay Area, and San Francisco's more sophisticated equipment.

At first, the lab crew at the house didn't have any luck. There was a momentary round of excitement when they discovered a rust-covered spot, but, after performing tests microscopically, microchemically, and running a spectrographic analysis they learned that it was just that—a rust spot.

The lab crew examined the bullet hole in a wall of the main bedroom. They pulled out a .22 slug and sent it to the lab table.

Then, in the same room, they found a diary.

The spiral bound book was tied to the springs under the double bed. After the lab crew lifted prints and photographed it, Ballard took the diary to his command post and began to read.

Ballard's jaw dropped in revulsion as he read. It was written by Leonard Lake.

Unbelievable, the sheriff thought. That bastard had hunted, raped, and killed all these victims.

He decided to postpone reading the diary. Right now he had a job to get done, to push for more evidence. He looked out at his battlefield. The officers were working their way up the trench.

Ballard went to the trench.

Irene Brunn said, "We just found a camera in site one."

The sheriff said, "Tag it and have the film sent down for development. Make copies of the film and send them on to Erdelatz in the City."

She held up a metal logo—it read Suzuki.

"Tag it," Ballard said. He watched Eisenmann pick up a small photo. He was helping collection, packaging, sorting, transportation, and identification.

Ballard asked, "What have you got?"

"It appears to be a photo of a small white baby." Eisenmann flipped the photo over. "It's very deteriorated, but I can make out some writing on the back: Stephanie Jennie Carr, three and a half months, 7–81."

Sickened, the sheriff wondered, how many are buried here? And babies yet!

Years earlier, his county had been a sleepy retreat for rural folk and retirees.

He thought, *Has our home turned into a graveyard?*

Chapter 4

The Dungeon

Eisenmann and Brunn stood at the open doorway of the bunker. The lab crew had finished its work.

Brunn pointed at the interior window and said, "There's got to be a way in there."

Eisenmann said, "There are no trick doors outside. The exterior is solid concrete cinder block." As he talked, he led them into the now lighted room. He said, "In this room there are three walls made of concrete block and—"

"A floor-to-ceiling bookcase," Irene completed excitedly. "The same bookcase that has the interior window facing the missing space."

They looked along the edges of the bookcase. A spring release catch was found behind the first-aid kit. Eisenmann pulled the lever and the bookcase swung out.

There was a door behind the bookcase. It had two hinges and two throwbolts, both secured. He peered at the two hinges. "These appear to have been bent, then pounded back into shape."

The bolts were thrown, and the door swung open.

Eisenmann squeezed in and began measuring. The room was three feet, three inches wide, seven feet, six inches long, and six feet high.

Eisenmann studied the tiny room. There was a roll of toilet paper on one wall, a single shelf with a one-gallon plastic water container, a dirty

The Balazs cabin near Wilseyville, with its ominous bunker, became the center of a massive investigation in June, 1985, when missing persons were traced to Lake and Ng's stay here. (Mike Maloney/*San Francisco Chronicle*.)

towel, a can of air freshener, and a can of ant repellent. There was a narrow wooden bed with no pillow and no sheets.

The back of the door was painted the same gray color as the other three walls. Tiny air holes were punched out in a row along the top, six feet high. There was blocking on the other side of the air holes, a clever system that allowed air to flow, but damped out any light coming from the larger room. When the door and the bookcase were shut one got the feeling of being entombed. No light, no sound, no air movement.

The floor was concrete. There were no outlets for electricity. Eisenmann ran his hands along the walls. The texture of the concrete block was the same, even on the backside of the door. The only break to the monotony of the walls was a small mirror on the wall.

This was two-way glass; on the reverse side was the interior window.

He stepped out of the tiny enclosure. With the bookcase open, letting some light in, one could see through the window into the small enclosure.

He asked Irene to go into the small room.

Eisenmann swung the bookcase shut. He noticed a small button, partially hidden under the window frame.

He pushed it and heard Irene say, "On the wall. Someone's written: Cliff, P.O. Box 349."

Eisenmann thought, without a flashlight in there, I wouldn't be seeing anything. So what's the purpose of this two-way window?

He thought for a moment, then took the Starlight Scope off the bookshelf. He opened the bookcase and asked Irene to shut off her flashlight. He closed the bookcase.

Looking through the interior window with the Starlight Scope he saw the eerie, purplish-pink shape of Irene. Even with the powerful military scope, the interior was vague. Just gray, dreary dark walls. Like a small crypt, or a tomb.

How long, Eisenmann wondered, could a person stand being locked up in that room?

He'd read articles on sensory deprivation. No sound and no light quickly brought a person to the brink of insanity.

How long were people kept in there? This was worse than solitary confinement, where at least you had light, air, and noise.

How long could I last?

A day? A week? A month?

Then would I be willing to do anything, anything at all, to get out? What sort of depravity went on here?

The sun was setting fast over the valley beyond San Andreas. Sheriff Ballard returned to his office at the Calaveras Government Center. He sat behind his desk and took out a legal-sized piece of paper.

Organization, he thought, I need organization. Each department must be utilized for what it could best provide.

He penciled in "Office of Emergency Services." Underneath he wrote: Need mobile van with its workstations.

Next he wrote: C.A.R.D.A.—California Rescue Dogs Association.

He reached in his desk and pulled out a standard form from the FBI. For this type of case it listed several possible areas of help:

1. Branch assistance
2. Develop federal fugitive warrant

3. Coordinate and supervise international search
4. Performance of ballistic tests
5. Conduct out-of-state and international interviews
6. Behavioral science psychological profile

Ballard pondered, who else can I tap for help? He carefully wrote:

California Department of Justice (DOJ)
1. Latent prints
2. Criminalistic lab
3. Missing Persons unit
4. Personnel
5. Facilities for processing evidence
6. Forensic lab
7. BOCI homicide analysis unit

Who else? Sheriff Ballard thought. Manpower, I need manpower. And money—lots of money. This thing is going to cost a bundle and no way can Calaveras County, with its fewer than thirty thousand citizens, afford to pick up the tab.

To his list he added a dollar sign.

Ballard decided, if the need arose, to tap into the California Department of Forestry. The CDF could provide some extra equipment, prison labor, and, maybe most important, reports of smoke or fire not connected to a permit in the Wilseyville area during the past two years.

He didn't think the people building an incinerator on Blue Mountain Road had bothered to take out a permit. Why would they? It might just call attention to them.

Then again, maybe they took out permits to avoid attracting attention to the smoke.

Have to check it both ways.

He wrote in California Conservation Corps, for possible labor for evidence gathering. He glanced at his watch and left his office.

He felt tired, both mentally and physically. And it's just beginning, he thought.

He arrived at the crime site. A team from C.A.R.D.A. had arrived. The three dog handlers and their German shepherds lined up in front of him. The men were yawning, the dogs barking.

The sheriff said, "I want the dogs on leashes at all times. I want the search methodical. The dogs' quadrants will be twenty yards by twenty yards."

An hour later, the dog handlers reported to Ballard that nothing obvious was being found, a few dead birds and a decayed fox carcass.

Ballard gave permission for the heavy digging to begin. A back hoe was ordered from the county road management department.

Leonard Lake's mother, Gloria Eberling, arrived unexpectedly at the mountain property. Looking frazzled, she asked to see Eisenmann.

He led her to the command post, offered her a folding chair, and asked why she'd returned.

"I'm frightened." She clenched her hands together in twin, balled fists. "I visited my son last night. The doctor told me he's brain-dead."

"I'm sorry."

"I came here because I'm terrified. Nearly two years earlier, my other son, Donald, went off on a gambling trip to Reno. He never returned."

"You haven't heard or seen Donald in two years?"

"I know something terrible happened. He always wrote."

"Did he ever write his older brother?" Eisenmann asked.

"When Leonard was in Vietnam."

"Leonard skipped bail about the same time Donald disappeared. Did he ever push Donald for money?"

"Leonard would never hurt . . ."

Eisenmann watched her hands. During the entire interview they never moved, they remained in her lap, fiercely interlaced. He decided it wouldn't help to tell this woman what he thought, and what he was very sure she thought: Donald's *dead*. Another one on a growing list of potential victims.

He asked, "Did you or Claralyn remove anything from the house?"

"I didn't."

"Did Claralyn take anything?"

"She took about a dozen videotapes out of the master bedroom."

What! Eisenmann thought. He remembered Claralyn telling him that she and Lake made videotapes of their pornography, but she had stated that she hadn't found any. Now I learn she found about a dozen?

Gloria said, "The doctor asked me for my permission to stop Leonard's life support."

"Did you?"

"No."

"Are you going to?"

"I don't know," she said. "It's hard, he's my son. Donald's missing and now I'm supposed to let Leonard die?"

"If the doctors pronounced him brain-dead, then he really isn't—"

"But I saw him. He looks like he's sleeping. So peaceful."

Eisenmann glanced around. Law enforcement personnel were everywhere, shifting dirt and photographing, tagging and analyzing the garbage they found.

"So peaceful."

Thursday, June 6, 1985, 1:00 p.m., San Francisco

Attorney Ephraim Margolin stared out at the bustling scene in Union Square. Secretaries on their lunch break jammed the park benches alongside panhandlers.

Margolin was a defense attorney. He was a past president of the Trial Lawyers' Association of America, an expert on the Constitution of the United States.

He had just received a phone call from Garrick Lew. Lew was a criminal defense attorney for many unpopular clients. Lew had spent his adult life defending people who had nowhere else to turn.

Margolin pushed a stack of file folders to the side of his desk and tried to recall the people he knew in law enforcement—preferably at the top. He flipped through his Rolodex. A United States Attorney at the local FBI office had been the sheriff of Santa Clara County years ago. Now there was a man he could trust; he had worked scrupulously with him on a false arrest case. He called the San Francisco office of the FBI.

Margolin said, "I don't have any idea why the FBI is on this case. All I know is that they've put out bulletins that the man is armed and extremely dangerous. The man then calls his attorney from God knows where, and says 'Hey, the FBI is going to kill me on sight'. He's scared, his attorney told me so."

Margolin listened patiently, then said, "The point is this: the FBI must have picked up that phone call. They barged into the attorney's office and demanded to know where his client was calling from. The attorney is Garrick Lew, an old friend."

Ephraim had the shock of silver hair of a Leonard Bernstein or an Albert Einstein. It was no secret to those who met him in a courtroom that he liked to borrow from music or even quantum mechanics to make a point.

Ephraim said, "Lew represented this client in a misdemeanor case several years ago. Shoplifting, something like that. He's now claiming he's innocent and isn't armed or dangerous."

"Has the FBI called you?" the U.S. attorney asked.

"No."

"Give me the name of the fugitive."

"Capital N, small g. Pronounced *Ing*. Charles Ng."

"Common enough Chinese name. I presume they gave a description in the bulletin."

"That's another point. I think all they have is his name and nationality. And already they've put him on the Most Wanted list."

There was another long silence. Ephraim felt the wheels turning. He could visualize the attorney pulling up names on his screen. Margolin said, "All I want is to get the FBI out of my client's office."

"You're right. Even if Mr. Lew knew the origin of the call, he could hardly divulge it."

Margolin drew some arrows on his scratch pad as he listened. I'm missing something here, he thought. Why was the FBI in Garrick's office in the first place? Could the investigation be so serious that Lew was discovered from that old misdemeanor case, then his phone tapped?

He asked the attorney at the FBI, "Sounds to me that Ng is already on the FBI blotter for something else."

"I'll call it in for any federal offense, plus any time in a federal penitentiary."

Thursday, June 6, 1985, 2:00 p.m., Blue Mountain Road, Calaveras County

Doctor Boyd Stephens, the chief medical examiner and coroner of San Francisco, arrived at the site on Blue Mountain Road at the height of the afternoon heat. He unloaded equipment, then examined the two bones found the day before. He pronounced the vertebra and leg bone as *human*.

An administrative decision was immediately made that the San Francisco Missing Persons case be turned over to the Calaveras County Sheriff's Office as a homicide case.

One of the dog handlers found a four-inch bone. He marked the spot with a stake. The stake had a white flag on it, not unlike a miniature-golf flag. The flag was marked with an assigned number.

The dog handler carefully wrapped the bone in plastic and carried it back to the command center.

"What quadrant?" Ballard asked.

"Thirty-three."

The coroner examined the bone.

"Human," Ballard asked, "or animal?"

"Human," Stephens answered after peering through his microscope. "And almost totally decomposed. This bone has been sawed off at both ends. There is some soft tissue present. I'll remove it for toxicological analysis. We're going to need an anthropologist. I recommend Doctor Heglar, he's a specialist in forensic odontology."

"I'll phone him right away."

"I won't need him for a few days," the coroner said. "Anthropologists like bones bleached and clean."

"What do *you* need?"

"Get me a soil sample from where this bone was discovered. That'll give me a general idea of how long decomposition took."

Stephens examined the bone more closely. The upper half was a grayish-white, the lower half brownish-black. He said, "The different colors indicate that this was only partially buried. That's probably why the dog found it."

The photographer took pictures of the bone. When he was finished, the coroner removed the rest of the tissue from the bone. He wrote down the location on the bone where he had gotten each piece of tissue, tagged it, and put it in a plastic container. When he was finished, he immersed the bone in a dilute aqueous solution of trisodium phosphate and household detergent.

The bone would be soaked for two days. The solution would remove whatever remaining tissue still clung to it. Once clean, the bone would be odorless and left to bleach in the sun.

Deputy sheriffs Steve Mathews, Norman Varain, Larry Copland, and Ron McFall bore the brunt of uncovering evidence in the telephone trench that afternoon.

The deputies faced each other in squatting positions. A long line of officers worked the telephone line trench for a few minutes at a time, checking their discoveries with McFall and Copland. Irene Brunn joined them.

Larry Copland asked, "How long have you known Eisenmann?"

"Ten years," Irene answered.

"He's soft-spoken."

"He's seen a lot. You wouldn't know it, but he's the top authority on child abuse and child pornography in Northern California."

"Tough duty."

"He handles it: the snuff flicks, the multiple child molesters, the mothers who suffocate their babies to get them to stop crying, the fathers who lock their kids in the closet."

"How does he stand it?"

Irene watched Mathews pull a T-shirt out of the disturbed earth. He dusted it off. It had the words "Guardian Angels" on the back. Another shirt appeared out of the crumpled dirt. It had a National Medical Home Care patch on the shoulder. He pointed. Above the left pocket was stitched the name "Scott."

Copland repeated, "How does Eisenmann stand it?"

"He believes what he does is more important than any other type of police work."

"Even homicide?"

"*Especially* homicide, as Tom likes to say. The victim's relatives notwithstanding: for the victim, the crime is over. You're dead. Period. In all other cases, from petty burglary to wanton rape, the victims are still breathing, still hurting and suffering."

"I never thought of it that way."

"Most people don't. And who suffers the most? And potentially the longest? The little kids. The kids Tom Eisenmann has spent his life trying to protect."

"You like him a lot."

"I like the way he works, and I like his guts."

"Why's he working a Missing Persons case?"

"We all pull a general-caseload weekend shift once a month. Cosner's case happened on Tom's watch."

Irene watched Mathews and McFall hold a window screen horizontally. A deputy shoveled dirt onto the screen. The two sheriffs' deputies, like 49ers searching for gold nuggets, shook the window screen; dirt fell through and what remained was examined: teeth, small bones, buttons, and an occasional buckle. The items were tagged, put in plastic bags, and, with a log of the chain of evidence, sent to the table where they were catalogued.

A green plastic garbage bag was unearthed. In the bag was a receipt dated July 24, 1984 from Captain Video, a rental shop in San Francisco. The receipt was for two movies and made out to Harvey Dubs. In the same garbage bag was a letter addressed to Charlie Ng.

"This is incredible," Copland said. "Usually, you're lucky to find a clue once a week. We're turning up dozens with each shovelful." He held up a pinstriped shirt. The name "Scott" appeared again—over the right pocket.

Irene thought, the clothes and bones filtering out of the dirt sifting through the screens aren't just objects to be scrutinized as clues, they belonged to someone.

A man? A woman? A *child?*

In her original investigation involving the Dubs family she had seen a family portrait. The wife, Deborah, long hair draped over a shoulder, eyes twinkling, mouth smiling, was cradling her son, Sean. The husband, Harvey, wearing a Film Festival T-shirt, had his arm around her. His hair was tousled; his head bent close to his wife. He looked happy, content, in love.

Real people. A real family. Missing for months.

Were they here? Did the tooth that the deputy sheriff just tagged belong to one of the Dubs family?

Mathews and Copland found a floor mat in the carport. It was for a Honda automobile. This was tagged, signed, dated, and sent to San Francisco.

The lab crew finished its examination of the dungeon at the rear of the concrete bunker.

The load of armament found in the bunker on Wednesday morning was being itemized.

Eisenmann would examine a weapon, then methodically list the stats and serial number in his notebook. Pistols, automatics, rifles, shotguns, hunting knives, butcher knives, and switch blades were carefully itemized.

Irene Brunn pointed at the growing inventory of lethal weapons. She said, "It's nice to be prepared."

"For what," Eisenmann said, "World War Three?"

Chapter 5

The First Videotape

Thursday, June 6, 1985, 4:30 p.m., Blue Mountain Road, Calaveras County

An officer stumbled down the hillside, his eyes wide with excitement. "Where's Ballard? We've found two bodies."

Two skeletal remains had been discovered in the telephone trench. A crowd quickly gathered, but was ordered back to work by Sheriff Ballard. A stretcher was brought, and the first skeleton tagged and sent to the table where the coroners were working.

The Calaveras County coroner, Terry Parker, studied the grisly remains. With him was San Francisco Coroner Stephens.

Parker said, "This body's been badly burned."

Thursday, June 6, 1985, 8:00 p.m., South San Francisco

At Kaiser Permanente Hospital, Mrs. Gloria Eberling signed the release form. The physician turned off the life support system that had kept Leonard Lake's heart pumping.

The respirator and the intravenous tube swinging from the bedside stand were snapped from their holders by a nurse and dropped into plastic bags for disposal. The woman did not look at the body on the bed. When she finished turning off the instruments of survival she walked quickly from the room and nodded to a policeman.

The officer entered the hospital room and gathered personal belongings from the table next to the bed, recorded the time, and copied a few lines from the physician's report that was on the patient's clipboard.

He removed a camera from his briefcase, hovered over the lifeless face, and pressed the button. The flash bulb popped. The film developed slowly, revealing Leonard Lake's face, captured in color, three minutes after his death.

Friday, June 7, 1985, 6:00 a.m., Leeds, England

The London train pulled into Leeds, Yorkshire. The Scotland Yard Inspector was on his way to interview Charlie Ng's former headmaster.

Tea was ready when the headmaster received the policeman, who asked, "The Yard did call and bring you up on why I'm here?"

"Yes," the headmaster said. "I do not want the school's name mentioned. The tabloids would—"

"We're not looking for Ng here. Just leads. His sister attended school here also?"

"Yes."

"Do you have any idea where she went after graduating?"

"Why don't you ask her uncle?"

"Her uncle? And Ng's uncle?"

"Of course, he teaches here."

Doctor Rufus Good was summoned. The Scotland Yard Inspector asked, "You're Charlie Chitat Ng's uncle?"

"Yes."

"Your last name is Good."

"Ng's father married my sister. What's going on?" Doctor Good learned what was happening and said, "That's why I had Charlie expelled from here."

"You expelled him?"

"Charlie demonstrated antisocial behavior very early in life. He developed a morbid fascination with cruelty. He drew pictures of women that made them look like mechanical robots with exaggerated sexual features. He came from a wealthy family, yet he constantly stole. An incident here at school, involving theft from a fellow student, was why I had him dismissed."

"Intelligent?"

"Very. Charlie cannot accept the world realistically, yet he knows the difference between right and wrong."

"We know Charlie has two sisters living in Canada. His father has business interests in Quebec, Toronto, Vancouver, and Calgary. The Bureau told us they've run checks on all four cities. Many Ngs, none related to Charlie."

"Easily explained. Charlie's sisters have married. They no longer use their maiden names."

Friday, June 7, 1985, 7:30 a.m., Blue Mountain Road, Calaveras County

Sheriff Ballard handed out his permanent assignments. Deputy sheriffs Mathews and Copland would run the crime scene. Mathews would process evidence from inside the residence; Copland would do the same for the bunker. Both men would oversee the fire pits and trenches.

Doctor Stephens had forbidden the back hoe to be used on the trench. He was worried about damaging the charred bones and fine bone fragments already located there. If there was more, he wanted them intact.

The back hoe would be used to excavate the ten-foot diameter of disturbed ground next to the bunker. When the cinder block structure was built, the bank was dug out. This dirt was back filled against the concrete building.

In that pit, articles of clothing had already been discovered. Parts of cloth had been above ground. Investigators merely had to tug on them and they came away intact.

* * *

Tom Eisenmann hung up the phone and muttered, "Incredible."

Irene asked, "What is?"

"Captain Philpott remembered a case, when he was head of Vice. A prostitute filed a complaint. She said a man hired her as an escort. He took her out to dinner. Then he took her to a motel in Sausalito. She went to the bathroom and opened the door. A naked Chinese man was standing there holding a knife. He raped her while," Eisenmann peered at his notes, "'all the time stabbing a knife into the mattress close to her head. The other man took photographs.'"

"Lake and Ng."

"Yes. Philpott had the prostitute rounded up this morning. Half the men in the photos were Caucasian, and half were Chinese. She had no problem pointing Lake and Ng out. Lake told her that he did this all the time, but usually killed the women afterwards, but he liked her. He took her driver's license and said he knew where she lived, and if she told anyone, he was going to torture her to death."

"Sounds like business as usual."

* * *

Just before noon the big break came by accident, as so often happens. A man leaves a piece of bread to mold; a new vaccine is discovered. An apple falls and hits the right head; a new set of physical laws becomes part of the scientific universe.

A county road maintenance worker stood by the edge of the driveway leading to the cabin. He was supervising the movement of equipment, the back hoes and bulldozers; directing traffic, guiding the heavy machinery into a staging area.

Coroner Stephens wasn't letting the big stuff in yet, not while the meticulous search continued.

A DC 10 bulldozer lumbered up the road. The county road worker stepped out of its way and the ground gave way slightly under his feet. He thought nothing of it, until he stepped on the same spot again, and the ground depressed again. He called Deputy Norman Varain and Inspector Tom Eisenmann over. "There's something buried, right there."

"How do you know?"

The worker pressed his boot down on the spot, then lifted his boot. The ground flexed back. "Ground don't work that way. If you compact it, it stays compacted, it don't keep popping back up."

Using a small entrenching tool, Eisenmann and Varain carefully scraped away dirt. They uncovered a round, white, metal surface three inches under the ground. Working painstakingly, they dug around the object and finally unearthed a white, five-gallon container, with the lid sealed.

Eisenmann placed the can in a plastic bag and carried it to the Command Post. He could hear something rattling around inside.

Eisenmann gave Ballard the five-gallon bucket. The sheriff pried the lid off. Inside were wallets, rings, bracelets, necklaces, credit cards, driver's licenses, and two unlabeled videotapes and a third video marked "M. Ladies Kathy/Brenda."

Ballard held up the videos and said, "What the hell?"

A deputy sheriff said, "I have a VCR at my house."

"Get it, and a TV."

Ballard began itemizing the rest of the contents of the pail. There was a checkbook with the name Scott Stapley on the checks. The address was 4755 Felton, Apartment 4, San Diego. Inside the checkbook was a Food Mart card with Stapley's name on it. Also inside the pail was a still photo of a dark-haired woman.

The sheriff said, "Someone make copies of this. We're going to need them to attempt identification on this woman."

The deputy returned with the VCR and TV. He asked, "Do you want this set up in the house?"

"No, the lab hasn't had time to go over it yet. Put your stuff at the cabin up the hill."

The nineteen-inch TV and VCR were hooked up.

County Sheriff Lt. Bob Bunning and Deputy Chief Joe Lordan watched the videotapes with Ballard.

Outside, police officers stood in a knot, speculating about what was on those tapes. The work around the site was at a standstill.

Sheriff Ballard left the cabin and called the entire task force together in front of Lake's cabin. He studied the mixed bag of uniforms, deputy sheriffs in green, the S.F. patrolmen in black, a variety of investigators in jeans and work shirts, the dog handlers in fatigues, coroners in butcher aprons, the pathologist in a suit.

The sheriff said, "I want the wasted energy and effort everyone is expending over the videotapes to stop."

"So let's see one."

"I am going to do just that."

They were suddenly a subdued, expectant crowd. They formed a semicircle around the TV.

Ballard held up a tape. He peered closely at it, then slid it into the VCR.

A dining room appeared on the screen. People sat on one side of a long table. It was a scene like the Last Supper, allowing the camera to pick up everyone's face.

Eisenmann recognized Leonard Lake, seated in the middle. Claralyn was on Lake's left; his mother, Gloria Eberling, on his right. It was soon learned from the conversation that two of the others present were Claralyn's parents, Louis and Grace Balazs.

A large turkey was in the center of the table, flanked by a ham, yams, mashed potatoes, cranberry, asparagus tips, and assorted white and red wines.

"What is this?" Irene asked.

Putting a finger to his lips, Sheriff Ballard pointed at the TV.

The assembled officers watched Lake and his extended family eat Easter dinner.

Lake said, "We're one step closer to a nuclear war."

"Why?"

"Those Reds are just itching to launch," Lake said, "I'll survive. You all know where to come when it happens."

"If it happens," Louis Balazs said, "I want to be at ground zero."

"Someone has to live, someone has to repopulate the earth."

Lake began to carve the turkey. He explained the inevitable coming of nuclear holocaust—the almost total destruction of the planet, and his future role as the new Adam. He explained how he intended to build a series of bunkers, each to house an Eve, the mothers of the new world order.

The videotape ended abruptly, the screen turning into a gray void.

"That's it?"

"Not quite," Ballard answered and shoved another tape into the VCR.

Leonard Lake appeared. He was sitting in a chair. He spoke like a talk show host. He talked about his fantasies: to kidnap a female and enslave her. She would take care of all his needs.

The screen turned snowy again.

"That's it?" was asked again.

"That's it," Ballard said. "Now will everyone get back to work: the real evidence is outside."

The officers filed out. Irene Brunn and Tom Eisenmann dawdled behind. When they were alone with Ballard, Eisenmann said, "I know why the sheriff showed those two tapes, to cut down on the speculation. But what's on the third tape?"

Ballard hesitated, "Tom, I know you found the tapes. I don't mind if you watch part of the third."

"Part?"

"Yes. Just to give you a flavor of what these two were up to."

Irene turned to the door.

Ballard said, "Stay, Irene. You two helped crack this mess." He stuck a tape into the VCR. The screen filled with snow, then cleared. A commercial broadcast appeared. The commercial ended. The screen went blank, then cleared, depicting a white woman sitting in a chair in what appeared to be the living room in the house on Blue Mountain Road.

The woman's hands were cuffed behind her.

A voice mumbled something, then became audible. "Money back, so to speak. Mike owes us. Unfortunately, he can't pay. Now we're going to give you a choice, Kathy, and this is probably the last choice that we're going to give you. You can go along with us, you can cooperate, you can do everything we tell you to do willingly, and in approximately thirty days, if you want a date to write on your calendar, the 15th of May, we will either drug you, blindfold you, or in some way or other make sure you don't know where you are and where you're going and take you back to the city and let you go. And what you say at that time, I don't care.

"My name you don't know. His name's Charlie, but screw it. You don't know where you are, and what you say, hopefully, can't hurt us, and by then, hopefully, Mike will have disappeared gracefully. Obviously, I'm telling you this because we'll have no control over what you say or how you say it once you're gone. If you don't cooperate with us, if you don't agree this evening, right now to cooperate with us, we'll probably put a round into your head and take you out and bury you in the same area that we buried Mike. We do this just because we admit we're scared, nervous.

"We never planned on fucking up, much less on getting caught, and we're not intending to get caught. It's the old no witnesses. It's a little crude, but that's where it's at. While you're here, you'll give us information on Mike in terms of his brother, bank accounts, who we need to write to make things correct. We'll probably have you write some letters to the guy that's storing his furniture, his step, or foster brother, whatever, telling him some bullshit story about how you and Mike have, uh, moved off to Timbuktu, and he's got a job doing this and that and doing something else and, basically, we want to phase Mike off, just sort of move him over the horizon, and, uh, let people know that, yeah, Mike moved off to God knows where, and we never heard from him again. That's semiacceptable. If anyone wonders, no one's going to wonder too hard.

"While you're here, we'll keep you busy. You'll wash for us, you'll clean for us, cook for us, you'll fuck for us. That's your choice in a nutshell. It's not much of a choice unless you've got a death wish."

The woman said, "No, I . . ." and her words trailed off.

Lake said, "Actually, Kathy, I like you. I didn't like lying to you. Whether you believe that or not, that's not important. The fairness of what we're doing is, uh, not up for debate. We're not worried about whether we're fair or whether we're good. We're just worried about ourselves.

Selfish bastards maybe. You'll probably think of worse names for us in the next four weeks, but that's where it's at.

"In the last twenty-four hours we've been tired, nervous, a little high strung, perhaps. We expect you to do something about that. Believe me, we both need it. If you go along with us, cooperate with us, we'll be as nice as we can to you within the limits of keeping you prisoner. If you don't go along with us, we'll probably take you into the bed, tie you down, rape you, shoot you, and bury you. Sorry, lady, time's up. Make your choice."

Kathy said, "Well, I have to be available."

"Spell it out for us on tape," Lake said. "I want to hear it from your own lips."

"I can't spell it out. I'll go along with whatever you want."

Lake said, "That's all we wanted to hear. Mike was an ass."

Kathy mumbled.

Lake nodded his head. "I understand. Either he lied to you or you lied to us. You can believe this or you don't have to believe it. It has nothing to do with anything. Mike was getting ready to drop you, so he said. He said you were clinging on to him, asking things of him that he didn't want.

"Today, was it today? Yesterday? He had some woman in the motel giving him a blow job. Again, this is what he said. Whether it's true or not, I don't know. He could have been lying to us."

Kathy mumbled.

"OK," Lake said. "Then maybe he just liked to talk big. He thought he was impressing us. He wasn't. He was disgusting us. But for whatever reason. Do you have keys for her cuffs?"

A high timbered voice offstage said, "Uh huh."

On the screen Lake began putting leg irons on Kathy's feet, then removed the handcuffs.

"Stand up, Kathy," Lake ordered. "If we're a little clumsy at this, forgive us. Stay on your feet. Undress for us. We want to see what we bought."

"Undress for you?"

"Take your blouse off. Take your bra off. They're not all that bad. Take your jeans off."

The voice offstage said, "Take her pants off." And then a shadow appeared on the screen. The man moved into the light.

Ballard said, "That's Charlie Ng."

Lake moved beside Ng. The two men studied Kathy. Lake said, "We'll run it through the shower."

"Should I go, too?" Ng asked.

"No," Lake said. "Oh, you want to take a shower with us? If you want to. Sit down, Kathy."

Ng said, "This is surprisingly cooperative."

Lake said, "Wisely cooperative, Charlie. We're prepared to do practically anything to get you to agree with us. I'm glad you've, uh, made all of that unnecessary. But a few ground rules, Kathy. We're real serious about this. Do what you're told, cooperate with us, and there won't be any problems. If you create any problems whatsoever, you could very well die."

Charlie Ng said, "Keep undressing, please. The piece is on the table."

Lake said, "I see it."

Ng said, "You didn't get the shower . . . time limits."

"No," Lake said, "I tried. Keep going."

Kathy fumbled with the buttons on her clothes. "Excuse me for being shy."

Lake said, "I can understand, but don't be shy. You're going to take a shower."

Ng added, "This won't be the first time. It won't be the last time."

"Don't make it hard for her, Charlie. Kathy, undress, please."

Kathy muttered, "Yeah."

"Panties, too," Lake said. "Kathy, I don't want to have to make an example of what we need to do to make you cooperate."

"I realize that."

"Then please cooperate. Go ahead, Charlie."

Ng muttered something.

Kathy mumbled something.

Lake said clearly, "When you get out put these slippers outside the—"

The TV screen went to snow.

Irene asked, "Is it over, I hope?"

"No," Ballard answered, "A bit more on Kathy."

The TV screen cleared. A bedroom. It showed a black-haired Asian on a bed with a white female sitting on his back. She began rubbing some sort of lotion on him. He then lifted his head and was easily identified as Charles Ng. He said, "Don't forget to . . . get my ass, too."

Once again the TV turned to snow.

Eisenmann asked, "Now is it over?"

Ballard answered, "Still a bit more on Kathy."

The TV screen cleared. An advertisement for a motel appeared. Abruptly, the scene cut to a bedroom. The background identified the location as the bedroom at the Wilseyville house.

Kathy Allen was strapped to the bed. Lake began taking photographs of her.

Lake said, "Not bad. Anyway, uh, I very much intended to keep my promise, and I couldn't say that I have. I told you there's a lot of things I'd like to do with you that I know you wouldn't like. Would you look over here, please? And even though it shouldn't make any difference to me in terms of what you like and what you don't like, I've tried to, I don't know, respect your feelings as best I can in these matters. On the other hand, when I tell you to do things, I tell you things that are very important to me that I want you to do.

"Can you, uh, turn, your head far enough around? Yeah, that's it. Just lay on the bed if you want. I really want you, or expect you, as a matter of fact, to do them. And, uh, you haven't, you didn't."

Kathy asked, "What haven't I done?"

"I'm referring to, uh, me telling you not to beat . . ."

"Oh, geez."

". . . to beat on the doors and make noise." Lake stepped over to the bureau and picked up a set of keys.

Kathy pleaded, "I didn't beat on it. It's just—"

"I'm afraid you did beat on it. Those latches were especially picked. Well, I don't know if you beat or pushed or whatever, but, picked because the metal, well, it would never break. It's relatively soft, and they were hammered out, well, yeah, they were hammered out flat, and now they're bent, so you must have put an immense amount of pressure, well, at least a fair amount of pressure on the door. This leaves me somewhat disturbed, and I realize no one heard you and probably if anyone had been around they wouldn't have heard you anyway, but, um, I showed you those cyanide pills, and I'm trying to tell you the truth when I showed you those, that they're never going to take me alive.

"Hopefully, no one's ever going to catch me at these weird things, but if someone ever did, um, I'd die. The fact that you'd die is immaterial right now. I don't want you to die, and I don't want me to die, and the best way to accomplish that is for neither one of us to get caught. So, I suppose my question is what do I do to prove to you that I'm serious about this? Furthermore, what can I do to you—"

"Are you asking me if you can hit me?"

"No, I'm not asking you if I can hit you. I can very much hit you, very easily. The fact that you can get out of these things is not going to stop us. I don't want to hit you, Kathy. Let me take this back. Erotically it would turn me on. I would get a great thrill out of it, but, but let's say I'm still trying to keep a little bit of your sanity, OK?

"I'm having a little war within myself, between what I want to do and what I think I should do, because I promised you I would, and what we might call is the decent thing to do. And, for the moment, the decent thing to do is, uh, rest. But I'm going to go hammer those hinges back flat again, and I don't want to find them bent again at all. I don't want to hear anything. Let me put this in the strongest possible terms. It was like the first night when I told you I wanted you to drink me. If it ever arises again, if there's any circumstance whatsoever that leads me to think that you're even attempting to make noises, immaterial as to whether I hear you or anyone else hears you, you'll be whipped very severely. Now tell me you understand."

"I understand."

"OK. Good. Some girls are into pain, Kathy, and I don't think you're one of them. If you were, I wouldn't feel so guilty about yielding to my lesser impulses. It's the fact that you're partially a stranger, that you don't know my name, and that you're going to go away, and I'm never going to have to deal with you again, unfortunately for you, you and me . . . What did I do with that other thing? Rats! That I can even talk to you like this. Needless to say, the, uh, common person on the street I, uh, don't confess my, uh, sadistic tendencies to. I don't know if you're flattered or not. There's no reason you should be. But, uh, if nothing else, I'm being honest with you. Oh, screw it. Can you, uh, take those straps off by yourself?"

"I think, yeah."

"Are they binding, tight?"

"That one's cutting off my circulation."

"OK," Lake said. "Take off your jeans and put these and this on." He gave her lingerie. "Take off the red panties, too."

She started to comply.

Lake said, "These are tight."

"Huh?" Kathy said. "Around the leg. The waist is still big. There's plenty of room. It's I have heavy hips and heavy legs. Now, how do you find, figure out which way's up? The elastic part's up . . ."

Lake snapped a couple of pictures and said in a rambling voice, "My first girl friend. I actually first met her when she was three years old. I was nineteen at the time and visiting her house. She got up at some ridiculous hour, and I took her out to play, but, of course, she was naked as a puppy when she came running into the room, so I put what I thought were her clothes on and let her go outside."

Kathy asked, "Is this inside out?"

Lake mumbled something, then said, "When she got back, though, her mother gave me this big lecture, and it seems that I had done everything wrong. I put her panties on backwards. I didn't know they had a front and back, and I put her shirt on backwards. I thought her shirts were like my shirts that buttoned in the front. Hers buttoned in the back. I put white trousers on her, which evidently is nothing to put on a three-year-old girl to let her go outside and play. In general, I blew it. OK, hop on the bed please. And I didn't see her again for twenty years, and, my, what twenty years will do for a three-year-old.

"I know you're not trying to do anything foolish, like smile, but you have such a pretty face that even when you're not smiling, you have sort of a sultry look about you, but, uh, well, the guys would find very attractive. OK. Take that off. There's only two more pictures, by the way, then I'll start playing this game, go out and have a cigarette. Notice I haven't done any full nudes."

Kathy said, "Uh huh."

"Personally, I don't find full nudes very attractive. I think a woman should always . . ."

"They don't leave nothing for the imagination."

"Right," Lake said and took another picture. "Yes, I agree, completely. Well, actually, I've done full nudes before, but . . . your pants. Some of the stuff I've just acquired. Try this on. It may actually fit you. It's small."

"It probably will."

"And . . ."

". . . Problem."

"That's all right."

". . . Years of practice."

"Experience," Lake said, "Yes . . . There, it's OK. Try to put this on. You told me awhile back that you were religious. Are you still so?"

Kathy put on new lingerie. She said, "That's what you heard me saying in the bathroom this morning when you walked in. Did you notice I was kind of mumbling?"

"Oh, yes. In fact that's what I went in to check on you for. I thought you were working up for a kamikaze wrist slash, and I was going to tell you not to."

"No, I was saying my morning prayer . . ."

"Jump in bed," Lake ordered. "Sit, please. Look at me."

Lake fiddled with a camera. He said, "Not a very flexible tripod. OK, stay there. OK, take your bra off."

She did as she was told.

Lake snapped a picture and asked, "Do you ever wear bras that fasten in the front?"

"Yeah, I used to. This one's kind of tricky though."

Lake asked, "Can I help?"

"Yeah, well, I don't know. It's got a little string that's stuck right now."

"OK," Lake said. "Put your legs out in front of you. Sit on the bed rather than lean on the bed. There you go. That's it. Lean back slightly."

He snapped a few more shots. "I should have these photos, well, obviously, I'll have these photos before you leave, whatever it's worth. You can see them. There you go. OK. Get your clothes on, get um, whatever you have to do to get ready to go outside, 'cause that's where you're going next."

Kathy put on her jeans.

Lake said, "Tell me, Kathy, you've given up smoking for four days or however long you've been here. Wouldn't this be a nice opportunity just to . . ."

Kathy said, "That's why I shake a lot. It's the nicotine that I want."

"Right. And what happens if you don't get it for a month or two? After a while you'll stop shaking."

"Yeah, I'll just quit, but I don't want to quit. It's not something I want to do."

"OK. I just want you to know that I'm giving this stuff to you under protest. Not that we care, mind you, but . . ."

Once again the screen went snowy.

Ballard pushed a button on the remote and the screen went blank. "That's it."

"You mean for now," Eisenmann said. "There were two names on that tape when I found it: Kathy *and* Brenda."

"Later, Tom, later."

Irene and Tom turned to go. Eisenmann paused, then asked in a quiet voice, "Sheriff, is the other half a snuff flick?"

Chapter 6

Bodies and a Diary

**Friday, June 7, 1985, Noon, Blue Mountain Road,
Calaveras County**

The incinerator that squatted by the concrete bunker had not been examined yet. The inside of the cinder block structure and its secret cell had taken priority.

The lab crew began work on the incinerator. The steel hatch was dusted for prints. The results were taken to Sheriff Ballard.

Next, the lab crew took samples of the fine powder in the bottom of the fire pit. The samples were put into glass jars, sealed, and sent on for microexamination at the sophisticated facilities in San Francisco. Samples were also forwarded to the FBI and the other law enforcement agencies.

Ballard asked, "Anything?"

The technician shrugged, "I doubt it. Whatever was burned in that thing was cooked at extremely high temperatures. But you never know. I'm looking at it with the naked eye, not a fifty thousand dollar microscope."

**Friday, June 7, 1985, 1:30 p.m., 136 Lennox Way,
San Francisco**

Having secured a search warrant for Charlie Ng's residence from Judge Phillip Moscone of the Municipal Court, Police Officer Jerome DeFillipo entered the premises. He began a careful search.

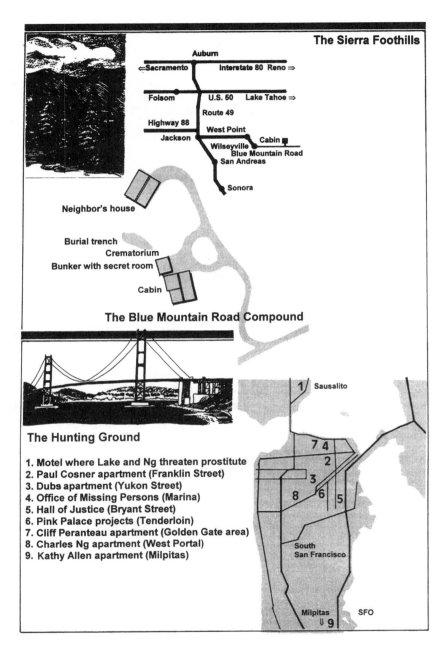

The Sierra Foothills

Auburn
⇐Sacramento   Interstate 80 Reno ⇒
Folsom   U.S. 50   Lake Tahoe ⇒
Route 49
Highway 88   West Point
Jackson   Wilseyville   Cabin ■
Blue Mountain Road
San Andreas
Sonora

Neighbor's house

Burial trench
Crematorium
Bunker with secret room
Cabin

The Blue Mountain Road Compound

The Hunting Ground

1. Motel where Lake and Ng threaten prostitute
2. Paul Cosner apartment (Franklin Street)
3. Dubs apartment (Yukon Street)
4. Office of Missing Persons (Marina)
5. Hall of Justice (Bryant Street)
6. Pink Palace projects (Tenderloin)
7. Cliff Peranteau apartment (Golden Gate area)
8. Charles Ng apartment (West Portal)
9. Kathy Allen apartment (Milpitas)

Sausalito

South
San Francisco

Milpitas   SFO

San Francisco Bay Area: Overview and index to various locales.

By the bed, in a letter rack on the floor, he found two street maps of San Francisco. On one he noticed that a red circle had been drawn around Yukon Street. He found a G.E. VHS connected to the TV. This was compared to the list containing the missing property from the Dubs residence. The G.E. VHS was listed as stolen.

In the top center of a black desk located on the south wall of the apartment was an envelope containing a First Interstate Bank credit card issued to Lonnie Bond.

The envelope with the credit card in it was partially torn. It was addressed to a Mr. Abe and Ms. Marsha, the cowardly Labradors. In the torn corner were the letters e–l–t–o–n, Number 4, and a zip code—92116.

He found another envelope. Inside was a check from the Dennis Moving Services, Suite 806, 16 California Street, San Francisco. The check was made out to Charlie Ng.

Officer DeFillipo found a photo album. Inside were pictures of a concrete building under construction and photos of Leonard Lake.

The officer found a Cross pen-and-pencil set with the initials C.R.P. monogrammed on it.

Officer DeFillipo found a box under a desk. Inside were videotapes. Some were labeled: KQED, KSAN, McCartney interview 20/20, Roberto Duran versus Sugar Ray Leonard, and TV Guide, 25 years, 10/79.

Two more tapes were labeled "Taboo" and "Vice Squad."

DeFillipo didn't have authority to play the tapes. He labeled them, signed the chain of evidence line on the manila envelope, and turned it into the San Francisco property room.

Friday, June 7, 1985, 2:00 p.m., Blue Mountain Road, Calaveras County

Ballard sat at his makeshift desk outside the mountain house. Leonard Lake's diary was in front of him. He opened it and read: "I plan to build a prison for sex slaves. It will provide a facility for my sexual fantasies. It will provide physical security for myself and my passions. It will protect me from nuclear fallout.

"The perfect woman for me is one who is totally controlled, a woman who does exactly what she is told and nothing else.

"There are no sexual problems with a totally submissive woman, no frustrations, only pleasure and contentment."

* * *

Dr. Roger Heglar arrived. Scholarly in appearance, with piercing eyes, he was a biological and forensic anthropologist at San Francisco State University.

Sheriff Ballard shook hands and introduced him to Coroner Stephens.

Heglar waved toward the long line of officers who were sifting dirt and said, "This is bigger than some of the digs on the Gaza Strip."

"I wish the bones were as ancient."

"Let's get at it. I need large quantities of dirt from wherever bones are found. Don't put the samples in sealed containers, just open buckets. I want to see what kind of insect larvae and pupae are in this area. That will help when I get around to analyzing and dating the time of death from the bones."

Doctor Stephens said to Doctor Heglar, "You're early, the first bone's not even bleached yet."

"I've got prep work to perform before even looking at a bone. How many have you found?"

Ballard pointed to the table where Eisenmann and Brunn were working. "Hundreds."

"The skeletons are disarticulated?"

"So far, most have been sawed into two- to four-inch pieces."

"Makes it rough. I'm going to have to match up parts, very time consuming. I'm going to need a large area."

"Will do," Ballard said. Had the business at hand been different, he thought, the command post might look like a circus encampment. Huge tents had been erected with netting around them, necessitated by the mosquito problem.

But the atmosphere here was anything but festive. If anything a grim feeling pervaded the entire area. In the trench various items were being discovered: magazines, soup cans, a suitcase, paper articles, clothing, burned ash, a vacuum cleaner, toys, children's coats, jewelry, hair brushes, bones, teeth. Each had belonged to a man, woman, or child, someone's husband, wife, boyfriend, girlfriend, or precious baby.

Soon, a small sealed pail was found. Inside was an envelope with the return address of the Philo Motel. Also inside was employment identification in the name of Kathy Allen, who had worked for the Safeway store in Milpitas, California.

This information was relayed through the command post. Investigators on the San Francisco end would follow through on this evidence. They had to keep a certain professional distance from this ghoulish atmosphere to be effective.

A partial skull was found in the telephone trench. It was brought to the command center.

Coroner Stephens held out the skull, like Hamlet holding Yorick's, and noted, "The walls of the cranium are thin, might be a man's skull."

"Why?" Ballard asked.

"Because men are not thick-skulled. The walls of men's craniums are thinner than the walls of women's."

The coroner pointed at the roof of the cranium. "The ossification lines are saw edged, very pronounced."

Heglar peered into the cranium and read the suture lines like a tree surgeon reading the age of a tree. "The lines, plus indications on parts of the interior wall, lead me to say thirty to forty years old."

Ballard thought, Charlie Gunnar was thirty-six; Lake's brother, Donald, thirty-three; Harvey Dubs, twenty-nine; Paul Cosner, thirty-nine. Was the cranium that of one of those missing persons? Or someone else's?

Heglar asked the coroner, "Are you going to do superimposing?"

"Sure," Stephens said. "I have photographs of all the suspected missing persons connected to this site."

"And the teeth?"

"Of course teeth. I've already requested dental records on the same missing people."

Heglar peered at the jaw of the skull. "Crowns are in pretty good shape. I'll know who this joker is soon."

"Kind of irreverent," Ballard said.

Heglar looked surprised, then grinned sheepishly and said, "Sorry, I forgot what's going on here. In my line of work, the skulls usually belong to someone who died ten thousand years ago."

"Forget I said anything."

"You don't look so hot, Sheriff."

"I've been reading a diary."

"You keep a diary?"

"I'm reading someone else's."

"Whose?"

"A sadist's."

* * *

By late afternoon, Sheriff Claud Ballard decided it was time to call in more help. He called the California Conservation Corps headquarters in

Sacramento. The director said that it would have to be voluntary; he couldn't order young people to help in a search like this.

Twenty minutes later he called back and said, "I have ten teenagers for you; they'll be up in a couple of hours."

Fine, Ballard thought. He was sitting at his desk. The thermometer read 101. The air was heavy, oppressive. He tapped a finger on the diary in front of him.

Bits and pieces, he thought, that's all I can stand reading at a time.

The sheriff flipped open the journal and read: "I hired PP1, PP2, and PP3 today and brought them here.

"Operation Miranda: I plan to build a network of bunkers, to stock each with weapons and food. Each fallout shelter will have a woman, to cook, carry, and serve, and perform sexual services. After the day of holocaust arrives, after the nuclear bombs have rained from the sky, these women will become breeders, the future of the race is in my loins."

What did "PP 1," "2," and "3" mean? What did "Operation Miranda" mean? There was a place named Miranda on the Avenue of the Giants, north of Garberville on 101. And, of course, the Miranda decision, involving reading a person his rights before arrest.

Ballard thought, there's another Miranda, and linked to something I've seen since I've been here. I can't put my finger on it.

He tried to blank out his mind, so that wherever the information was stored could have a chance to rush to the surface. He thought, it'll come.

* * *

The lab crew, which had been working directly with the officers sifting dirt, was now finally ready to examine the house.

Kaiser Permanente Hospital had sent up a sample of Leonard Lake's blood. The Marines had given them Charlie Chitat Ng's blood type. The various Missing Persons Units involved—San Francisco, Calaveras, Humboldt, Mendocino, and San Diego—had sent up copies of their files; part of the information contained was each missing person's blood group and type.

The mattress in the master bedroom had already been examined. The bullet in the kitchen floor and the bullet in the living room wall were extracted. They were both .22 slugs. A section of the ceiling, dotted with small red stains, was removed.

* * *

In the stifling heat of the late afternoon, Ballard stood beside Terry Parker, the Calaveras coroner. The doctor examined one of the hundreds of small bones on the table.

Ballard asked, "Have you made an identification yet?"

"No, and if by some miracle I do, I'll tell you."

"Miracle?"

"Isn't it obvious, sheriff? The bodies were systematically hacked up. The bones were sawed, some with a hack saw, some with an electric skill saw. Look at this bone."

The ends of the bone were smooth, like a chain-sawed log.

The coroner said, "It's almost impossible to get any information from a bone this size. And the people who did this must have known it, otherwise why go to all the trouble?"

Ballard went back to his desk. Irene joined him. She said, "A police courier just gave me two manila envelopes. One's from the Marine base in El Toro, the other's from the San Francisco Police Department. Both contain Ng's background."

Ballard opened the Marine file and read, "Born: December 24, 1961. Christmas Eve! What a travesty."

"What's next?" Irene asked.

"Enlisted in Marines, October 12, 1979." Ballard remembered something Eisenmann had told him. He opened the S.F. file and placed it beside the Marine file. He read from the S.F. file, "In Sept. 1979, Ng lived in San Leandro, Alameda County. He drove into a telephone pole and left the scene. He was arrested for hit-and-run. Charge dropped after Ng's enlistment in the Marines. That's probably why he signed up." He continued reading, "Place of birth, Bloomington, Indiana."

"What?" Irene said. "The S.F. file states: place of birth, Hong Kong."

"Let's compare files. Marine file: family lives in Belmont, California."

"S.F. file: family scattered throughout Commonwealth."

"Marine file: high school education in Yorkshire, England."

"S.F. file: high school education in Yorkshire, England."

Ballard read, "On October 13, 1981: Ng robbed the Marine station armory at the Marine Corps Air Station at Kaneohe, on Oahu. He and three others stole two machine guns, three grenade launchers, a night-sighting scope, and seven pistols. Value: $11,406.00.

"Nov. 11, 1981. Ng went AWOL after being questioned over robbery. One of his accomplices led military police to the top of a hill and showed them where Ng buried the weapons.

Remains of victims were catalogued at the site for shipment to San Francisco for further tests to determine age and sex. (Mike Maloney/*San Francisco Chronicle.*)

"April 29, 1982. Ng arrested with Lake by an FBI SWAT team at Indian Creek Ranch Motel, in Philo, Mendocino County.

"Aug. 15, 1982. Ng convicted, sent to Leavenworth. Released June 29, 1984."

Irene held up the S.F. file and read, "Oct. 16, 1984. Ng charged with petty theft by Daly City police for shoplifting a fifty-dollar waterbed sheet from a Mervyns Department store.

"Oct. 17, 1984. Claralyn Balazs puts up $1,000 bail for Ng."

"What?" Ballard said. "Claralyn bails Ng out? When did she divorce Lake?"

Irene shuffled through the growing mountain of paper on the desk. She compared various dates. "October 17th was after she and Lake were divorced. On October 17th Lake had already skipped bail and was a fugitive living here in the mountains."

"How many people do you know who would post a thousand-dollar bail for you?"

"Most of my friends are cops, they're broke all the time."

"Were Claralyn and Ng sleeping together back on October 17, 1984. Last week? Ever? Three years ago?"

The volunteers from the California Conservation's Corps piled out of a truck. Renee Nolan came over and introduced herself to the sheriff as the trainees' leader.

Ballard directed her to Bob Bunning, who explained he wanted the crew to assist deputies in their inch-by-inch search of the property. They were going to crawl on their hands and knees, looking for bones.

Saturday, June 7, 1985, 9:00 a.m., San Francisco

The press finally pierced the security clamp on the case. Someone mentioned something to someone else and the news rippled out that there was something incredibly sordid and evil going on in the mountains. The press showed up, the news went out.

In *The San Francisco Chronicle,* Police Chief Con Murphy was quoted: "This may be a case of mass murder or a cult situation. Right now we don't know. A cult case is a possibility we're not going to exclude at this time."

Grace Balazs, Lake's ex-mother-in-law, was quoted: "I don't believe Lennie did anything. What kind of fool would someone have to be to burn bodies where you live?"

When asked about Ng, Grace said, "He just showed up one day to see Leonard. Lennie said he never met Ng before that day. I don't believe Lennie killed anybody. He wasn't that kind of person. . . . He loved animals. He was good to children."

* * *

The crime lab in San Francisco had viewed most of the tapes seized from Ng's residence on Lennox.

The tapes marked KQED and KSAN had been viewed. They were normal commercial TV programs. The Roberto Duran versus Sugar Ray Leonard was just that—a copy of the fight.

The tape labeled "Vice Squad" was started. One of the investigators shouted, "Wait a minute, play that back."

"What?" the projectionist said as he looked at the commercial TV program roll across the screen.

"There was something at the beginning—just a flash, that looked like it was shot unprofessionally."

The tape was rewound and started again. There was a picture of a woman sitting in a chair.

The tape was rewound, played, and frozen this time.

"We need to take this to the Department of Justice. Plus send still copies out to the various Missing Persons units involved."

The frozen image on the screen portrayed a woman chained to a chair.

The next video, "Taboo," was inserted. Again a brief flash of amateurish image came on before the commercial program started.

This time the half-second image showed a heavy-duty, construction-type bluish wheelbarrow.

The projectionist said, "That looks like a body in that wheelbarrow."

"In rigor."

"Full rigor, it's lying straight across the barrow. Full extension. It looks like it's wrapped in something."

"Yeah, some sort of plastic, like a garbage bag."

"Is that a second body next to the wheelbarrow?"

On the ground to the right of the wheelbarrow was a second form, definitely shaped like a human being. It also was covered in plastic.

San Francisco Detective Gary Hopper showed the observant clerk from the South San Francisco lumber yard a photo lineup. The clerk pointed at Ng's picture and said, "That's the man I saw shoplifting the vise."

The clerk signed the photo identification form with the number of the photo he picked, picture number four.

Saturday, June 7, 1985, 1:30 p.m., Blue Mountain Road, Calaveras County

The ten trainees from the California Conservation Corps were assigned to search a large slope covered with Mountain Misery. Mountain Misery is a small weed that flourishes throughout the Mother Lode. The plant, with tiny, fernlike leaves, is quite attractive. It gets its name from its ability to spread like a wild fire, not from its appearance.

Irene Brunn studied the group of CCC volunteers in front of her. Ballard had delegated her to warn them what was to come. She said, "This is a difficult task. Young people like yourselves have active enough imaginations, without this sort of thing. I want you to try and think that what you're searching for is evidence, not just bones. And that the evidence may help identify a missing person."

A teenager asked, "Why would anyone really want to know for sure a loved one is dead?"

"They do, believe me. The torture comes from not knowing. The dead can never be mentally laid to rest until the living know for sure. That's where the ancient ritual of a wake and an open casket comes from. We see, we know, we begin to heal."

"Why are we searching here?"

"Doctor Heglar, the anthropologist, noticed something. This whole slope has been recently fertilized. Now who would fertilize a plant like Mountain Misery?"

A CCC trainee said, "To cover something up?"

"Yes. And they should call this whole place Mountain Misery."

* * *

Eisenmann went to where Irene was sifting dirt and said, "Captain Philpott just called. The wallpaper at the South City Juvenile Hall matches exactly that in the background of two of the twenty-one photos found in the bunker. Plus, he found out that Claralyn works there as a teacher's assistant."

Irene said, "Is she here yet?"

"Not yet, she is being driven up this morning."

"Is Sheriff Ballard doing the—"

"Yes, he's doing the interrogation."

"This news should help."

Eisenmann went back to work. He added another entry to the long list of bones being brought from the area where the CCC workers were combing.

Ballard asked, "Want to take a break?"

Eisenmann stretched. "Do I ever."

"Not really a break. There's a mother and her teenager down at the barricade. She wants to make a statement."

Eisenmann walked down the road, learned it wasn't the mother who wanted to make a statement, but her child, Scott Mosher. He led them both to an area that had been set aside for just this purpose. A few comfortable chairs and a coffee table were under a stand of trees. Mosquito netting protected the area.

Scott Mosher was a good-looking fifteen-year-old. He said, "I answered an ad and—"

Eisenmann asked, "When?" Interviewing teenagers was tough. They had a tendency to blurt out everything as fast as they could, no matter how incoherent the statement sounded.

"Last January," Scott said. "I knew the man who ran the ad, he was called Charlie Gunnar. I saw his picture in the paper this morning, he's really Leonard Lake."

"What did he want?"

"He hired me to help him and his friend build a tool shed." Scott pointed at the fallout shelter. "I saw a carton by the project. It was marked 'one-way glass'."

"What happened next?"

"One day it rained. Lake said that instead of working we could watch a video. The tape was of women undressing. There were also nude men. I asked, 'can I go home now?' After I got home I cried. Those videos really shook me up. I can't get the images out of my mind."

Eisenmann thought, another of Lake's victims.

* * *

They found an intact corpse.

Sheriff Ballard paced around the autopsy table. He watched the doctor take samples from the body.

Coroner Parker said to the photographer, "Taking initial shots of bones is all that's usually required, but this is a full-fledged corpse. I need someone taking videos of what I do. Normally we'd do the postmortem at the hospital. There I have cameras to record what I do, but this is fieldwork."

Ballard said, "I have a camcorder in my vehicle."

The camcorder was set on a tripod and focused on the bloated body resting on the butcher paper on the table. Eisenmann and Brunn walked up and watched.

Coroner Parker said, "Chief, I finally have something to work with. Even though this body has been burned, I think I'll have our first identification very soon."

Parker removed a tape recorder from his briefcase and asked Sheriff Ballard, "What information do you want first?"

"Was the victim alive in the fire?"

"I think, because of what's going on here, we can rule out alcoholic intoxication, sedatives, poisonous drugs—"

Ballard interrupted, "Don't rule out anything."

"Then let's start with a surface-body search. There doesn't appear to be any antemortem burns, only postmortem. Antemortem trauma is destroyed if the fire continues for any length of time. If this body was burned in that incinerator beside the bunker, then—"

Eisenmann said, "If that corpse was burned in that incinerator you'd have only white powder and small fragmented bones left."

Parker pointed at the blackened hulk of the burned corpse. "That's edema and erythema. Doesn't that prove circulation? You can't have blood pumping in a corpse. Except, look at the vesicles. They're different than those formed by a live body."

Irene said, "I saw a body that looked like this once. It had been burned on a funeral pyre."

"Like a Viking?"

"Exactly. The part of the body on the flame cooks differently than the part facing away."

Eisenmann said, "So what's the answer? Was this body burned before, or after, it was dead?"

An exasperated Irene said, "Exactly. Give us something concrete."

"Concrete?" the doctor said.

"Evidence."

"Come back in a few hours. These things take time."

Two hours later Irene and Eisenmann returned. They asked the doctor what he had learned.

Parker said, "There's no thermal damage in the pharynx, or the epiglottis and the larynx. Which means he was dead when burned."

"He?"

"Yes, and also, I'm fairly certain, black. See the lower border of the nasal passage? We're not saying we're positive this is a black man, but at the very least of mixed origin."

* * *

Claralyn Balazs arrived at the property. Escorting her were two detectives with the San Francisco Police Department.

Ballard didn't waste time with any formalities. He knew what tack he wanted to take: right in her face. She had already been read her rights. He said, "What was on the twenty tapes you took from here?"

"I didn't take twenty."

I know, Ballard thought, I read Eisenmann's report, your ex-mother-in-law said about a dozen. He said, "How many did you take?"

"Twelve."

"You want us to believe that all twelve are of just you cavorting with Lake?"

"Yes, that's what's on them."

"Why did you drive up before us?"

"I told you, I wanted—"

"Why didn't you wait and come with us? You could have explained about the tapes. We could have had a woman, like Irene Brunn, view them. Your privacy would have been protected."

"I didn't think of that. Why are you treating me this way? You act like I did something."

"Did you?"

"No, I keep telling you—"

"We matched the background in two of the twenty-one photos we found. Those shots were taken at the South City Juvenile Center. Where you work. And yes, I think you did something."

"I want my lawyer."

"You've hired a lawyer?"

"Yes."

"Why?"

"I want immunity."

"From what? You said you didn't do anything."

"I'm not saying another word. I want to be taken back to San Francisco."

After she left, Ballard said, "Damn, I blew it."

"No, you didn't," Eisenmann said.

"No? Now she wants immunity."

"You tried the ramrod approach," Irene said, "and it didn't work. At least it saved time. I don't think any other interrogation tactic would have."

"Thanks," the sheriff said, "I'll have to think about it when I write my— Miranda!"

A pleased look flooded Ballard's face.

Irene asked, "Miranda?"

"I know why Lake called this place Operation Miranda. It's nothing to do with Miranda rights. It just clicked. I saw John Fowles's book, *The Collector*, on the bookcase the first time I went into the bunker. I thought nothing of it then."

"What's it mean?"

"You're not familiar with the novel?"

"No."

"It's the story of a butterfly collector, Ferdinand Clegg, who kidnaps a woman. He keeps her in the cellar. The entrance to the cellar is behind a false bookcase."

Irene asked, "So the woman's name was—"

"Miranda Grey."

"Nice bit of deduction, except it doesn't do us much good."

"It does me some good; trying to remember where I got that name has been driving me crazy."

Sunday, June 9, 1985, 6:00 a.m., Saint Joseph's Catholic Church, Calaveras County

Irene slipped into the rear pew. She was raised in a strict Hispanic household. She noticed a considerable number of other officers, both from San Francisco and Calaveras, throughout the church.

The priest started Mass.

Irene had been working twelve-hour shifts since Tuesday. She faced another one today, Sunday. It didn't seem right, going to that terrible place on the Sabbath.

The priest read the gospel, then said, "I know many of you here think that this should be a Requiem Mass, but I am saying the Mass of Resurrection."

Mass of *Resurrection?* Irene thought.

The priest said, "The shocking depravity that has hit our small community has brought us all to our knees. We are faced with the very essence of evil. But we are a community, and together we must work and pray to heal these terrible wounds. And the Christian message is a fierce one. We must even pray for murdering sadists."

Chapter 7

Corpses: Men, Women, Children

Sunday, June 9, 1985, 11:00 a.m., Greenwich Street, San Francisco

Captain Diarmund Philpott, head of San Francisco's Missing Persons Unit, was working on a Sunday.

Born in County Cork, Ireland, he had come to America as a young man. He had been with the police force for more than twenty years. His first assignment was walking a beat in Chinatown and he became the first non-Oriental officer in the City's history to learn the rudiments of the Chinese language.

Sifting through the papers on his desk, he found the Ng file was growing. Among the many weapons found in the bunker was a Ruger. A Ruger is a single-action revolver—based on the Western-style guns of the frontier days.

Investigators had traced the Ruger found in the bunker to the Accuracy Gun Shop located at 3651 University Avenue, San Diego, California. After checking his records, the owner stated, "On March 30, 1985, Robin Scott Stapley, apartment 4, Felton, San Diego, purchased a used Ruger, .22 caliber, semi-automatic pistol, serial number 12-70329."

But the real reason Philpott, a devoted Catholic, was working on the Sabbath was a phone call from Calaveras County. A new name had been added: Kathy Allen.

Investigators from San Francisco had contacted the Safeway Store in Milpitas. That lead had come from the envelope with the Philo Motel return address found in the telephone trench. Inside were items with Kathy Allen's name on them.

The investigators talked to Andrea Medrano, a fellow employee at the Safeway Store.

She stated, "The last time I saw Kathy was on April 14. She told me she had received a phone call that her boyfriend had been shot."

"Who's her boyfriend?"

"Mike Carroll. Kathy said she had to go up to Lake Tahoe because of this."

The investigators talked to James Baio, a friend of Kathy Allen's. He said that the last time he saw or talked to her was April 14. "She said she was going to Tahoe, that Mike was in trouble. I asked her to call me when she got there. She never called."

Investigators interviewed Monique Mavraedis, another coworker of Kathy's. She stated, "On the evening of the 14, 1985, at about 7:30 in the evening, Kathy Allen left with a man in a copperish-looking Honda automobile. The man had been waiting for her since about 5:30 or 6:00."

Investigators talked to John Gouveia, the foster brother of Mike Carroll. He told them that he had received a letter from Kathy Allen, Mike's girlfriend, stating that some people will be by to pick up Mike's property.

The investigators next checked with Pacific Bell. Phone records for the Wilseyville residence indicated that on April 14, 1985, just after 1:00 in the afternoon, a phone call was placed from that house to the Safeway Store in Milpitas, California.

Phone records revealed three more phone calls made to San Francisco: on April 14, at 4:19 in the afternoon; on April 15, at 7:42 in the evening; and again on April 15, at 7:57 in the evening. The first number was discovered to be the residence of Dennis Goza. The investigators learned that Mr. Goza was the owner of the Dennis Moving Service Company. The second two numbers were Mr. Goza's business phones.

The investigators interviewed Dennis Goza. Charlie Ng had been an employee of the moving company. Employment records revealed that Ng did not work on April 14, 15, or 16, 1985.

Of course, Captain Philpott thought, Ng was in the mountains.

Sunday, June 8, 1985, Noon, Blue Mountain Road, Calaveras County

Another intact body was unearthed in the telephone line trench. Fifteen minutes later there was a second one. One minute later, the corpse of a small child was discovered. Ten minutes later, a fourth one.

Coroner Terry Parker asked Ballard for more tables.

After a cursory inspection of the corpses, Ballard asked, "Anything?"

"I'm sorry to tell you, Sheriff, two are women, the third a child, the fourth, another black male."

Ballard went back to his desk. Ng's court-martial transcripts had arrived from Hawaii. The sheriff opened the thick file, and began making notes. A picture of Ng's life was emerging.

He read: Statement by Ng to a Navy Investigator, "While I was living with Lake, he and I shared an interest in weapons. He bought me a semi-automatic pistol. With my knowledge of weapons, I filed . . . to make it an automatic weapon. I also made a silencer from ordering parts from various catalogues. I asked Lake to get me an AR-15, which I wanted to convert into an M-16, and he did."

The Navy investigator asked, "Did Lake know you were a fugitive?"

"I told Lake that I had embarrassed the government in a big way, but nothing more."

Ballard flipped through the pages, scanning the text. He read: "A psychiatric evaluation of Ng was done during the court martial. He was pronounced sane.

"The investigating naval attorney said that Ng told him, 'I consider myself a good liar. They never know who you are. Your best friend is your best enemy. If you want to kill someone, make him think you like him, then it will be easy.'

"The Navy lawyer said Ng told him he put potassium cyanide in the salt shakers in the Marine mess hall, but no one got sick, and Ng couldn't figure out why not."

Semper fidelis, Ballard thought.

The sheriff read: "The attorney stated that Ng tried to kill a staff sergeant. He used a grenade launcher but it failed to detonate. Ng claimed to have blown up two cars, and said he enjoyed military operations, as long as he planned them.

"The Navy investigator asked, 'Why did you steal the weapons?'

"'I feel I am a born fighter, and I like to plan tactics and try to perform clandestine operations, so I was thinking I could be a good elite soldier. I was basically in charge of the execution. My main feeling is just to prove that I can do something nobody did before.'"

*   *   *

At the autopsy table, the San Francisco and Calaveras coroners worked on the four new cadavers. They stopped for lunch. Brunn, pitching in as a substitute photographer, snapped one more picture of the wound Heglar pointed out. Then she went in search of Eisenmann.

She couldn't wait to ask him a question that had been nagging her all morning. She found him and said, "Why didn't you arrest Claralyn yesterday?"

"For what?"

"Look at the evidence," Irene said. "She came here before us and took God knows what. What else do you need?"

"You forgot the credit cards."

"What credit cards?"

"Ballard told me this morning. Before driving Claralyn up here yesterday, she was interrogated in San Francisco. The fraud detail did a trace on all credit card charges on cards owned by missing persons. Claralyn's signature matches on two bills, both for meals at restaurants. She admitted to treating Ng and Lake, but said Lake gave her the cards."

"All this isn't enough for an arrest?"

"No. She turned over the twelve videotapes. They *were* homemade pornography of her and Lake."

"What about the two photos? She had to have let Lake into the juvenile center. Or else she took them herself. How else could he get photos with the nursery-rhyme wallpaper in the background?"

"She refuses to talk about that. But so what? We don't know who any of those women are yet, let alone if they're missing. Claralyn also said that Lake told her Ng killed a gay San Francisco disc jockey named Don Giulletti. Charlie was to go into the apartment and rob these two men and call Leonard, and Leonard was supposed to come. Charlie went into the apartment and ran into one of the men and got nervous with his gun and shot and killed one of the gay men."

"What about the other man?"

"Supposedly, Ng shot him, also, but the man didn't die. He recovered."

"An eye witness?"

"An eye witness. Lake also told Claralyn that he and Ng had discovered their neighbors, Robin Stapley; Lonnie Bond; his common-law wife Brenda O'Connor; and their child, Lonnie Bond, Jr., shot to death in the cabin next door. Lake claims they were cooking amphetamines over there and someone bumped them off for the cash and the drugs. Lake said he and Charlie disposed of the bodies by burning them Indian-style on top of some wooden, built-up thing and then they buried them. Leonard said he got rid of the bodies because he didn't want the police snooping around."

"Lake told her that," Irene said, "and she didn't say anything to us. Arrest her for withholding evidence and previous knowledge of a felony. We got her on conspiracy."

"I think her interrogators must have assured her that she was immune from any stuff she was aware of, but did not participate in."

Irene glanced around the area. The sun was filtering through the surrounding trees. A faint breeze had picked up, rustling leaves and branches. In the distance she heard the chirping of birds. Two squirrels chattered at each other.

Any idyllic beauty easily vanished as the workers persevered on their gruesome quest. The CCC trainees had covered almost half the slope filled with Mountain Misery.

Almost simultaneously, much was happening. The coroners were bent over a small corpse. Roger Heglar held a vial up toward the sun and stared at it. Dozens of officers dug in the telephone line trench. Sheriff Ballard sat at his command post poring over documents.

Brunn thought, this place looks like postwar Dachau.

Sunday, June 9, 1985, 1:30 p.m., Greenwich Street, San Francisco

Captain Philpott opened another file and read the report.

Ballistics expert Richard Grzybowski had examined Paul Cosner's car. He retrieved spent bullets from the headliner above the passenger seat and from the passenger door. Both were .22 caliber.

The sun visor found at the Wilseyville property had been forwarded to San Francisco. Grzybowski took the sun visor and placed it in its proper position in the Honda Prelude. The bullet hole in the sun visor and the bullet hole in the headliner matched up. The trajectory appeared to be the same.

Philpott put the file aside and opened another one.

Down the San Francisco Peninsula, investigators spoke to a George Blank. They tracked him down through the Wilseyville phone logs. Mr. Blank stated, "On April fourteenth, I received a phone call from Leonard Lake."

"Did you know Lake?"

"Yes, I did. Leonard asked me to pick up and repair a car. He said that a man named Charlie would be delivering the keys. Two days later, on April 16th, my two children, Deborah and Ryan, met an Asian man in his early twenties named Charlie at the bus station in San Jose. He gave my kids instructions on where to find the car and the keys. I went to the parking lot of the Safeway Store in Milpitas, California, and picked up a 1974 Mercury Capri."

"Do you know who the owner was?"

"The pink slip was registered to a Mike Carroll."

Monday, June 10, 1985, 10:00 a.m., Blue Mountain Road, Calaveras County

A Deputy sheriff told Eisenmann, "There's a private dick that wants to talk."

Eisenmann went to the barricade, met private detective Henry Meister, and led him to the interview area.

Meister showed his P.I. license. "For almost a year I've been searching for a Jeffrey Askren, of Sunnyvale. His parents live in Indiana. They're the ones who hired me. Jeffrey was an electronics engineer."

"What makes you believe that he's part of—"

"Let me finish. Fourteen months ago, Jeffrey told friends he was going on a photography excursion. He said he was first going to West Point, take some pictures, then stay at the Sutter Creek Hotel."

"He never arrived?"

"No, but he did make reservations. The sheriff's department found his locked car seven miles from where we're now sitting. The cops think his car got stuck in a snow bank. Remember, this was at the end of March, '84. They think he tried to walk out. One of them said that it happens once in a while, and the bodies always turn up when the snow melts."

"And Jeffrey didn't turn up when the snow melted?"

"No, he's never turned up. It may have gotten dark and he lost his way. He was not a camper, not wood-wise."

"Was he married?"

"I thought of that," Meister said. "Sometimes people just drop out. I talked to the people he worked with in Santa Clara, and I couldn't find a reason why this guy would drop out."

"You think he's here?"

"Yes, and the reason's really strange. His parents kept bugging me to get a psychic. Last November I hired Catherine Glashan, who lives in Sacramento. The scary part is, back then, six months ago, Catherine told me she felt Jeffrey had something to do with bones, and a married couple with a kid. She felt him calling, 'come and look for my body right now, I am not alone.'"

"What do you want from me?"

Meister opened a briefcase and gave Eisenmann a file. "This has Jeffrey's dental records, pictures, medical history, photographs, last—"

"Thank you," Eisenmann said, "I'll let you know immediately if we learn anything." He carried the file back to Ballard's desk and added it to the growing number of missing persons files that were coming in from all over the country.

* * *

The police had done a good job of keeping the lid on the case. But the local people were talking. The press found out. The police kept the early arrivals behind the yellow caution tape. But the crowd from the fourth estate was growing—and becoming restless.

Ballard asked Eisenmann to fill in for him at today's press conference.

Tom assembled the four dozen reporters in front of the Blue Mountain Road house and said, "As different evidence is uncovered, we bring in different specialists. Calaveras County has a fourteen-person force on the case. San Francisco has a three-man homicide team, a ten-man tactical investigation unit, two missing persons officers, a handwriting expert, and a link analyst."

"What's a link analyst?" a reporter asked.

"He links the victims to the suspects. We also have five special agents from the Department of Justice here. We have fingerprint experts, crime lab experts, forensic experts, pathology—"

"Why did you wait so long to inform the press?"

Eisenmann thought, here comes the old First Amendment Rights. "We were hoping to capture Ng. If he didn't know we had discovered anything, then—"

A stout reporter, with a full beard not unlike Leonard Lake's, interrupted with, "Maybe if we had run Ng's photo on the front page of the papers he'd be in custody now."

"You ran his photo on the front page of your papers Saturday and he's not in custody."

A female reporter shouted, "This case is being carried out with the speed of a snail."

Another reporter added, "A snail with a bowling ball tied to his tail."

Eisenmann flipped open his notebook. "You want an official opinion? Glen Craig, director of the Department of Justice's law enforcement division said this about the handling of this case. And I quote: 'There has been some criticism about slow movement, but you basically know who the suspects are. There's no point in trying to move so fast that you make mistakes that would damage any potential prosecution. It takes time to make a strategic plan. And I don't know of any evidence that's been destroyed or lost.'"

Friday, June 14, 1985, 11:00 a.m., Blue Mountain Road, Calaveras County

Another grueling week of work had passed by on the rural property.

People started to come forward with strange stories involving the property. Eisenmann escorted a woman, about fifty, plump, wearing a colorful peasant dress and a straw hat, to the interview area.

The woman settled into a chair. She kept unzipping and zipping her purse. She said, "I've been so worried since I read the papers."

Eisenmann asked, "Why are you worried?"

The woman opened her purse and pulled out a strand of pearls. "I'm worried about these."

Puzzled, Eisenmann examined the necklace, then gave it back to the woman. "Do you think they're fake?"

"No, but I bought them here."

"Here?" Eisenmann said.

"Here. I saw a notice at the Academy Club, that's a bar in West Point. The notice was on the bulletin board. It was for a yard sale, giving this address. I also bought a ring."

Eisenmann eyed the strand of pearls the woman was twisting nervously in her hand. He said, "A ring?"

"Yes."

"What about the pearls?"

"I bought them here a couple of months ago. At another yard sale. I thought the man's name was Charlie Gunnar, but when I heard on the—"

"How many times have you been here?"

The woman frowned, concentrating, then, "Six, maybe eight times. About once a month."

Eisenmann thought, Lake held yard sales to peddle the jewelry he took off his victims. He was selling the merchandise while standing on top of their graves.

The tormented woman said, "I don't know what to do. I keep thinking, these pearls might have belonged to one of those poor women who died here. I can't sleep at nights, and . . . I don't know why, but I feel guilty."

Transference, Eisenmann thought, and it caused heavy-duty guilt. He asked, "Are you religious?"

"Catholic."

"Make a donation to your parish church, light a candle to the Blessed Mother."

Saturday, June 15, 1985, Noon, San Francisco

Claralyn Balazs' attorney, Stan Pozanski, told the press, "We have decided before she makes any further comment she must be granted full state and federal immunity. In recent days, there have been death threats against our client."

Claralyn Balazs said, "I have cooperated with the police to the best of my ability. I wish to express my concern to the people affected by this situation."

Claralyn Cricket Balazs' other attorney, Chris Carroll, said, "The ball is now in the various agencies' courts. We will settle for nothing less than blanket immunity."

Saturday, June 15, 1985, 2:00 p.m., Blue Mountain Road, Calaveras County

Sheriff Ballard stood by the autopsy table. Coroner Parker pointed at a skull. There were tufts of hair popping out in a random pattern. "See the bullet hole."

The sheriff saw the small, circular hole, just behind where an ear once was.

Parker said, "One bullet, right behind the ear." The coroner bent down to within a few inches of the skull. "It looks like the size of a .22. Then it would just tumble around, smashing and tearing. No way would it have oomph to go all the way across the brain matter."

Ballard sighed and returned to his command post. Ten minutes later Doctor Parker stood in front of him. His hands were stuffed into his pockets. He was hunched slightly forward, peering over his wire-framed glasses.

"Yes?" Ballard asked.

"I've made an ID."

"Who?"

"Jacobson."

"Who?"

"Randy Jacobson."

Sheriff Ballard pawed through his files and found the inventory of identifications found in Paul Cosner's Honda Prelude. Under the front seat was a First Interstate Bankcard in the name of Randy Jacobson.

Parker said, "We got Randy Jacobson's fingerprints from S.F. Missing Persons. No question, the guy on our table with a bullet in his head is Randy Jacobson." He handed over the file.

Ballard read: "Randy Jacobson, white, thirty-five, Vietnam War veteran. Missing for six months. Last known address: The Pink Palace, San Francisco."

"Pink Palace," Parker said. "I know that place. It's a rundown project near the Haight–Ashbury District."

Ballard continued to read: "Two other residents of the Pink Palace, Maurice Rock, thirty-eight, and Cheryl Okoro, twenty-six, disappeared at the same time. An investigator learned from other residents of the housing unit that Lake frequently stayed there too. Last February, Lake hired the three people to finish a job he was working on in the mountains."

Three more. *Pink Palace.* Ballard rubbed his chin. There was a connection between the Pink Palace and three more bodies. Wait, he thought, it will come, just like the Miranda connection had come.

Sunday, June 16, 1985, 10:30 a.m., Father's Day

It was now two full weeks since the case broke. Criminal investigations the size of Blue Mountain Road's killing fields inevitably bog down. It was becoming compartmentalized. One officer did nothing but itemize, another sift dirt, another photograph.

Brunn remembered the two photos taken at the juvenile hall. Were any of them identified? Were any of them missing? She found Ballard by a flat bed truck. The truck was filled with evidence being shipped to San Francisco. She asked about the photos.

Ballard said, "You mean you haven't heard? The papers ran the photos. We've been able to identify seventeen of the twenty-one photos. And the wonderful news is, they've located all the women. All seventeen are alive and fine."

"Then why were the photos taken in the first place?"

"We'll find out; we're plowing our way through puzzle after puzzle. We'll learn everything in the end."

Irene thought, we have positive proof linking Paul Cosner, the three Dubses, Charlie Gunnar, Donald Lake, Robin Stapley, Randy Jacobson, Maurice Rock, Cheryl Okoro, Lonnie Bond, his common-law wife Brenda O'Connor, their kid, Lonnie Jr. to this place. And we have physical evidence, driver's licenses, credit cards, linking twelve more here, like Michael Carroll and his girlfriend Kathleen Allen.

She said, "Hopefully, we've already learned everything."

Ballard said, "Let me read you something from Leonard Lake's diary." He read, "Leonard Lake, a name not seen or used much these days. My second year as a fugitive, mostly dull day-to-day routine, still with death in my pocket and fantasy my major goal. I'm older, fatter, balder, and not much wiser. Interesting to see where I go from here. Hopefully, no one's ever going to catch me at these weird things, but if someone ever did . . . I will die."

Irene said, "Quick death was too good for him."

"Advocating bringing back some medieval torture?"

"Just fantasizing."

"About?"

"Crime and punishment. Lake got away with murder."

"Not if there's a heaven and hell."

Chapter 8

Evidence, and More Evidence

Wednesday, June 19, 1985, 10:00 a.m., Sacramento

Claralyn Balazs's attorneys requested blanket immunity in return for her full cooperation.

The petition was denied at all levels: federal, state, and county.

California State Attorney General John Van de Kamp said, "This is an overwhelming case, so enormous that systems, including computer access, have to be developed to deal with it. The problem is one of magnitude. You have to continue the investigation to find out how big it really is. This thing went from burglary to atrocities."

Sunday, June 23, 1985, 2:00 p.m., Central Standard Time, Toronto, Canada

The manhunt for Charlie Ng continued. Law enforcement representatives followed up reports from places throughout North America.

Ng's relative's houses in Toronto and Calgary were staked out.

Through a tip, Sergeant John Clarke of the Metropolitan Toronto Police, in a joint statement with the Royal Canadian Mounties, said, "Charlie Chitat Ng is hiding in one of the three Asian communities in our city."

Monday, June 24, 1985, 8:00 a.m., Blue Mountain Road, Calaveras County

Another grueling week had passed for the officers working the bizarre and unholy cemetery in California's Mother Lode. Using an infrared camera, the crime lab found a hot spot directly under the bunker.

"About six by six by six feet," the technician informed Ballard. "In the center, directly under the reinforced floor. We did a couple of core samples. That floor's made of rebar, wire mesh, and concrete."

"Tear it down."

"The whole bunker?"

"Yes, but get an architect here and have him sketch the layout. Have him build a miniature replica, and get Marlene to photograph every angle on that thing."

"What do you think's under there, Sheriff?"

"After spending weeks here, I wouldn't be surprised at anything we found."

* * *

The following morning the architect had finished his drawings. A back hoe was used to scoop dirt from the rear of the bunker. An eight-man crew of officers, four from Calaveras and four from San Francisco, started to dismantle it, cinder block by cinder block.

Eisenmann's field phone rang. A voice whispered, "I don't want to get involved, but you guys should know about—"

"Who are you?" Eisenmann asked.

"None of your business," the husky voice said. "I just want you to know that Jeff Gerald and Cliff Peranteau have been missing for months."

"What does that have to do—"

"They both worked for the Dennis Moving Company. That's where Ng worked."

"Why do you think Ng was involved?"

"I don't think, I know. I was standing there when Ng asked if they wanted to pick up extra cash. I've never seen them again."

"Thank you, are you sure you can't tell me who you—"

"No way. Just you and the other cops start doing something and get off your fat asses."

Thursday, June 27, 1985, 11:00 a.m., San Francisco

Investigators interviewed the employees of the Dennis Moving Services Company. One of them was Hector Salcedo. He said, "I dropped Clifford Peranteau off at his house. Cliff was supposed to go to work that afternoon. That was the 19th of January this year. He never showed up for work again."

"Did you try to contact him?"

"I tried to call his house a couple of times. No answer. I went around to his house in mid-afternoon. Cliff had a Suzuki motorcycle. It was there on the 19th, but Cliff wasn't. A few days later the motorcycle was gone."

* * *

That afternoon the oak-framed mirrors that once hung in the spare bedroom of the house on Blue Mountain Road were identified as belonging to Mr. Peranteau. The Cross pen-and-pencil set monogrammed with the initials C.R.P. that was found in Ng's apartment on Lennox was also identified as belonging to Clifford Peranteau.

The film in the camera found in the telephone trench was developed. It showed a nondescript scene from a window. The investigators showed it to Cliff's fellow employee, Hector Salcedo. He didn't recognize the scene.

The investigators spoke with Jerry Gonzalez, another employee of Dennis Moving, and his brother Robert. They identified a turntable found at the Blue Mountain Road property as one that they had sold to Cliff Peranteau.

Jerry Gonzalez said, "I heard Ng and Peranteau quarreling, back around Thanksgiving. Cliff called Ng a goddamned Chinaman. I remember Cliff saying, 'I should never have gotten you this job.'"

The photo of the nondescript scene was shown to Gonzalez. He did not recognize it.

Mike Fitzgerald, another employee, said that he also heard Ng and Cliff arguing, except that it was in January. Ng was angry because he thought Peranteau was sluffing off on the job.

Kenneth Bruce told the investigators that Cliff was to watch the Super Bowl with him and Rick Doedens.

Rick Doedens told the investigators that Cliff Peranteau never showed on Super Bowl Sunday. "However," he added, "I got a letter from

Cliff on January 28th. In it was a stamped, self-addressed envelope. Cliff wanted me to send him his winnings on a Super Bowl bet."

Investigators asked if Mr. Doedens still had the original envelope. He gave it to them. It was postmarked Wilseyville, California. The self-addressed envelope was made out to P.O. Box 349, Mokelumne Hill, California.

The investigators showed both Rick Doedens and Kenneth Bruce the scene found on the film developed from the camera discovered in the telephone trench. Neither recognized it.

Calaveras investigators contacted Wanda Davis, the postmaster of Mokelumne Hill. Her records showed that a post office box, 349, was opened on January 20, 1985, in the name of Clifford Peranteau. The box was subsequently closed.

Investigators talked to a Cynthia Basharr, a friend of Cliff Peranteau's. She had not seen or heard from him since January 15. She said, "Cliff said he was going to Tahoe with Charlie."

She also did not recognize the scene on the photo.

The investigators spoke once again with Dennis Goza. He didn't know where the photograph was taken. He did tell the investigators that during this time there was only one Charlie working at Dennis Moving and that was Charlie Ng.

Clifford Peranteau had been scheduled to work on January 19, but he didn't appear.

Goza said, "I did receive a letter from him later. He wanted his last paycheck to be sent to a post office box. He wrote he had a new girlfriend, a new job."

"Did you send the paycheck?"

"No. How could I know the letter was from Cliff?"

"Did you keep the self-addressed, stamped envelope?"

Goza rummaged in his file cabinet. "Here it is, P.O. Box 349, Mokelumne Hill, California."

"Do you know where Mokelumne Hill is?"

"Up in the Mother Lode somewhere."

"It's a few miles north of San Andreas."

Monday, July 1, 1985, 2:00 p.m., FBI Building, San Francisco

The FBI held a press conference and formally accused the Pentagon and the Navy of malfeasance. Ng was born in Hong Kong, he was a British subject, and he should have been deported after serving his prison term for stealing weapons in Hawaii. Also, as a British subject Ng should never have been recruited by the Marine Corps in the first place.

An information officer for the FBI said, "Who knows, if he was sent back to Hong Kong, maybe none of this would have happened, or at least not in this country."

The Pentagon's response: No comment.

Tuesday, July 2, 1985, 10:00 a.m., Blue Mountain Road, Calaveras County

Sheriff Ballard saw Deputy Copland on top of the hill covered with Mountain Misery. He waved at the sheriff.

Copland said, "I was probing the ground with a rod and hit something. He pointed. At his feet, still recessed into their holes, were three pieces of Tupperware. He knelt and pried the lid off one. It was filled with silver dollars. The second was also filled with silver dollars.

The area around the Tupperware was dug up. A white, five-gallon, plastic bucket was found. More silver dollars. A metal pipe twelve inches in diameter was found, with an AR-15 inside. In all, 1,863 silver dollars were counted, plus wallets and credit cards. A social security card in the name of Jeffrey Gerald was found.

The sheriff ordered several deputies to search on ever-larger concentric sweeps from ground zero. On another piece of property approximately six-tenths of a mile from the Balazs house, a small section of ground was disturbed. Another rectangular-shaped Tupperware-type container was unearthed. Inside was an envelope with the return address of the Philo Motel. The name Cosner was written on the outside. A pair of glasses were found. Also inside the container was an AAA automobile Club card, a Pac Tel card, a Banker's Life Insurance card, and some business cards for Marin Motors of San Rafael, all in the name of Paul Cosner.

Finally, Ballard thought, we've found an ID for Cosner. We haven't identified a body as Cosner's yet, but he's here. Somewhere.

Also in the Tupperware container was a Ruger Mark II .22 caliber semiautomatic handgun. The serial number had been ground down. There was a holster. There was a clip of twelve rounds of .22 caliber ammunition. Also inside was a silencer.

* * *

The next morning the shoptalk turned to the "hot spot" found under the bunker by infrared camera. The concrete bunker was gone, dismantled block by block. The reinforced floor was gone, jack-hammered up. The back hoe had dug an enormous hole.

There was nothing. Even infrared sometimes leads nowhere. The "hot spot" was rotting timber.

Eisenmann sank into a chair and rubbed the back of his neck. The muscles were tense, rock hard. He was emotionally and physically exhausted.

Sheriff Ballard and Irene Brunn joined him.

Eisenmann said, "Sheriff, you look pleased with yourself."

"I just figured out what PP1, PP2, and PP3 refer to in Lake's diary. PP stands for Pink Palace; one, two, and three for the three people Lake recruited to help build the bunker: Jacobson, Rock, and Okoro."

"When will it end?" Irene said.

"It will end. In a way it already has. Lake and Ng get nailed June second, one dies, the other flees. Neither comes back here again. When you guys arrived, the dungeon's empty, no one is chained to the bed in the house. Coincidence? I don't think so."

"What are you driving at, Sheriff?"

"I think they were in the Bay Area on a hunt. We've identified all but two of the twenty-one photos of women found in the bunker. They're alive, accounted for."

"You think they were photos of potential victims?"

"That's what I think, except they never got to them. Officer Wright deserves a medal."

Friday, July 5, 1985, 11 a.m., Sacramento

The California Legislature unanimously approved giving a half a million dollars to Calaveras County to help defray the cost of the criminal investigation.

Senator John Garamendi, Democrat, Walnut Grove, said, "Calaveras just don't have the resources to fund even a part of that investigation." He added that these funds were not to be used to cover the costs of a trial.

* * *

In San Francisco, Lloyd Cunningham, who worked for the San Francisco police force as a questions document examiner, was performing a series of tests using the Olympia typewriter found at the Wilseyville property.

He compared the typewriting on the letter that had been sent to Rick Doedens and the self-addressed envelope containing the request for Cliff Peranteau's Super Bowl winnings. He also compared the type with the letter received by Dennis Goza, owner of Dennis Moving, requesting Cliff's wages.

Cunningham wrote out a report stating: "In my opinion all the letters I examined were typed on the Olympia typewriter."

* * *

At noon on the day of the vote in Sacramento, two more five-gallon buckets were uncovered near the spot where Larry Copland found the Tupperware. Inside one was a first-aid kit, ammunition, and a knife. Inside the other was an electric skill saw, a three-foot tree trimmer blade, and a hatchet. All three were covered with a maroon stain.

The crime lab determined that the maroon stain was human blood.

Another partially decomposed body was found. Coroner Parker established that it was a white woman, dead less than a year, and that she was not Brenda O'Connor, Kathleen Allen, or Deborah Dubs.

The FBI obtained a search warrant for six P.O. boxes, all believed to be "mail drops" of Ng and Lake's. Two boxes were at the Wilseyville post office, two in Pioneer, one in Railroad Flat, and one in Mokelumne Hill.

Fifty pieces of mail were seized.

* * *

In San Francisco, the police department obtained a search warrant for Claralyn's parents' house. They removed six bags of evidence, among which were duplicate copies of the photographs taken of women in various stages of undress at the juvenile hall. There were also whips, leather restraints, two vibrators, a chain, and audio cassettes. They were taken to the Hall of Justice's property office at Seventh and Bryant in the city.

Claralyn Balazs was not home at the time. She was on a cruise ship sailing through the Mexican Riviera.

Saturday, July 6, 1985, 1:10 p.m., Calgary, Alberta

Two FBI agents sat in the car of Special Agent in Charge Karen Alexander. They were half a block away from Ng's sister's house.

"Do we interview the sister?"

"No," Karen said, "just stake out the front and rear of the house."

The two agents got into their own car. Karen turned on the radio and headed toward downtown Calgary.

The radio blared, "In San Francisco last night, Stan Pozanski, one of Claralyn Balazs's attorneys, said he was advising his client, 'not to take the oath at her upcoming Grand Jury investigation, and to invoke her Fifth Amendment rights. I'm also advising her to invoke marital privilege.'"

A reporter said, "I thought they were divorced."

"Some of this involves things that happened during the time they were married."

Karen pulled her car onto the MacLeod Trail, got in the fast lane, and sped toward downtown Calgary.

Special Agent in Charge Alexander thought, the legal battle is beginning; parry and thrust, lunge and retreat. The complex issues involved, besides proof of guilt, are enormous.

How difficult would it be to extradite Ng back to the United States? She vaguely remembered a treaty signed years ago, in the early seventies, between Canada and the United States. Extradition rights had been part of that treaty.

Saturday, July 6, 1985, 1:30 p.m., Hall of Justice, San Francisco

During their interview with Dennis Goza, San Francisco investigators learned that another fellow employee of his was missing. Jeffrey Gerald worked at the Dennis Moving Services Company with Charlie Ng. His roommate was a woman named Terry Kailer. ·

Kailer said, "On February 24th, Jeff received a number of phone calls. He told me they were from Charlie, a guy he worked with. Charlie wanted him to go to Stockton to help somebody move. The pay was a hundred dollars. He took a bus up there. I've not seen or heard from him since."

"Can you think of anything else?"

"On February 27th, I came home around six o'clock in the evening. Most of Jeff's stuff had been taken from the apartment."

The work jacket found in the rear of Paul Cosner's car was identified as having belonged to Jeff. Also identified as Jeff's were the guitar and guitar case found in the Wilseyville residence. The book discovered at Ng's Lennox apartment by Officer Defillipo was identified as belonging to Jeff Gerald.

Investigators took the nondescript photograph that had been developed from the camera found in the telephone trench. They matched it to the scene outside Gerald's apartment window. No luck.

They showed the photo to Kailer. She said, "I know that place. That's the view out of Jeff's *old* apartment."

* * *

DA investigator John Crawford had been trying to find out whose child was in the photo found in the telephone trench. He had two clues. Her name was Stephanie Jennine Carr, and a date, 7/81.

He contacted the California Department of Vital Statistics. They checked their records for a possible match to the photograph.

Nothing.

Crawford sent letters to the remaining forty-nine states. He received an answer from Pennsylvania. A police officer with the Abington Police Department, Joseph Dalton, called. He placed Crawford in contact with Donna Mullen.

Stephanie Jennine Carr was Donna Mullen's daughter. She told Crawford she had dated Cliff Peranteau from 1978 to 1981. She had given Cliff a picture of her daughter, the one found in the telephone trench.

* * *

The Calaveras DA's office received a phone call from Tori Doolin. Investigator John Crawford flew to San Diego and went to her home.

Tori explained that she was a friend of Robin Scott Stapley and that she had had occasion to visit Lonnie Bond and Brenda at their place off Blue Mountain Road. She had seen Leonard Lake's photo in the papers and knew him as Charles Gunnar.

She said, "On April 24th, 1985, at 8:30 in the morning, a man named Charles Gunnar and an Oriental male, who I later found out is Charlie Ng, came to my door. They rang the doorbell. I said, 'Who is it?' The reply was, 'Charles.' I asked, 'Charles who?' because I didn't know any Charles. He said, 'Charles from up north.' I recognized him as the man that I had seen at the house next door to Lonnie's. I opened the door. Gunnar came in and said his friend would rather wait in the car. Ng left and went back to the car."

"What happened next?" Crawford prompted.

"Gunnar told me that he had found the three of them, Lonnie Bond, Brenda O'Connor, and Robin Scott Stapley dead. He said he and his friend,

Ng, cleaned up the mess and then burned the bodies Indian style. He said the baby was missing."

Crawford asked, "How do you know Lake was referring to Ng when Lake said he and his friend had cleaned up the bodies?"

"Lake referred to Ng as a good friend from the Marines, and that it was him, the good friend from the Marines, who was there and helped them clean up the mess."

"What happened next?"

"He said there were clothes all over the place. There was no ID left on any of the people. He said no guns were found there. He told me he wanted to make it look like Scott moved, so that the police wouldn't come snooping around up there where he lived."

"And you didn't report this to the police at the time?"

"I was terrified. Lake wanted the pink slip on Scott's truck. He wanted Scott's diploma. He wanted Scott's favorite bike. He wanted all of Scott's clothes. He wanted the receipt for a gun Scott had bought from him when he had been up there on vacation."

"Did you give him those items?"

"I told him I couldn't get into Scott's safe. He gave me Scott's keys, which allowed me to get into the closet where Scott's safe was. I let Gunnar take Scott's clothes. I didn't know where the receipt for the gun was. I later found the receipt."

She handed the receipt to Crawford, who read: "Sold to Scott Stapley, a Walter pistol, model PPK/S, 9 millimeter, Serial Number 1562315." The receipt was signed Charles Gunnar.

He asked, "What did the man you knew as Charles Gunnar do when you couldn't find this receipt?"

"He became very upset, about the receipt and the other things he wanted. He said, 'Well, if you find them, will you please call me or will you send them to me?' He asked for the pink slip to the truck."

"Did you give it to him?"

"No. And he got very upset. He told me the truck had been in an accident. And he had driven the truck to San Diego. I walked out to the truck with him. He showed me where it had been wrecked. Ng walked around the truck with us and never said a word. The truck looked like someone had hit a tree up by the left front, the driver's door."

"What was the license plate number?"

"It was personalized: AHOYMTY. I remember it because there are a lot of sailors here in San Diego."

"Meaning?"

"Ahoy matey. Navy lingo." She gave Crawford a receipt for repairs to a camera owned by Scott, Serial Number 5022594.

A check was run. It was learned from the Calgary police that a camera had been discovered on Ng at the time of his capture. The serial number: 5022594.

*   *   *

Investigators interviewed Judy Emerson, the landlady of Robin Scott Stapley. She stated, "Last April 18th I saw Scott loading his pickup—"

"What kind of pickup?"

"A gray Chevrolet. I again saw Scott the next day around noon. He told me he was going to the mountains. That's the last time I ever saw him."

"Do you know the license plate of the Chevrolet?"

"Yes, it was personalized: AHOYMTY."

A highway patrol check was run. On April 23, 1985, Kern County Highway Patrolman Wood Hicks made a report of an accident involving a Chevrolet truck with the license plate AHOYMTY. Hicks identified the driver as Charlie Ng.

*   *   *

Dennis Goza, owner of the Dennis Moving Services Company, was contacted. His employment records showed Charlie Ng took off work from April 22 to April 27. There was a note in his files stating that Ng had phoned, saying that his parents had been in an accident in Los Angeles and he needed time off.

Phone records were again checked. At 7:21 on the evening of April 21, 1985 a call went to Dennis Goza's home phone from the Blue Mountain Road residence.

Saturday, July 6, 1985, 4:00 p.m., Blue Mountain Road, Calaveras County

Sheriff Ballard studied the time sheets lying on his desk.

This thing is killing my department, he thought.

Every one of his patrolmen not assigned to the Ng case was working a twelve-hour shift, seven days a week. The Ng task force was working more than twelve hours a day.

My department's facing bankruptcy, he thought. The state had allocated a half million, but they were parceling it out like Simon Legree. Even though Assemblyman Norm Waters and Senator John Garamendi, with an assist from Mayor Diane Feinstein, had helped push through the request for state funds, Calaveras County was to pay a percentage of the initial cost, called a platform. After the platform was reached the state would pick up 90 percent of the costs.

The platform was based on .0125 percent of the full value of taxable property in the county, and totaled $70,746.00.

The sheriff was granting days off to his personnel on a review of each specific request.

But he had received a great deal of help from other agencies. An enormous number of telephone calls were coming in. FBI agents had been sent to handle the overload, as well as two Department of Justice agents.

A media hotline had been set up. A prerecorded message of the latest information was available.

The Office of Emergency Services had provided a van with five mobile work stations. These lines were dedicated to law enforcement calls only.

Even with the extra help, the county was still facing an enormous economic shortfall.

Sheriff Ballard pushed aside the problems of money and opened Lake's diary.

He read: "May, 1983, Operation Fish completed—the murder of Charles Gunnar."

Investigators on the Ng task force had learned that Lake had formed a guardianship for Charles Gunnar's children. Lake explained that their dad had moved to a desolate mountain cabin and would never return. He took letters from those children to their dad, and brought letters back purported to be written by their dad. He asked for money from them.

They never saw their father again.

* * *

At the Wilseyville property, more personal items were found at various sites.

A key was unearthed. An ID for Mike Carroll was found. The key was tested and found to open Mike Carroll's house.

A small Buddha figurine was found. Near it a ceramic fish and a candlestick holder were unearthed. A Pennsylvania license plate with the personalized plate CINDY was dug up. All were traced back to Cliff Peranteau.

* * *

That afternoon a top ranking law enforcement agent for the state delivered a profile of Lake and Ng to Sheriff Ballard.

He studied the file.

It was not from the Behavioral Science Unit of the FBI. They got involved only to profile a suspected serial killer and identify the potential psychological makeup of the suspected perpetrator.

Lake and Ng were already known entities.

Ballard studied the two sheets of paper.

Leonard Lake, white male adult

1. Studied survivalist activities.
2. Lake would raid marijuana plants from the growers in many counties: Humboldt, Mendocino, and Calaveras.
3. Lake was a member of the Society for Creative Anachronism (SCA). This was a cult based on medieval worship involving sacrifices.
4. Lake wanted to totally dominate and control females. He was more interested in psychological domination. He played mind games, using degradation, both psychological and intellectual, so they knew he was in control.

Charles Chitat Ng, Asian male adult

1. Considers himself a survivalist.
2. Studied the following:
   a. Martial arts
   b. Nuclear warfare
   c. Firearms
3. Suspect displays a deep hatred toward blacks, women, and children.
4. Has intense need to physically abuse as well as dominate females.
5. Favorite sayings:
   a. "No kill, no thrill."
   b. "No gun, no fun."
   c. "Mommy cries, Daddy dies, baby fries."
6. Suspect believed to be agent for many homicides in which victims were shot. Of the two, he is considered to be *The Executioner.*

Chapter 9

The Second Videotape

Saturday, July 6, 1985, 2:00 a.m., Blue Mountain Road, Calaveras County

Sheriff Claud Ballard motioned for Detective Tom Eisenmann and Policewoman Irene Brunn to join him. He asked, holding up an ice chest, "Would you guys like a drink?"

"We celebrating something?"

"It's Saturday. I just want to relax."

Irene pointed at the cabin up the hill. "How about the porch?"

The three went up to the porch. The sheriff poured the drinks, three beers, and settled into a deck chair.

Eisenmann looked at the sky. A hawk circled in a lazy pattern. "A predator, just looking to do its thing."

"The natural order," Irene said.

"Like Lake and Ng?"

The sheriff drained his beer, opened three more, and said, "I want you to see the video marked Brenda. Then tell me if there's anything natural about Lake and Ng."

They entered the cabin. Ballard inserted a videotape into the VCR. He fast-forwarded past the Kathy Allen portion. The tape slowed as a woman appeared in the Blue Mountain Road bedroom.

Ballard said, "That's Brenda O'Connor; she, her husband, and child, rented the Carter place next door."

Brenda's hands were handcuffed in front of her. Charlie Ng, wearing no shirt, stood beside her. On the other side of the chair stood Leonard Lake.

Lake said, "If you must know, I didn't do anything with him."

Brenda asked, nodding at Ng, "What'd he do with him?"

Ng said, "I didn't do anything."

"Did you guys kill him?"

"No," Lake answered, "we didn't kill him."

"Are you going to let us go soon?"

Lake said, "Probably not."

"Never?" Brenda asked. "Are you going to kill us?"

Lake answered, "That's sort of up to you, Brenda."

"Charles," Brenda said, "what are you going to do to us? Why are you doing this?"

Lake answered, "Cause we hate you."

"What did we do to you?"

"Shut up," Lake said. "Ooh, what a hairy day."

Brenda mumbled, finishing with ". . . me my baby down there."

"Your baby is sound asleep," Lake said, "like a rock. Brenda, the neighborhood doesn't like you. The neighborhood doesn't like you, the neighborhood doesn't like Lonnie, and we haven't liked you since you moved in."

"So we'll leave."

Lake said, "Oh, you've already left. We've closed you down. The Star Route Gang, if you want to call it that. We got together, and we took you away. We took Scott away. Lonnie's going to earn a decent living for the rest of his life, hopefully."

"I know he is."

"Your baby is going to be taken away."

Brenda put her head on her chest. She mumbled something, finishing with, ". . . taken away."

Lake said, "There's a family down in Fresno that doesn't have a baby."

"You aren't taking my baby away."

"They've got one now."

Ng added, "It's better than the baby's dead, right?"

Brenda said, "What do you mean they've got one now? That's my baby."

"Brenda," Lake said, "you have a choice. We'll give it to you right now."

"What?"

"You can cooperate with us. By cooperating with us, that means you will stay here as our prisoner, you will work for us, you will wash for us, you will fuck for us, or you can say, 'no, I don't want to do that', in which case we'll tie you to the bed, we'll rape you, and then we'll take you outside and shoot you. Your choice."

"I'll cooperate."

Ng mumbled something.

Lake laughed and nodded. "That was fast."

Ng mumbled something again.

Brenda asked, "Are you really going to take my baby away from me?"

Lake answered, "Yes, we are. Personally, I don't think you're a fit mother."

"Where's Lonnie at? Where's Scott at?"

"They've been taken away. There's a place up in the hills where they'll split wood for the rest of their happy lives."

Brenda asked, "You mean you haven't killed them or anything?"

"No," Lake said, "I haven't killed them, although if they die, that's their problem. To be honest, I couldn't care less. They had better cooperate, too. They're getting the same choice you're getting. To be honest, for all I know, maybe they're dead right now."

Brenda said, "Is that why you invited us over here for dinner?"

Lake said, "Uh huh."

Ng added, "It's part of the game."

Lake said, "You guys have been such assholes, Brenda. You in particular. You know, Lonnie hasn't been all that bad, I'll give you that; except for his shooting and his drug factory over there, he hasn't been all that bad. But you've been an asshole like I can't believe. You have been so damn rude and for no reason that I can figure."

"Cause I can't stand it up here," Brenda said. "It's in the middle of nowhere."

"Ah."

Ng said, "Explain those letters."

"What letters?" Brenda asked.

"The letters you wrote to Lonnie while he was gone."

Brenda asked, "What about them?"

Lake said, "They weren't particularly flattering."

"You read them?"

"Of course, every bit of them."

"How'd you get to read them?"

"No sweat," Lake answered. "You broke the window, remember?"

"Oh. Are you going to keep me up here the rest of my life or something?"

"No. To be honest with you, I probably won't keep you here for more than a few weeks, but, after that, we'll probably pass you around. There's other—"

Brenda blinked and looked up at an overhead light fixture. "The light's hot."

"Suffer," Lake said. "There's people that are going to want to know that we did our job. There's already some guys that took away Lonnie and Scott."

Brenda asked, "Why do you guys do this?"

"We don't like you," Lake answered. "Would you like me to put it in writing?"

Ng said, "It's done. Just take whatever we tell you."

"I can't take . . . this."

Lake said, "We're going to sit back and enjoy ourselves. It's been a hectic day, and you are going to learn the true meaning of fuck face. That's me, if you haven't gotten that." Lake turned to Ng. "Where are the manacles?"

Brenda held up her hands and rattled the chain that linked her metal handcuffs together. "Can you loosen these?"

Lake said, "We're going to take them off in a minute."

Brenda buried her head in her hands. She mumbled something, ending with, ". . . hurt Lonnie."

"Well," Lake said, "to be honest, we weren't gentle with him, but I'll tell you that at least he was alive when he, uh, walked out of here."

Ng said, "Since you say you're hot, I'll take it off of you."

"What?" Brenda said.

"Well," Lake said, "she could actually take it off herself, but—"

Ng said, "With the cuffs on it's hard."

Lake said, "I was going to have you take the cuffs off."

Brenda said, "I'm not hot."

Lake asked, "Where are the manacles, Charlie?"

"It's in the—"

Brenda sobbed, "Would you please just go get my baby?"

Lake said, "I'm going to—"

Ng interrupted him with a mumble.

Lake pointed. "It's under there, Charlie."

Brenda said, "You can't keep my baby from me for sex."

Ng asked Lake, "Where did you say they were?"

"It's right here." Lake held up leg manacles. "Put them on her. I'm going to take the handcuffs off. I'm taking your baby because your baby is an innocent in this."

Brenda said, "So am I."

Lake said, "Huh?"

Ng echoed, "Huh?"

"You two are crazy."

Lake said, "Maybe the whole neighborhood's crazy. The point is you haven't been particularly innocent while you've been here, Brenda. In fact, you've been something of a first-class asshole. However, we are going to give you an opportunity to make up for it."

Using a knife, Ng cut the T-shirt off Brenda. She had on a bra.

Lake said, "You're so crude, Charlie. I actually like that T-shirt."

Ng waved the knife. "Let's see what we're buying."

Brenda said, "What are you going to do, sell me or something?"

Lake said, "No, as a matter of fact. We're not going to sell you at all. We're going to give you away."

"Don't cut my bra off."

Ng said, "Nothing is yours now. It'll be totally ours." He cut the strap of her bra and tossed the undergarment away.

"Take her handcuffs off, Charlie. She'll never get out of that." Lake pointed at the leg manacles.

"OK," Ng said, "You can cry and stuff like the rest of them, but it won't do you no good. We are pretty, ha, cold-hearted, so to speak."

Lake laughed. "Frankly, I'm as hot as they come. Take the cuffs off of her."

"All right," Ng answered.

Lake said, "Please."

Ng leaned close to Brenda. "I'll get my weapon handy in case you try to play stupid."

"I ain't going to play stupid. I don't want to get killed."

Ng placed what looked like a stun gun on the table. "Yeah, that—"

"Stand up," Lake ordered, "Brenda, Brenda, stand up."

Brenda held out her wrists, the handcuffs were still on. "Will you get these off?"

Lake said, "I thought he already had them off."

Brenda's face perspired. "Light, it's so hot . . . sick."

"Suffer," Lake said. "See this, Brenda? I'm only going to show it to you once." He held up a black coiled whip.

"What are you going to do, beat me?"

"It's a very vicious . . . As a matter of fact I just might, but if you do exactly as you're told, without any fuss, no. Now what's it going to be, full cooperation?" Lake pointed at Ng. "Are you ready for your shower, kid? Take them off then and run her in."

Ng mumbled something unintelligible.

Brenda asked, "I'm going to take a shower?"

Lake said, "Uh huh."

Ng added, "Clean you up."

"Actually," Lake said, "you're both going to take a shower."

"Yep," Ng agreed, "I always do that. It's luckier."

Lake said, "See, Charlie owes me one, so I get you first, but he's got his heart set on taking a shower with you, so who am I to turn him down?"

Ng asked, "You want her to take a shower with the leg irons or—"

"No, take them off." Lake pointed at Brenda's face. "I think she believes us. You better believe us, Brenda, or you'll be dead."

Ng added, "Right."

"I believe you."

"Take your jeans off," Lake said. "In fact, take your panties off, too, while you're at it."

Ng mumbled something.

Lake ordered again, "Stand up and take your jeans off, Brenda."

"Can I do it over there? The light's—"

Lake shook his head. "Right there."

"Right there," Ng said.

"I'm getting dizzy."

"I don't care," Lake said. "Do what you're told."

"I'll pass out. I'm afraid, I'm real dizzy."

Ng said, "If you don't do it, I'll do it for you."

"Wait till I'm not dizzy no more."

Ng said, "Okay, I'll give you a few seconds."

"Actually, Charlie, I can move the camera over to the couch. Move over to the couch, Brenda. That's away from the heat."

Ng pointed at the couch and said, "Sit down."

"Yeah," Brenda said, slumping onto the couch, "I'm real shaky and real dizzy."

Ng said, "Okay."

"I'm going to pass out. I guess from that light or something."

Ng said, "You can pass out, but we're going to wake you up."

Lake said, "Brenda, I have a lot of animosity against you, and I would just as soon start you out with a nice firm whipping right now to make you believe how serious we are."

Ng mumbled something.

Lake grinned. "How did you know?"

Ng laughed.

Lake pointed at Brenda's jeans. "Slide them down, and then sit down."

"I'm just, just too dizzy."

"Slide them down. All right. Charlie."

Ng said, "Yeah, that could be the truth. Yep, sure. Her lip's turning pale."

"Her lips are pale, anyway. You got the, uh, OK."

Ng asked Brenda, "Feeling better? You want some water?"

"I'll take something to drink. I've been sick all day, real bad." She pointed at a pack of cigarettes.

"You know," Lake said, "you don't want to smoke that. Did you give up smoking?"

"No."

"You have now."

Brenda vomited. Then she mumbled something.

Lake said, "I'm sure you don't. You did it, you clean it up."

"Well . . . dizzy and sweaty and sweaty, hot—"

Lake said, "It is very hot. Charlie, will you turn that light on that's over the kitchen table? The switch is right on it. No, over the kitchen table. The switch is on the light itself, Charlie. Over the kitchen table. The switch is on the light, Charlie."

"You mean this one?"

"Yes."

Lake said, "Thank you. Now tell me, isn't she a little better than Kathy?"

Ng studied Brenda's body. "Sort of, a little, basically the same."

Lake pointed at Brenda's midriff. "She just had a baby. She looks OK."

"She's younger," Ng said, "that's why."

"No, she's a year older."

Brenda said, "All I can hear is shush in the top of my head."

Ng asked, "Do you want some aspirin?"

Lake waved a hand. "No."

Brenda sobbed, "Like this the rest of the days of my life. Like I'm pregnant or something."

Ng said, "Not the right time for that shit. We told you what's going to happen to the baby. Just don't ask us or else it'll be history. I don't want to hear nothing about it."

"Give my baby to me. I'll do anything you want if you—"

Lake said, "You're going to do anything we want anyway, and you don't want to have a dirty house around with the baby."

Brenda said, "He can't live without me."

"He's gonna learn," Lake said. "Come on, stand up. Jeans off. Panties off and everything else. Shove them down. Watch that she doesn't fall over in the shower and split her head."

Ng said, "Oh, yeah, yeah, I won't."

"I don't need a shower," Brenda said. "I took a shower."

Lake said, "You do, too."

Ng said, "Make sure you're clean before we fuck you. That's the house rule. Traditional."

The three people disappeared off the screen. The sounds of a shower running water blocked out most of the conversation.

Brenda mumbled something.

Lake said, "Gobble down."

Ng said, "Let me make sure there's towels and all that other shit."

Lake said, "Give me your hand, Brenda, give me your hand."

Brenda's words were blocked out by the sounds of running water.

So was Lake's response.

Brenda mumbled something else.

Lake said, "Take good care of Charlie. Charlie, see if you can not get her hair wet. Just wash her body."

The running water blocked out Brenda's words.

Lake said, "Not that you have to worry about it—"

Ng said, "You have to worry about."

Brenda's words were drowned out by the sound of running water.

Lake said, "I don't know. Maybe he does, for all I know. I don't care."

Ng mumbled something, then his voice cleared. "Something's wrong with this showerhead. It pisses me off."

Brenda's voice could be heard, but it was impossible to make out any words.

Ng said, "OK, OK."

Lake said, "Take care of her now, Charlie."

Ng's answer was inaudible.

Lake instructed, "Make sure she brushes her teeth and uses mouthwash."

Ng's voice rose above the sound of rushing water. "What the fuck's wrong with this shower? Taking a shower . . ."

The video ended.

Eisenmann opened three more beers. He said, "I'm no lawyer, but this appears irrefutable."

"Lake's there," Irene said. "Captured by camera. Ng's there. Both immortalized."

"Even the defense can't contest the identifications on the videotape."

"Whether Ng pulled the trigger and killed Kathy Allen, or was the one that exterminated Brenda O'Connor's life, there's one undeniable fact: he was present. He knew. He participated in kidnapping, in rape, in slavery."

Ballard said, "But did he commit murder?"

"And does it have to be proven he actually did, or is being an accomplice enough to warrant the death penalty?"

Saturday, July 6, 1985, 2:00 p.m., Calgary, Alberta, Canada

John Patrick "Sean" Doyle, forty-six, a part-time security guard at the Hudson Bay Department store in Calgary, was halfway through his shift. He worked full time as an English, art, and science high-school teacher. He picked up extra money as a guard during the busy ten days of the Calgary Stampede.

He stood next to another security guard. They had both been watching an Asian man, wearing a light blue knapsack, steal the store blind.

So far the man had taken two cans of fried herring, one can of baked beans, a Swiss Army knife, two boxes of cookies, a braided cord, three miniature packs of Vitabath, and a packet of breadsticks.

The two guards watched him slip a can of lighter fluid and a wedge of cheese into the knapsack.

Sean said, "That bloody thing holds a lot."

The second guard said, "He's as oblivious to us as if we were on the moon. How long do you want to wait?"

The Asian man slipped a bottle of Pepsi Cola into his knapsack.

"You want to do it, or me?"

"I'll do it," Sean said. He approached the man and said, "Please, I'd like to look into your knapsack."

"No, that's mine."

Sean grabbed the bag.

"No! That's mine."

"You've been shoplifting. I watched you put things in the bag."

"Let me get my wallet," the Chinese man said, and reached into the knapsack.

The second guard shouted, "Sean, he's got a gun."

Sean saw a black shape being pulled from the knapsack. He grabbed the gun. The two men grappled for it for a moment, then there was an explosion. The bullet lodged in an overhead fixture.

The two men fell to the floor, still fighting for the gun. Sean looked down. The barrel was being forced toward his chest.

Sean felt strength come with a surge of adrenaline. He shoved with all his energy, forcing the gun to the floor. There was another explosion; Sean felt a flash of heat in his hand.

His partner swarmed over them and got a choke hold around the shoplifter's neck.

Sean stood up, but felt dizzy. He held a .22 caliber Ruger in one hand. His other hand was bleeding bright red. He had been shot.

Two hours later, at the Calgary Metropolitan Police Station, Sean learned that he had helped apprehend Charlie Chitat Ng.

Chapter 10

Jailhouse

Saturday, July 6, 1985, 4:30 p.m., Blue Mountain Road, Calaveras County

Sheriff Ballard put down the phone and shouted, "They got him, the Canadians captured Ng!"

Officers rushed in from all sides. Ballard gave them the details, then ordered, "Let's call it a day." They raced for their cars and the nearest bar.

Surrounded by officers, Ballard drained his beer. Relieved, he declared, "It's all been worth it."

"Every agonizing minute."

"When do you think they'll ship him back, Sheriff?"

"No problem, just a few days for the paperwork. Ng was caught committing a crime in Canada; they'll have to straighten that mess up first. But the FBI said extradition proceedings have already started."

A deputy asked, "Who you going to send to get him?"

Another deputy added, "I'll volunteer, and I'll do it for free, I'll even pay for my trip out of my own pocket."

"Me, too," chorused the group.

Ballard held up a hand. "I'll make that decision when the time comes. I want to congratulate all of you on a fine job. But Ng's capture doesn't mean the work's finished. Enjoy yourselves. Tomorrow we're back in the trenches."

* * *

Officers who had been exhausted twenty-four hours earlier filled the dawn with happy talk.

Calaveras County sheriff's deputies Larry Copland, Steve Mathews, and Bob Bunning drove down a dirt road adjacent to Blue Mountain Road. They noticed the ground had been dug up. They got out of the car. Then they noticed the smell.

Mathews got a camcorder out of the trunk of the car. He set it up on a tripod. Using the car's radio, Bunning called the command post and filled Ballard in.

The sheriff sent Coroner Boyd Stephens, Irene Brunn, and Tom Eisenmann.

They drove the six-tenths of a mile from Lake's house. Coyotes had clawed at the dirt. The two cadavers were only six inches underground.

The degenerative process that the body undergoes after death had proceeded normally. The bodies decomposed slowly. The stench was trapped underground.

The coyotes performed their partial exhumation. An acrid odor contaminated the mountain air.

The law enforcement team began a careful excavation. The first body was found at a shallow depth.

Doctor Stephens carried a tape recorder. The bodies had attracted hundreds of giant bluebottle flies.

The coroner said, "Corner's Case Number 2521-85. Body enclosed in a blue-colored sleeping bag with a zipper across two sides. Bag is tied around the head region with gray-colored duct tape. Similar tape is about the ankle and lower region."

The sleeping bag was moved. Another sleeping bag was below the first. Doctor Stephens said, "There's no dirt between the bodies. This suggests they were buried at the same time."

The sleeping bag was removed from the first body. Stephens spoke into his tape recorder, "Body clothed in a shirt, an undershirt, pants, and socks. A green plastic garbage bag is enclosing the head and upper trunk. The hands are handcuffed at the back. The ankles are tied with rope."

The green plastic garbage bag was removed. Doctor Stephens bent over the corpse and said, "Around the neck there is a leather cord, which contains a red rubber ball, which has been made in such a fashion as to be consistent with a mouth gag. There appears to be a single gunshot wound to the head."

The coroner turned to the second sleeping bag. "Coroner's Case Number 2522-85. Body enclosed in a red-colored sleeping bag. Bag is quite damp."

The red-colored sleeping bag was opened. Stephens said, "The feet and hands are taped together with gray duct tape. There are two plastic bags about the body. The first is a large-sized garbage liner that's been cut open, and the cut portion of the bag is adjacent to the left anterior surface of the body. The second green-colored plastic garbage bag is across the head and shoulders."

The garbage bags were removed.

Stephens said, "Around the neck is another leather thong holding a red rubber ball mouth gag."

The coroner knelt and examined the face. "There appears to be a close contact gunshot wound to the dental ridge. A second gunshot wound is located just above the right eyebrow. A third gunshot wound through the right supraclavical space and clavical." With his right forefinger he traced the two slender bones, each articulating with the sternum and a scapula and forming the anterior part of the shoulder.

"A fourth gunshot wound involves the right lateral fibula and tibia." He pointed at the corpse's calf.

He leaned to within inches of the leg. "The route of the projectile appears to be across the left posterior parietal region, approximately two and a half centimeters lateral to the vertex and slightly behind it. By aligning across the repositioned calvarium, the most likely area of impact, the course of the bullet would be from up to down, from back to front by approximately ten degrees, and from left to right by approximately forty degrees. The wound is consistent with those made by a .22 caliber firearm."

"What do you make of it?" Irene asked Eisenmann.

"I don't like to guess, but if I had to venture something I'd say that the bullets in the leg and shoulder were fired first, while the victim was on the run. The shot came from behind, the shooter on high ground and to the left of the victim."

"Then head and mouth shots administered the coup de grace."

Monday, July 8, 1985, 1:00 p.m., Calgary, Alberta, Canada

Provincial Court Judge Edward Adolphe removed his glasses and peered at the three-page document presented by the prosecutor. "Mr. Delong, may I ask why you have asked for a psychiatric examination?"

"There have been a number of troubling reports in the press about the state of mind of Mr. Ng. We intend to charge him with crimes of a most serious nature. It is our belief that it is in the interest of justice to establish Mr. Ng's mental fitness before he is charged."

"Is there any objection from counsel?"

Brian Devlin, in a flowing black robe topped by white, starched collar, rose and bowed respectfully to the bench. "Your Honor, my client has no objection. We are familiar with Dr. Feinman's credentials."

Judge Adolphe referred again to the document. "You state that you can conduct this examination in less than half an hour?"

"Quite," the psychiatrist answered.

"Then we will have a thirty-minute recess. Please clear the courtroom. And again I warn you gentlemen from the news media that no cameras of any kind are permitted in this room and I expect civility from you at all times."

Thirty minutes later the psychiatrist delivered his report to a full courtroom. "Mr. Ng is mentally competent to stand trial."

Charles Chitat Ng sat impassively in the handsome wood-paneled docket. His pitch-black hair was tousled. His face was squat, almost pudgy. His eyes were jet-black.

The cuffs on his wrists were joined by a short chain in front of him, limiting the range of his arms to his lap. His legs were restricted at the ankles by manacles. His pajamalike, gray clothing was in stark contrast to the robes of the prosecutor, Manfred Delong, of the Judge, and of the defense attorney.

The prosecutor listed the charges. "Attempted robbery. Robbery. Possession of a firearm. Attempted murder."

Tuesday, July 9, 1985, Noon, Blue Mountain Road, Calaveras County

A hushed group of officers huddled around the radio.

The radio announcer said, "Charlie Chitat Ng's defense attorney, Brian Devlin, stated Ng is using his option to be tried before a jury in the Queen's Bench Court. Devlin said, 'The charge of attempted murder of the Hudson Bay department store's security guard is ludicrous; they're really holding Ng for shoplifting. I am requesting bail be set.'"

Brunn said, "What bullshit."

"Don't worry about it," Eisenmann said, "it'll never happen."

The radio announcer continued, "Len Westerberg, Canadian immigration spokesman, said, 'No action against the gentleman will be taken until court in Canada is completed.'"

"The gentleman?" Ballard said in a dull voice.

The announcer continued, "This story just broke a few minutes ago; Canadian Justice Minister John Cosbie will face a huge legal problem if our southern neighbors charge Ng with a capital crime. In the 1976 treaty with the United States, Canada has the right to refuse extradition of someone accused of a capital crime that carries the death penalty. We Canadians feel strongly enough about barbaric state-sanctioned executions to have outlawed them in our own country."

"Sheriff, does that mean what I think it means?"

"I think so."

Irene said, "That's why Ng fled to Canada."

"Yes," Eisenmann said, "no death penalty."

"This can't possibly be happening."

"It is." Ballard snapped the radio off.

"Is Ng," Irene asked, "going to hide behind Canada's laws?"

The sheriff shrugged.

"You mean there's a possibility that we may never get him back?"

Eisenmann added, "That he may never stand trial here?"

"That's a possibility," Sheriff Ballard said.

"Law enforcement is almost finished its job. It's time for the legal order to take over."

"Here come the lawyers," Irene said. "It kind of makes you long for the good old days when you just tossed a rope over the sturdy branch of an oak tree."

Sheriff Ballard said, "Law enforcement's come a long way since then."

"Too bad criminals haven't."

Part II

Order

Your Honor, what we used to call astronomy we now call megaphysics. This case we should properly call a megacase. Plain common sense suggests that we break the rules.

—EPHRAIM MARGOLIN, *The People vs. Charles Ng*

Chapter 11

Man in Orange

Monday, July 10, 1985, 9:00 a.m., Union Square, San Francisco

Ephraim Margolin seldom had occasion to read *The Sacramento Bee,* but now it was the basic source of information on how criminal proceedings against Ng were going in Calgary. He thanked the young reporter, who had driven from Sacramento for this interview, for bringing him up to date.

Murder, sex, torture—the stuff of page one news. And now an international legal challenge.

He had been out of touch with the case since the FBI had ended their investigation, in mid-June, of Garrick Lew, his client and court-appointed attorney for Ng. But this was clearly a news story that was not going to evaporate. With a smile, he handed the woman's credentials back to her. "To answer your question, yes, I have appeared in extradition cases."

"You've seen what the state deputy attorney said about extraditing Ng?"

"I haven't. Which deputy attorney?"

"Nelson Kempsky. I'll quote from the *Bee.* 'It could take a few months, and at the fastest, it's unlikely to take less than a month.'"

"When did he say that? Does he know something the rest of us don't know?"

"Last Monday, after a press conference, he used the occasion to bring up John Belushi—"

"What's the reference?"

"Belushi died more than three years ago, in a Los Angeles hotel room. I covered the story for the *Bee*. It was a Canadian gal that spent the night with him, and supposedly fed him heroin and cocaine."

"She fled to Canada?"

"Back to her home in Toronto. Cathy Evelyn Smith was her name. And Kempsky pointed out in that newspaper story that Smith fought off extradition for a year and a half."

"So what's this talk about a few months?"

"That's why I'm here. What do you think?"

"I've appeared before the tribunal in The Hague."

"The world court?"

"Yes. On extradition cases."

"Involving?"

"Capital crimes. Death penalty cases. I tell them we are not a lawless country. I tell them we have a strict code of law, we have constitutional rights for the accused. You'd be surprised how tough it is to get through to them. When we electrocute people here, they imagine we're still in the Wild West. My job is to tell them, quite simply, 'We are not a barbaric nation.'"

Monday, July 10, 1985, 10:00 a.m., Calgary, Alberta, Canada

Canadian defense attorneys Brian Devlin and Don MacLeod gathered their papers at the conclusion of Charles Chitat Ng's arraignment. Provincial Judge Edward Adolphe left the courtroom, satisfied that the charges of attempted murder of a Hudson Bay guard, after an attempted robbery, were fully justified by the facts. Devlin turned to the spectators, mostly reporters, but among them were visitors from California who were still groggy from an all-night plane trip, and announced a press conference in five minutes.

With bailiffs flanking him cautiously, Ng shuffled off the stand. He was wearing the familiar orange jumpsuit that was quickly becoming ubiquitous for prisoners in courtrooms.

The shrill accents of the judge's voice echoed in Ng's ears: "Motion by the defense to delay the first hearing until September: granted. Motion by the defense for a 'ban on publication': taken under advisement."

"There's nothing unusual about a 'ban on publication'" MacLeod told the reporters in the crowded hallway. "At this stage, I'd request it for any of my clients."

"Would that include foreign press?" an Associated Press reporter asked.

MacLeod hesitated. "You've got a point. I don't suppose anything you printed in the States would affect potential jurors here."

"You're going to ask for a jury trial?"

"Before the Queen's Bench."

"How long is that going to take?"

"As long as it takes."

Monday, July 10, 1985, 11:00 a.m., San Francisco, Hall of Justice

Attorney Stan Pozanski, leading his demure client, Claralyn Balazs, strode down the steps of the Hall of Justice. This 1960s block-style building had all the charm of government housing, and a freeway connecting to Interstate 80 curved above its parking lot in an unending reminder that this was "South of Market." Five blocks away, six months earlier, it was a different story: at San Francisco's replica of the Capitol in Washington, City Hall, Mayor Diane Feinstein had announced a $50,000 reward for information as to the whereabouts of Paul Cosner and the Dubs family. The same knot of reporters who had covered this press conference in Civic Center now waited on the sidewalk of Bryant Street for some finality to the story.

"How'd it go?" a reporter from *The San Francisco Chronicle* asked.

"There's not much we can tell you," Pozanski answered. "We advised our client to refuse to take the oath."

"You mean she took the Fifth again?"

"Plus, she cited marital privilege."

A reporter from *The San Francisco Examiner* jumped in. "You've got to be kidding; she divorced Lake long ago."

"A grand jury doesn't set time limits to their questions." Pozanski shrugged. "You'll recall that my client has already given hours of testimony to the San Francisco police."

The reporter persisted. "Have you seen where Ballard says Ms. Balazs is a suspect?"

"Ballard?"

"Claud Ballard, Sheriff of Calaveras County."

"Ask him to talk to the San Francisco police."

"Ms. Balazs," the reporter asked, "why did you bail Ng out? And did you buy his plane ticket to Chicago?"

"Those are inflammatory and insulting questions," Pozanski answered. It was the last time, over the next thirteen years, the questions would be asked.

Wednesday, July 12, 1985, 2:30 p.m., Calaveras County Court House

Justice Court Judge Douglas Mewhinney was a familiar figure in San Andreas. Tall, thin, almost gaunt, with a well-trimmed mustache and beard, and black hair barely tinged with gray, he was Lincolnesque to some and a humorless monk to others. But no one could fault his judicial bearing.

The arraignments each morning involved the usual DUIs and domestic violence cases. But more and more, there were drug busts and execution-style killings. In the sixties and seventies, real estate promoters from both the San Francisco Bay Area and Southern California had sold retirement homes here like junk bonds. Nowadays, there was a good chance that the proverbial "cabin in the woods" would turn out to be an amphetamine factory.

Now serial killings.

Mewhinney studied the warrant drawn up by the district attorney's office. DA John Martin and his deputy, Ron Krelle, had worked on it feverishly since Monday, taking cues from deputy sheriffs in Calgary about how the case was proceeding there.

Things were happening "lightning fast" for a county that always seemed on the verge of going back to its horse and buggy days. It was difficult for prosecutors who had dealt mainly with domestic violence cases or bar fights to calculate what effect the warrants might have on an international case of extradition.

Mewhinney entered the courtroom on schedule and wasted no time in signing the warrants, ordering their transmittal to Calgary. Charles Ng's San Francisco attorneys were in court to receive copies. Garrick Lew had represented Ng long before, and ever since his visit from the FBI in early June he had been expecting this day. Michael Burt had been appointed to the case from the San Francisco Public Defender's office.

Mewhinney's declaration began: "Charles Chitat Ng is charged on two counts of violation of Section 187 of the Penal Code of the State of California, a felony." He cited the murders of Brenda O'Connor and Kathleen Allen and then a litany other charges, as reporters scribbled furiously.

Before closing the hearing, Mewhinney reminded the court that he had issued a gag order the day before. "All investigators, detectives, patrolmen, and officers of the court are forbidden to discuss this case."

Friday, July 14, 1985, 10:00 a.m., San Francisco, Hall of Justice

Coroner Boyd Stephens was at his lab desk in the basement of the San Francisco Hall of Justice, trying to establish some order among the bags of evidence that had been brought down from Calaveras County. As chief medical examiner of the city and county, he was now in charge of the most complex and confusing assignment of his career. He opened a metal wall drawer and pulled out the shelf. With help from an assistant, he transferred the body to a metal table. He studied the toe tag on the corpse, numbered Coroner's Case 2521-85.

Using an overhead microphone, he slowly read pertinent information into a recorder. Satisfied that he had established a solid base, the medical examiner bent and peered at the body. Bits of red dirt were scattered about the decaying flesh. Using a small scalpel and medical tweezers, he obtained pieces of epidermis with friction ridges.

He washed pieces of skin from the fingertips of the deceased, then put them on his own fingertips. He rolled on ink, then rolled his fingers onto fingerprint cards.

The results were faxed to Cheryl Steuer, who worked in the Criminal Identification & Information section of the State Department of Justice. Steuer had been asked to make a search for the prints of a possible victim in the Ng case.

Steuer had copies of Lonnie Bond's fingerprints from the state's arrest records. This significant bit of information was made possible by Section 11105 of the California Penal Code, which mandates that law enforcement agencies send arrest and booking information, dates of arrest, charges of arrest, the arresting agent, and fingerprints of those arrested to C.I. & I. The primary purpose of this database is to keep records on sex offenders or other criminals who might apply for jobs that are sensitive to criminal behavior. This time, the reason was different.

Steuer compared the original fingerprints with the faxed copies sent to her. She found ten points of similarity between the fingerprints of Coroner's Case 2521-85 and the known fingerprint of Lonnie Wayne Bond, date of birth 12–2–57.

Meanwhile, in another state office, connected to the Department of Motor Vehicles, Lieutenant Thomas Murphy, who for ten years had taught fingerprint identification at the City College of San Francisco, examined a transparency that had come from a driver's license. Murphy recorded information on the card: Robin Scott Stapley, DOB 8-16-58, California driver's license Number N, Nora, 4547300.

He placed this card next to a fingerprint card faxed to him by Coroner Stephens that morning.

They matched.

The two bodies found on the Heale property in red and blue sleeping bags had been positively identified.

Chapter 12

Gunpoint

December 15, 1985, 10:00 a.m., Calgary, Alberta, Canada

Charles Ng was brought before Court of Queen's Bench Judge Allen Sulatycky. Ng's defense suddenly unleashed a new tactic: His attorneys
waived a jury trial and asked the judge to hear the case instead. It turned
out to be a shrewd decision.

It was becoming apparent that the attempts of California jurisdictions
to file extradition papers were optimistically premature. The State
Attorney General's office now realized it would be at least a year before all
the charges from Calaveras County could be assembled and presented to
the Calgary court. The "order" of "law and order" had made its first mistake, and it colored events that followed.

The defense had no advantage in delay. By moving swiftly they could
secure a short sentence on a reduced charge. And that prospect was a very
good strategy for protecting Ng from extradition to California, where he
would certainly be up for the death penalty. In short, the plan was to get
Ng to trial and into a Canadian jail as quickly as possible.

Then the prosecution made a second mistake. Two of the four charges
brought before the Queen's bench were severe: attempted murder and
robbery while armed. Either could result in life sentences. Perhaps because
Calaveras County had originally rushed two murder charges, again for
good causes, against Ng, although unquestionably deserved, and because
six more had been added since July 15, the Canadian prosecutors per-
suaded themselves they had a major capital case on their hands.

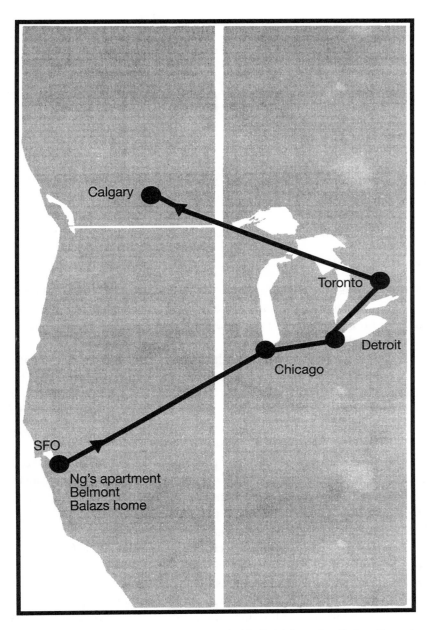

The escape route taken by Charles Ng in his flight from South San Francisco to Calgary.

"Canada has rightfully refused," defense attorney Don MacLeod told reporters, "to extradite anyone facing capital punishment for at least twenty-three years. The 1976 treaty with the United States leaves no doubt about our future intentions. As this is our law, we intend to argue for it vigorously."

The Queen's Bench proceedings moved so swiftly that MacLeod had no reason to bring up extradition. His matter-of-fact presentation of the case was designed simply to get his client behind bars on the least charge possible.

Prosecutor Manfred DeLong opened his presentation to the judge by introducing seven law enforcement officers of various jurisdictions as witnesses. Their demonstration of the events of five months ago was mercifully brief, mirroring repetitions of the case in the local press. John Patrick "Sean" Doyle, the affable security guard and part-time teacher who had pinioned Ng in the Hudson Bay store, had told his story many times over.

After the noon break, sparks began to fly. Doyle was subjected to a curious line of cross-examination from MacLeod's defense partner. "During the struggle with the defendant," Brian Devlin asked, "could you tell where your hands were?"

"My hands were wrestling against the gun he was trying to point at me," Doyle answered, bewildered.

"But can you tell us for certain whether your hands were on the gun handle, on the barrel, or perhaps on the trigger?"

Now the point was obvious. "They were not on the trigger—"

"Do you know exactly where your hands were, Mr. Doyle?"

"No."

The prosecution felt no damage had been done, and rested its case. MacLeod and Devlin asked for a recess to consult with their client. They returned in a few minutes to announce, "The defense elects not to call any evidence." Ng would not be put on the stand.

Devlin focused his summation on the fact that Ng was armed, but not pointing a gun, during the scuffle. Was it attempted murder? If a gun goes off in an altercation, he argued, surely there is no premeditation.

"If a person steals from a newsstand and happens to have a gun in his coat, for whatever reason," Devlin asked, "can it be called armed robbery?"

The reporters in the courtroom had already accepted the inevitable: it wasn't going to stand as "robbery at gunpoint." The prosecution had been snookered into an exaggerated charge of attempted murder. They didn't attempt to press that point, and as a result "robbery at gunpoint" also appeared weak.

The following morning, Judge Sulatycky ruled that Charles Chitat Ng was guilty of shoplifting and assault, for which he would serve a prison term of four and a half years in the Prince Albert, Saskatchewan provincial prison. In Canada, four and one-half years meant exactly that. Together with the nearly half year it had taken to get to trial, it would be five years since the crimes in California were committed, or 1990, before Ng would be released.

Eight days later, the defendant celebrated his twenty-second birthday in an Edmonton provincial prison to which he had been remanded. It was on Christmas Eve.

January 25, 1986, San Andreas, Calaveras County Court House

Just over a month after Ng began serving his sentence, District Attorney John Martin announced a possible breakthrough in the problem of extraditing Charles Ng. He had discovered that the Canadian Minister of Justice had set a precedent in scheduling the extradition of a convicted murderer back to the United States. The man was Joseph J. Kindler, who had escaped from a Philadelphia jail in 1985, and later was arrested for burglary in Montreal.

Martin was apparently unaware that the Kindler case was already the subject of intense debate in Canada. Over the next five years he would learn how determined the Canadians were to defend virtually anyone from the death penalty.

February 26, 1986, Austin, Texas

Another month, another possible breakthrough. Calaveras DA investigator John Crawford had followed up on a lead about an eyewitness to the murders—a Tori Doolin, now living in Austin, Texas. Last year Crawford had interviewed her in San Diego, California.

Crawford faxed the data to Sergeant Russell Schmidt of the Austin Police Department, who in turn tracked down Doolin. Leonard Lake and Charles Ng had supposedly told her about the deaths of Brenda O'Connor, Lonnie Bond, and Robin Stapley. Lake had later visited her apartment in San Diego with an Asian male.

The Texas policeman got permission from Doolin to show her a line-up of possible accomplices of Lake's. He spread six photos of Asian males on her coffee table. ˉ

She studied them, then pointed to the one numbered 15350-F. "That's the man I saw in my apartment with Leonard Lake on April 24, last year."

"Are you sure?"

"Well, I thought his name was Charles Gunnar at the time."

"No, I mean the Asian. Can you place him?"

"Yes, that's Charlie."

"Do you remember anything you forgot to mention when you last spoke to the police?"

"Yes. Lake actually told me where he found the bodies. He said, 'Brenda was found in the house, Lonnie was found—'"

"What house?"

"Lonnie's house, next door to Lake's. He said, 'Lonnie was found on the front balcony, and Scott was found outside the back door. There were no guns or drugs around.'"

The report of this identification was sent back to Detective Crawford, in San Andreas. He notified the sheriff, placed it in the files, and wondered what it meant about Lake's brazenness, or about Ng's role in the crimes. The files were beginning to bulge.

May 26, 1986, San Andreas, Calaveras County

Sheriff Claud Ballard called a press conference to respond to criticism from the press about lack of progress in extraditing Charles Ng. "It's been almost a year since these ghastly things happened," he told reporters at the County Administrative Headquarters. "But we now have a break-through in extradition evidence."

The reporters pulled out their notebooks. It was a far cry from a year ago. Ballard noticed the regular reporters among the press, but there·was no one from San Francisco or Los Angeles, let along the national media.

"I'm happy to announce," he began, "that we are going to release videotapes to Canadian officials responsible for holding Charles Ng." He noted that the State of California was now working with the U.S. State Department to put pressure on Canada for extradition.

"Videotapes? How many?" the reporter from *The Sacramento Bee* asked.

"One. We believe that is enough."

"What about capital punishment in California?"

"We intend to show that the nightmare in California and in Calaveras County overrides any objection against bringing murder charges with possibility of execution."

"On what grounds?" the reporter persisted.

"The public has a right to self-defense against this kind of sheer viciousness."

Friday, February 27, 1987, Ottawa, Canada

The "Brenda" videotape of torture, an Ottawa newspaper reported, was included in more than one thousand pages of evidence submitted by the U.S. State Department to the Canadian Department of Justice. There were eyewitness identifications similar to the one Tori Doolin gave in Austin, Texas.

The counsel for the Canadian Department of Justice told reporters, "We are prepared to recommend to the Ministry of Justice, after we have had a chance to analyze these records, that the Court of Queen's Bench issue a warrant to Edmonton to release prisoner Ng to us for extradition to the United States."

In Calgary, attorney Don MacLeod, still representing Ng fourteen months after the trial, demurred. "We're dealing with very complex issues here. Very complex. When you're looking at the nature and number of the charges here, and how serious they are, you can expect both sides to look at every issue carefully."

"What do you see as the next step, and the outcome?" a reporter asked. "Serious charges should get serious attention."

"The Fall of 1987 will not be the end of it."

Monday, September 26, 1991, Ottawa, Canada

The Fall of 1987 wasn't the end of it. Except for Sheriff Claud Ballard, who died on Christmas Day in 1987. The Ng case moved on through the Falls of 1988, 1989, and 1990. Month after month, representatives of the Canadian government and of the U.S. State Department argued over Charles Ng in memos passed back and forth through their embassies. Under cover of bureaucratic posturing, Ng was safe, serving his four and a half year sentence in relative comfort. The story of the horrendous charges against him had vanished from the headlines for years.

Charles Ng, transferred to Saskatchewan Penitentiary, in Prince Albert, was now an informal student of the law. He knew that when his four and a half year sentence was over, he would be in limbo between Canada and the United States, and he was preparing for that eventuality.

These were long years for the families of the victims who had come to Calgary for the trial. Some had exhausted their life savings on the interminable trips. In all of their nightmares appeared the face of the accused— the plump boyish face with the upturned, defiant chin and lips, the steady emotionless black eyes, the mop of hair falling in bunches over his forehead. And above all, the demeanor of intensity, of self-containment in the face of the most lurid accusations in memory.

It had taken years, as lawyers had predicted, for the final extradition papers to arrive on the proper Canadian bench. But now, in the Fall of 1991, years after his flight to Canada, the matter had finally come to a head. This time the Conservative Party in Canada had approved a resolution asking for the return of the death penalty. As in many of the states, public opinion polls in several provinces favored the return of justice based on "an eye for an eye."

Minister of Justice Kim Campbell had ruled that the extradition papers were persuasive, but her decision was subject to a Supreme Court ruling. Defense attorney Donald MacLeod had made sure of that. He had cited the Charter of Rights and Freedoms Act, passed in 1976. MacLeod argued it would violate Ng's constitutional rights to subject him to cruel and unusual punishment, and the method of execution in California at the time, by lethal gas, was exactly that.

Amnesty International had mounted a campaign for Ng ever since June of 1990, but now Minister Campbell decided enough was enough. Ng's case was going to Canada's high court with a lawyer from Montreal, Julius Grey, to argue it.

Campbell's predecessors as Ministers of Justice, John Crosbie and Douglas Lewis, had rebuffed efforts to assure the United States that the death penalty would not be an option after extradition. Both of them argued that Canada would become "a haven for murderers trying to escape justice."

At ten o'clock in the morning, reporters made their way through the demonstrations to hear the Court's ruling in person, and interview some of the justices.

"The ruling is conclusive," said a spokeswoman. "The Court has concluded that Ng may be extradited to the United States without assurances that he will *not* be subject to execution."

"What was the vote?" a reporter asked.

"The vote was four for the majority with three dissents."

In Calgary, reporters were waiting at MacLeod's offices. He was non-plused. "We still have a final appeal."

"Higher than the Supreme Court?"

"We are going to the United Nations," he said. "The Committee on Human Rights has agreed to hear our case. We intend to pursue all the avenues open to us."

September 26, 1991, 10:30 a.m., Saskatchewan, Alberta

Calaveras County Sheriff Bill Nutall waited in the Canadian warden's office for a phone call.

The first news was already in: the Supreme Court had voted 4–3 to "refuse to condemn the death penalty," as the media was framing the decision. Now, as Nutall had anticipated, the real decision would come.

The ball was now in the court of the Justice Minister, Kim Campbell. She could act on the Court decision, or she could demur, as did her predecessors.

The phone call came. "Release the prisoner to United States authorities."

At first there was pandemonium in the prison, as the California officials swarmed around Sheriff Nutall. Nutall had already reserved a flight at the airport. He signed the documents allowing him to take custody of the prisoner. A car was brought around. The prisoner was led through a side door. Soon they were at the airport.

Ng shuffled to the waiting aircraft.

The speed of Campbell's decision and the subsequent immediate flight of Ng out of Canada caught even the attorneys by surprise. The Royal Canadian Mounted Police were back at their stations before MacLeod could denounce the haste of the exit. MacLeod took comfort in one of the dissenting opinions of the Supreme Court: Justice Peter Cory had written that morning, "This amounts to an indefensible abdication of moral responsibility."

September 26, 1991, California, Canada

Paul Cosner's sister, Sharon Sellitto, had harried the press and the police over the injustice of the interminable delays. She had not endeared herself to either with her frank criticisms of how the search for her brother, Paul Cosner, had been carried out. She was still unrepentant in her outrage. Her vivacious, outgoing manner gave her easy access to reporters, and she used them to try to find some recompense for her brother's disappearance and death.

His body had never been found. She said, "All I want for Ng is to tell us, by God, where they buried my brother. Then maybe we can give him a proper burial. Watching Ng go through the legal system is like running a triathlon. The first leg was the horror of the murders. The second was the horror of the Canadian justice system and how long it took to get him back here. The third and final leg will be getting the justice system started in California."

In Canada, Sharon's words were echoed by police associations and public organizations demanding the death penalty.

In Oakland, California, close to some of the crime scenes, a national group, Citizens for Law and Order, jumped on the decision to support victims' rights. "For some of these people, it's not even over when the trial is over," said the president, Phyllis Callos. "For some, it has to be the final sentence. For others, it's not over until the death sentence is carried out."

"Time isn't the problem," she continued. "Each person needs the final act that will set him free."

Tuesday, November 5, 1991, "Inside Edition," New York

The release of Charles Ng to the prison at Folsom, California, after more than six years of detention in Canada, had again excited interest in the sexually violent case.

"Inside Edition" broadcast a controversial segment over many national stations. It featured graphic details of the sexual torture of several women by the accused Lake and Ng. But a new aspect of the case was the introduction of a further compelling player—a former cellmate of Ng's at Fort Leavenworth, Kansas.

The unidentified ex-prisoner claimed he was a friend of Ng's during several months in 1982. Ng was sentenced there for stealing military weapons in Hawaii and later fleeing to Philo, California. After he left Leavenworth, Ng hooked up again with Leonard Lake in the infamous survivalist bunker.

Yet the "Inside Edition" segment stirred up the Ng mania once again, after years of quiet. A former cellmate of Ng's said Ng bragged about using pliers and other common tools to disfigure women as they screamed in agony. He enjoyed the screams, he said. There was a semblance of credibility in the report that went beyond jailhouse talk. "He had sex-slave fantasies . . . but I don't think sex to him was very important. . . . The torture, the pure terror, he wanted them to see terror. He wanted to see them beg, to plead."

Prison confessions that cannot be authenticated by any records are worthless, most law enforcement people said. But there was speculation. "There is even talk about this guy being a key witness in the trial that's coming up in Calaveras County," a Sacramento officer argued in a television interview.

"I doubt that," another rebutted. "It's part of the hype."

Perhaps the most compelling information from this television tabloid show concerned Ng's personality. Until now, Ng was an enigma. He sat stone-faced in court in Canada. There were reports of his studies in prison, some signs of humanity. But now the Leavenworth story painted a different and frightening picture. "He seemed like he hated everyone and everything," the former cellmate said. "Gays, drug users and dealers, ethnic groups . . . . He can kill and not even think about it."

The fear that he instilled rang true. "In prison, people would whisper and move away from him. People were scared of him." The former convict mentioned that Ng had called him after he got out, continuing to describe his escapades of violence. "He's behind bars, I know. But I'm paralyzed with fear. . . ."

Wednesday, November 10, 1991, Edmonton, Canada

As the appearance of Ng at the preliminary hearing in Calaveras County loomed, further damning reports came from another ex-inmate, this time in Canada. Attorneys close to the case discounted, however, the possibility that this kind of testimony would ever be allowed in an American court.

The Edmonton Journal published a complete version of the story, including drawings that Ng purportedly made in his jail cell. "It's pretty damning stuff," one of the sources of the information said, "but whether it can be used is a question."

Ng's fellow prisoner in Canada claimed that Ng had bragged that he would never be returned to the U.S., "even at gunpoint." He was quoted as saying that he would kill a guard or a fellow prisoner first.

That offense would bring a potential twenty-five years to life in Canada.

The fellow prisoner from eight years before, in Leavenworth, had said that, when he knew he was to be released, Ng tried to hire him. Charlie gave him a list with seventy-seven names on it—judges, law enforcement officials, and lawyers.

He wanted them killed.

"Charlie had a reputation when he came in," said the inmate. "He was the best martial arts guy I've ever seen, and he would do a lot of showboating, spin kicks and all that."

"This was in 1983. I contacted the FBI when I got out in January," the informant said, "and told them Ng was going to contact me and we would begin operations."

The "operations" were described as having a compound, "out in the woods somewhere" where they would have a torture chamber, the "whole nine yards." Photos sent by Leonard Lake reportedly confirmed that the plan was already underway.

The similarity of the Canadian revelations to those from Leavenworth also raised some eyebrows. "It's like a bombing," a psychologist said. "Everyone wants to get into the act. The pictures do exist, as do the titles, but as bizarre and shocking as they are they are only the product of an idle mind, in a prisoner facing death."

The FBI responded vigorously to the suggestion that the complaints of a former inmate of Leavenworth went unheeded in 1983–84, and thus led to the Wilseyville massacre at Lake's compound.

The FBI spokeswoman told the news media that "talk is no crime." An agent in the Kansas City office said, "There's really nothing you can do until a trial starts and the convict can testify under oath."

Before Ng would go to trial, the Canadian informant would be dead as a result of a traffic accident.

Chapter 13

Megacase

Monday, March 4, 1992, 8:00 a.m., Highway Four, Calaveras County

There's something wrong here, something I'm missing, defense attorney Margolin thought. There's something about the proportions of this case, something about breaking the boundaries.

He headed toward Angel's Camp. The two-lane road wound slowly up toward the western reaches of the Sierra, over washed-out gullies and around red-dirt bluffs from the last Ice Age, a desolate landscape of scrub trees and granite outcroppings. San Andreas was another thirty-five or so miles north, on Highway 49.

He was going to argue in court on behalf of a man accused of the most heinous murders in the history of the state. He was prepared to say that justice could best be served by allowing the accused to choose his own attorneys. Garrick Lew and Michael Burt had represented Charlie Ng seven years ago, in San Francisco, in San Andreas, and to a lesser degree in Calgary. Judge Douglas Mewhinney had ruled, when the accused serial killer was brought back from Canada to stand trial, that new attorneys were needed. He had appointed Thomas Marovich and James Webster, whose offices were in Sonora some miles down Route 49. His arguments seemed unimpeachable.

The judge's reasoning: Lew had never defended a capital case, let alone one this extensive. Burt was traveling back and forth from San Francisco to Los Angeles, representing the so-called Night Stalker. Charlie

147

Ng claimed vociferously that Lew and Burt could represent him best, but Mewhinney balked.

Was the judge worried about further delay, further obfuscation by the accused? Ephraim Margolin was prepared to argue that there was already something hideously wrong about new attorneys having to go through tens of thousands of pages of documents and research some six hundred witnesses.

What if Mewhinney countered that they had already done that work in preparing for the preliminary hearing?

The skeleton of the case now formed in his mind. He had to search for a parallel, a comparison in some other field to the enormity of this case. He couldn't approach the bench and say, "this is different." He had to specify how different.

He drove into the parking lot. Four deputy sheriffs, carrying rifles, were on the roof of the courthouse.

He drove to the rear parking lot. A white van was parked with its doors nuzzled against the back entrance of the courthouse. A Folsom prison guard lounged by the van, an Uzi slung over his shoulder.

Margolin went through a metal detector and entered the courtroom.

Judge Mewhinney entered precisely five minutes late—the prerogative of all judges.

"Your Honor," Margolin began, "we are all aware of the danger of bringing certain attorneys into a case." He noticed that Mewhinney was chary of smiling. The seriousness of his demeanor was a danger sign: humor was not the answer.

"I represent two attorneys, whom the accused, Charles Ng, wishes to reinstate. I fully realize that you have already ruled on Mr. Ng's request to be represented by these two attorneys. I realize that you have appointed the present attorneys, and that they have just completed their preparations for the preliminary hearing. These attorneys are Garrick Lew and Michael Burt. I need not mention that I know both these outstanding defense attorneys, and that I have represented them since the very beginning of this case."

The judge raised an eyebrow. "This was when Mr. Ng had been apprehended in Calgary?"

"Before that, Your Honor. You see, Mr. Lew had been Charles Ng's attorney for some time prior to that. There was a traffic case, I believe. When an all-points bulletin went out for him in 1985, Mr. Lew was de facto Mr. Ng's attorney."

"But Mr. Burt's appearance in this case dates from 1985."

"Yes."

"You intend to argue to reinstate this counsel."

"Exactly, and I would like to begin by reviewing your argumentation at that time. I will be brief, Your Honor. Three minutes should be enough."

The judge nodded.

Margolin said, "A man is about to go on trial for his life. We gassed one less than a year ago at San Quentin. A man in this danger should have his day in court. I'd like to emphasize, Your Honor, that the request I am about to make runs counter to what I or any other sane defense attorney aims for in a case of this kind."

Mewhinney raised both eyebrows. The handful of onlookers were silent. Margolin let the thought sink in for a few seconds.

"We all know," Margolin said, "what the defense in a capital case usually aims for. Delay. The longer the delay, the greater the chance that the defense might break down the case. And that the defendant might live."

He paused for effect.

"Instead of delay, I'm going to ask you to speed this trial up. I'm moving that we avoid further delay. I could argue point by point why my clients—attorneys Lew and Burt—have no problem with workload or lack of experience. I could try to make my case by reviewing the almost eight years of experience that my clients have had with this case. But I'm not going to do that."

The attorney paused just enough to let the judge know something new was now coming. "For centuries we were content as a human race with the ordinary laws of physics. Sir Isaac Newton laid out the principles of gravity, which explained the movement of every heavenly body."

Mewhinney peered over his glasses at the bushy haired, husky attorney.

Margolin steamed ahead. "Two thousand years before Newton, Euclid showed us proofs of geometry. All these things have served us well. Then along came Einstein. My point is obvious. Just as in physics we had to abandon the ordinary rules to deal with the macroscopic world of Einstein, so here we have to deal with a case that breaks all the boundaries by making decisions that also break normal boundaries."

Mewhinney nodded.

"We now think of astronomy as megaphysics, Your Honor. This is a megacase. Plain common sense recommends that we break the rules you have cited and abide by the request Ng has made. Your Honor, I move that Garrick Lew and Michael Burt, in the interest of speed and justice, be reinstated as counsel for the defense."

Margolin pulled back his cuff and looked at his watch. His statement had taken exactly three minutes.

The following morning the court ruled that Charles Ng's original attorneys be reappointed to the defense.

Judge Mewhinney knew that attorneys Webster and Marovich were virtually required to appeal. The appeal was made to the California Supreme Court.

With uncharacteristic speed, however, the high court voted against the lower court ruling. It was a close vote—4–3—but just as binding as 7–0.

Attorneys Lew and Burt were out. Webster and Marovich were in.

The attorney general's office in Sacramento reacted immediately to the decision.

"We're obviously pleased," said spokesman Dave Puglia. "The attorney general and the district attorney will be seeking a new date for a preliminary hearing in Calaveras County. . . ."

Margolin was aghast at the court's action. "The people of California want capital punishment, and certainly the Ng case is not a pretty case, but I do not think the people of California ever authorized or wanted a wholesale abandonment of fairness in preparation for trial. The people aren't that bloodthirsty."

A reporter muttered, "You want to bet?"

Chapter 14

A Sherlock Holmes Mystery

Thursday, October 8, 1992, 5:00 p.m., San Andreas, Calaveras County

After Webster and Marovich were allowed six months to prepare, the preliminary hearing began.

The attorneys challenged the affidavits introduced in the Canadian extradition hearings. The defense was following a textbook strategy in a capital crime case. Stall—the judge must take the time to honor every challenge.

Time—it was all about time. People die. Like Sheriff Claud Ballard, his affidavit now stricken. Affidavits are not accepted in a trial, only a preliminary hearing. The reasoning: the defense has the right to cross examine, which is impossible if the witness has died.

As the court proceedings ended its first week, the Dubs case—the disappearance of an entire family—hung over the testimony like a Sherlock Holmes mystery. A man leaves work, goes home to his wife and child, and two minutes later there is a huge void: none are heard or seen again. What evidence was found in the apartment? Was there blood? Were there weapons? Knives, shell casings? If there were no weapons, how did they die?

According to Missing Persons officer Irene Brunn's testimony, the neighbor across the street, Katherine McAuliffe, identified Ng as the Asian man she saw leaving the Dubses' apartment. She also said the house remained dark that night, with no lights clicking on or off, and that was very unusual. The tenant downstairs, Barbara Spolter, also said Ng was the Asian man who left the apartment that day. But no physical clues were found in the flat. Not a drop of blood. No one saw bodies hauled out.

Then what did happen? The Dubses' bodies were never found. Even with observant neighbors such as Katherine McAuliffe and Barbara Spolter looking on, it may have been easy to spirit away a year-old infant. But not two adults as well.

Irene Brunn and Tom Eisenmann had gone to the Dubses' house at the first call to Missing Persons. Long before they had any idea that this case was part of a larger killing spree, they had tried to construct a reasonable chain of events to explain this mystery.

One possibility they considered: Harvey Dubs leaves work at the Graphic Company and heads home. He has a potential buyer coming at a quarter to six. He parks his car in front of his house on Yukon Street. He's eager to see his son. Sean has infused his life with a new joy this last year. Every expression, every giggle, every moment of wonder at a new life flows from the animated face of his son and fills Harvey's heart.

Harvey enters his house. His wife, Deborah, waves at him. She has the telephone cradled under her chin as she bustles about the kitchen preparing dinner.

"Are you talking to Karen Tuck?" Harvey calls.

"Yes."

He grins. Very few people, besides her parents, have known Deborah as long as Karen Tuck.

Harvey goes to the bathroom and washes his hands.

Deborah stirs the stew she's cooking. She listens as Karen excitedly tells her what happened to her that day.

The doorbell rings. Deborah says, "Karen, got to hang up. The people who called about the video equipment are here." She goes to the door, Sean still on her arm.

Was Leonard Lake at that door? Was Charlie Ng?

Whoever was there, what happened next?

Deborah sees who is there. The potential buyer, or buyers, enter, the door swings shut, then a bullet is fired, without warning, into her head? Then another bullet crashes into Harvey's head as he rushes from the bathroom? Then a final bullet extinguishes the baby's life?

For what? A camcorder? Impossible. But what else made sense?

Deborah Dubs was alive at 5:45—that was Karen Tuck's testimony. The house remained dark that night—that was Dorice Murphy's testimony.

The Dubses weren't selling a car, like Paul Cosner. A car allowed mobility, misdirection, and seclusion. But video equipment?

Three lives snuffed out for a few bits of electronics?

Possible. But where were the bodies? And how were the bodies brought out of the house? And not seen?

Was it possible that Harvey, Deborah, and Sean had been led away from the scene, alive? Then killed later, at a different location?

Possible. Even with such attentive neighbors. The timing would have to be lucky, not intentional.

Another potential sequence envisioned by Missing Persons: the Dubs family is led down the stairs, at gunpoint. Katherine McAuliffe takes that particular moment to turn her attention to the dinner she is cooking. Barbara Spolter takes that particular moment to take a shower, and cannot hear the tramp of many footsteps on the stairs of the flat overhead.

Possible. But improbable.

The only other explanation is that the Dubses were killed in their apartment. Then their bodies moved.

But then there would have been physical evidence left in the apartment. It was impossible to kill three people and not leave some trace evidence.

No matter how Brunn and Eisenmann twisted and turned the facts, no matter how many times they tried to recreate the scene, Officers Brunn and Eisenmann had no answers.

Friday, October 9, 1992, 9:30 a.m., San Andreas, Calaveras County Court House

Security was more in evidence now than when the preliminary hearing had begun. A plainclothes policeman was obvious to all the journalists in the first row of the spectators' seats. Another officer, not in uniform, sat alone in the jury box. His weapon, a black Uzi, was held at port arms. Two uniformed deputy sheriffs stood at the rear door, another at the door that gave access to the judge's chambers.

Three more uniformed men sat in a triangle around the accused. Each had a side arm, each stared unwaveringly at Charles Ng. The defendant was shackled to his chair. His head was bent over a thick file on the table in front of him.

The courtroom players were all in place: next to Ng were his two lawyers, Thomas Marovich and James Webster. To their right was another table, for Sharlene Honnaka, Deputy Attorney General of California, and

John Martin, District Attorney of Calaveras County. The court reporter was Linda James.

The fifth day of the hearing began. Defense attorney Marovich stood. "Your Honor, Mr. Ng has indicated to me he has not had a hot meal since the preliminary hearing started. He had indicated he had cold pancakes and milk for breakfast on Tuesday. Of course, he got a bag lunch in court. When he got back to Folsom, it was cold meat stew and cold rice. Yesterday morning, he had a sweet roll and milk. Again, a bag lunch here, a cold chicken patty, mashed potatoes when he returned last night. This morning he indicated he had scrambled eggs, which were cold, and some sort of scalloped potatoes, which were the same. As I understand it, all his food is precooked, and it comes into administration segregation where it is supposedly heated up. He is on a different schedule than ninety-nine percent of the other inmates in 'ad seg' because of the early rise to get to court, and since the start of the preliminary hearing, the meals have been cold."

At each mention of a food item, Sharon Sellitto, Paul Cosner's sister, grimaced.

Three men went into a huddle on the bench: Judge Mewhinney, a representative from the Department of Corrections, and a defense attorney. They thrashed out a solution to Ng's meals.

The judge explained their solution and announced, "That may solve the problem."

"Part of the problem," Marovich said. "We want Mr. Ng being able to, when transported, to have a view of the horizon as to avoid motion sickness."

"Jesus Christ!" Sharon Sellitto thundered from the back of the room.

The judge looked befuddled, vacillating from wanting to make an admonition to a victim's relative and realizing how it would look in the press. He paused for a moment, then motioned to Marovich to continue.

The defense argued that Mr. Ng's dependency on Scopolamine, to avoid car sickness, was making him drowsy.

Marovich added, "Mr. Ng indicates his feelings of anxiety, confusion, shakiness, and psychological effects every time he arrives and is put in the cage. This affects his concentration, his ability to fully prepare and communicate with his attorneys."

As a security precaution, Charles Ng, when not in the courtroom, was held in a thick, wire meshed cage, six by four by three feet—not unlike those used in a zoo to hold vicious predators.

Charles Ng had told U.S. Magistrate Peter A. Nowinski that he felt like an animal when he was put in the cage. The morning papers carried

During preliminary hearings in San Andreas in October, 1992, Ng was confined in an extraordinary cage when not in the courtroom—a practice termed barbarous by a federal magistrate. (AP/Wide World)

the magistrate's reply in a sidebar to the photograph of the cage. "The cage is beneath any concept of human dignity worthy of a civilized society except under the most demanding circumstances demonstrated by clear and convincing evidence of necessity."

The judge refused to deny use of the cage, for security reasons.

Marovich said, "Judge, the photo of Mr. Ng in the cage, we believe, is very relevant information. A type of excessive unconstitutional confinement is being applied to him."

Webster stood. "I saw videotapes of the bunker on TV last night. All the information that the news media had received up to the filing of the gag order was from the prosecution. On the other hand, as the Court is I'm sure aware, it is not normal procedure for a defendant to put on any evidence at the preliminary hearing. So the total effect of this is that the—the news media is getting more of the prosecution's case and none of the defense side, even when we file a declaration as to why we need a continuance."

Mewhinney nodded. "I'll reconsider that declaration."

Webster held up a newspaper. "I think that the bottom line is that we don't want this case tried in the press."

Judge Mewhinney raised his eyebrows. "I definitely do not. I'm trying to prevent both sides from being tried in the press. I can only prevent that which has not occurred yet. I cannot go to the past and remedy those things."

Finally, Judge Mewhinney came to the word everyone had been waiting for.

Videotape.

A hush came over the room.

"Ladies and gentlemen," the judge said, "other than Mr. and Mrs. Stapley, if the remaining people will leave the courtroom, then we are going to show a videotape. The tape is labeled 'M. Ladies Kathy/Brenda.'"

Webster responded, "Fine, Your Honor. As a matter of fact, for this portion of the preliminary hearing, under 977, Mr. Ng would—well, actually—if possible, Mr. Ng would waive his presence, as well."

The judge was flabbergasted. "I can't do that. 977 specifically exempts his being excluded."

Webster and Marovich sat down.

The judge continued, "The first portion of the tape does not deal with Mr. Stapley or Ms. O'Connor. And on that basis, I'm going to have you excluded from the first portion of the tape. When the second portion is played, you will be present and are entitled to be present. And a member of the bailiff's staff will be out to have you step in at that time."

The Stapleys both said, "We understand."

"Thank you, sir. Thank you, ma'am."

Outside the courtroom, the press surrounded Sharon Sellitto. Microphones were thrust in her face. Random questions were fired—

"What about Ng's food?"—"What about Ng getting sick?"—"What about the cage?"

Sharon's face was fixed in a battle between rage and humor. She said, "Actually, for Ng the cage may be a little too large and roomy."

Chapter 15

Bombshell

**Friday, October 9, 1991, Noon, San Andreas,
Calaveras County Court House**

The courtroom doors swung open. The deceased Robin Stapley's father, Dwight, walked out. His face was ashen. He supported his wife, who was crumpled against his chest. She leaned against the wall, pressing her face against the cold concrete. Her shoulders visibly shuddered.

The press congregated around Dwight and Lola Stapley. A dozen different voices fired questions simultaneously. A reporter asked point blank, "Why did you decide to view the video?"

Dwight Stapley, the retired school teacher he was, gave a measured answer. "We're like people who are waiting for someone who is late, and we over-imagine what we don't know. We had to know. We knew it was going to hurt."

His wife, Lola, added, "To me, not knowing is the worst thing in the world. I had no idea what to expect."

Kathy Allen's sister had decided not to view the videotape.

Outside the courthouse a mob of the media surrounded Diane Montemurro, Kathy Allen's sister. She said, "I don't want to see the pain that she went through. Hearing about it was bad enough."

The preliminary hearing reverted to legal swordplay after the videotapes were played. The press, with its curiosity sated after viewing the tapes, all but evaporated. By October 20 the only media in the courtroom were reporters from the *Calaveras Enterprise* and *The Sacramento Bee*.

159

**October 20, 1985, 9:30 a.m., San Andreas,
Calaveras County Court House**

The bailiff called the courtroom to order. The judge took his seat behind the bench.

Defense attorney Marovich stood. "Mr. Ng has indicated to me when I first saw him earlier this morning, when he was in the cage, that he's feeling ill at the present time, feeling nauseous. From my personal observations he does appear not to be mentally alert, as I've frequently found him. But he does appear to be having some mental problems, and he's told me of physical problems."

The judge asked, "Mr. Ng?"

"Yes."

"You're feeling nauseous at this time?"

"I'm just . . . I'm feeling kind of sick . . . I think I've got the flu, I don't know, but I feel weak and tired, I can't concentrate. I wasn't able to sleep last night, because of nightmares of being in a cage."

"Mr. Ng," the judge asked, "you feel you have the flu; is that correct?"

"I've got a runny nose and I might have a temperature—I have a toothache, too."

"And have you sought medical attention for the toothache?"

"Yes, I did, Your Honor, the doctor in the prison told me that he won't give me any medication, because he doesn't want me to feel drowsy. So I didn't get any medical attention."

"You indicated you have a runny nose?"

"Yeah."

"And what other symptoms that you conclude that you have the flu from?"

"Headache, nausea, stomach problems."

"Mr. Ng, the Court is going to proceed today. If you feel that you need . . . if you feel nauseous, feel like you're going to throw up, if you'll just notify either of your attorneys at that point, then we'll recess at that point, gentlemen. On the—"

"Judge," Marovich interrupted, "for the record, we'd like to object to proceeding at this time. Obviously, given Mr. Ng's statement . . . and frankly, Judge, given my own personal observations at first having contact with him at quarter after nine this morning, I basically feel he is not really in any condition right now to meaningfully participate and assist us."

Webster added, "Your Honor, we've submitted two declarations, as the court is aware. They're short. I've just given them to the district attorney. As far as the security motion that we have been doing in closed session, we have an additional . . . at least one additional exhibit, which we would be presenting to the Court. I've just given a copy of the two to the District Attorney."

The judge said, "Well, let me deal with one thing at a time." Mewhinney ordered the Court to proceed. Within a few minutes Charlie Ng fell asleep at the defense table.

Once again the hearing was mired in cross-examinations and re-cross-examinations.

Highway Patrolman Hicks testified to having been called to the scene of an accident involving a pickup truck with the license plate AHOYMTY.

Mr. Crawford was cross-examined on the investigation he conducted involving Tori Doolin, the friend of Robin Scott Stapley who had moved to Austin, Texas.

But the groundwork had been cleverly laid. The bombshell was now ready to drop.

Wednesday, October 28, 1984, 1:30 p.m., San Andreas, Calaveras County Court House

Defense Attorney Marovich rose. "Your Honor, Mr. Ng has a civil case he wants to file. He requests an order from this Court that he be allowed access to the Superior Court Clerk's Office. The Clerk could come down to the security area and deliver the papers to the Superior Court Clerk so that he can file the civil action on his own behalf."

The judge said, "Have Mr. Ng hand it to the Bailiff, and I'll direct that the Bailiff hand it to the Clerk in whatever form it is currently in."

Marovich continued, "The civil suit names myself and Mr. Webster as defendants. It's a civil suit for malpractice, wherein substantial damages are sought."

Ng was suing his lawyers for one million dollars.

When the court reconvened, Judge Mewhinney addressed the defendant directly. "In regards to the civil suit, Mr. Ng, is it acceptable to you that I look at the Civil Complaint filed against your attorneys?"

"No," Ng said, "Your Honor, this Court has no jurisdiction, because I'm filing the matter in Superior Court."

"I understand that. It's a document of public record, Mr. Ng. The reason I want to look at it, is to determine whether it should be treated as a Marsden Motion in addition to whatever else it's being treated as. I just want to make sure you do not wish this Court to consider it for purposes of a Marsden Motion; is that correct?"

Ng said, "I believe the items I mention in the lawsuit, some of them already have been mentioned or complained of in my previous Marsden."

In California, a Marsden Motion considers the defendant's right to substitute counsel when questions of incompetence arise: *People v. Marsden* (1977) 2C3d 118.

Webster said, "We ask the court to review the lawsuit. It's now a matter of public record. I have been served, and Mr. Marovich has been served."

The judge said, "On what basis would the Court be reviewing it, to determine whether there is a conflict, or, what are you asking me to review it for?"

Webster continued, "The Court has made a finding, and it's in regards to the finding as already made on the record. And that is to the effect of the Court feels that this, the filing of this lawsuit against Mr. Marovich and myself, is another attempt to remove us as counsel, and in other words, it's a Marsden Motion through another avenue, which the Court has indicated is not the proper way to proceed on Marsden. The Court made that finding without reviewing the lawsuit."

"That is correct."

"I would also ask the Court to allow us a day to do two things. Mr. Marovich and myself both need to find an attorney to represent us. This suit obviously has to be answered, and possibly a demurrer within thirty days of today. We also would like time, a malpractice attorney may also be able to advise us on the ethical problems. But I don't know if we'll be able to get in touch with anyone this afternoon. I know how it is trying to get a hold of lawyers. Half the time they're not in their office, you have to wait until lunchtime for them to get back."

Charles Ng now had succeeded in having his lawyers describe how they needed representation, and how hard it is to get a lawyer on the phone when you want one.

"The Court will take judicial notice of it. In light of the allegations in the Complaint, the Court does not, at this time, relieve Mr. Webster and Mr. Marovich. The Court finds there is not a conflict created by the filing of the lawsuit. After review of the lawsuit, it is consistent with Mr. Ng's statements here in open court that the issues previously raised by

Marsden, by way of Marsden Motions are raised by way of this lawsuit. It is, in fact, an attempt to revive those Marsden issues in a non-Marsden form. It is not the basis for removal of counsel. This is an end run of Marsden, and the Court is not going to relieve counsel on the basis of the filing of the lawsuit—"

Ng interrupted the judge with, "On the Marsden hearings, there was never any kind of evidentiary hearing as to—"

The Judge interrupted, "Do you want to do this in chambers as part of a Marsden Motion, or do you want to do this in open court, Mr. Ng?"

"Open court."

"Okay. Because you have a right as to a Marsden hearing to have that in camera. This is not a Marsden hearing. This is a civil lawsuit that you have filed. The Court has stated its findings. Now, Mr. Ng, are you going to be arguing a Marsden Motion to me now or are you going to be doing something else?"

Ng answered, "I want to make the record clear that on the Marsden Motion, this Judge never has granted me an evidentiary hearing so I can present evidence. You're making summary rulings finding that these two counsel are competent without giving me a chance to present the facts or the evidence; whereas, in this forum, I'm demanding this to be, even though it's the same allegation, I'm able to present evidence and to prove that the Judge's findings are incorrect."

"Anything else, Mr. Ng?"

"And on that basis, I don't think that's an end run, because this Court has consistently told me in the Marsden Motion that there's also appeal afterward, the suffer-now-and grieve-later policy, as it were.

"As of right now," Ng continued, "all the Marsden issues that I have raised are still outstanding, that the Complaint has not been redressed. And this Judge is basically saying the Marsden is an appellate remedy, rather than immediate remedy. This suit is my only chance of immediate remedy on the cage, on shackles, on the failing of the lawyers to do the tasks they're supposed to do, to competently represent me. I can differentiate that very clearly to you. One of my points in the lawsuit is that counsel failed to file a disqualification statement to this Judge on time, and because of that, this Judge has ruled that as untimely. I think that there's a conflict of interest here that will prohibit these two counsels from effectively representing me, if forced to do so."

"Anything else, Mr. Ng?"

"Not at this time."

"The Court's ruling will stand. Mr. Webster, and Mr. Marovich, I'm going to proceed with the case at this time and allow you to consult with counsel; those are two things that can occur simultaneously."

Webster asked, "The Court is ordering us to proceed."

"I am ordering you to proceed."

"I suspect that if I don't proceed contempt proceedings will be instituted against me."

"That will be a logical progression."

Ng shot back, "I've got a disqualification motion. Can you give me a minute to finish it up?"

"Certainly," the judge said.

Ng now proceeded to read a motion to disqualify Judge Mewhinney.

The judge read the disqualification paper and said, "The Statement of Disqualification For Cause under Code of Civil Procedure Section 170.1, et seq . . . copies will be made, and it will be received by the Court and filed by the Court.

"The basis of the disqualification is . . . in Paragraph 2, filed a statement of disqualification against Douglas V. Mewhinney because appointed counsel Webster and Marovich have failed or refused to do so because of a conflict of interest."

"Reading Footnote 1: 'There appears to be a symbiotic relationship between counsel and Judge in this case.' Paragraph 3: 'The reasons for disqualification of Judge Mewhinney are as attached three-page to Complaint About A California Judge. This Judge should recuse himself because a Complaint is about to be,' it appears that the word is launched, Mr. Ng, 'against him with the commission on judicial formally' I just need you to read that language. I want to make sure that I'm not misreading it, if you'd please read Paragraph 4."

Ng's high-pitched voice cut him short. "This Judge should recuse himself because a Complaint is about to be launched—"

The word "recuse" hadn't been part of normal English until lawyers popularized it in the Irangate investigation. Now it was Ng's jargon.

The judge said in a puzzled voice, "Launched?"

Ng continued, "—with the commission on judicial . . . it should be performance."

"Performance," the judge repeated. "The Complaint, and it's three handwritten pages, are also included and attached. Under Code of Civil Procedure Section 170.4(b), the motion, on its face does not state a basis for disqualification. It's ordered stricken. Copies will be made for Mr. Ng and for both counsel."

Ng looked puzzled.

Even for a layman who had spent years in his cell studying the law, the language of the courtroom could be a mystery.

"So my motion" Charlie Ng finally said, "to request appointment of conflict-free counsel to rid this disqualification statement is denied?"

"Yes."

Chapter 16

Corpus Delecti

Thursday, November 12, 1985, 9:30 a.m., San Andreas, Calaveras County Court House

At the end of the preliminary hearing each side had the right to submit a summation of its case.

Prosecutor Martin rose and assembled papers in his hand. "Your Honor, it's the People's intention to discuss each of the homicides under two separate topical headings. The first will be corpus delecti, and the second will be probable cause to believe that this defendant committed the homicides.

"Starting with corpus delecti, the basic rule is succinctly stated in *People v. Ruiz,* R–u–i–z, a 1988 case at 44 Cal. 3d 589, and the quotation I am going to read is on page 611, which states: 'The corpus delecti rule is satisfied by the introduction of evidence which creates a reasonable inference that death could have been caused by a criminal agency, even in the presence of an equally plausible noncriminal explanation of the event.' Their real meaning was inside the statement: you don't have to have a body to prove someone was murdered. And this rule applies even when, as some of the counts in this case have indicated, there is not a victim's body that has been located. The rule logically applies to such cases; otherwise a murderer who destroys or successfully conceals a victim's remains would escape any type of criminal liability."

The prosecutor had established for the record that, even though some bodies, like Paul Cosner's, had not been found, a murder count still was valid.

"Count IV involves Lonnie Bond, Sr. and Count V, Robin Scott Stapley. As the evidence has shown, both of those victims have been positively identified by their fingerprints.

"Concerning Mr. Bond, the evidence has shown that the cause of death was a gunshot wound to the head. Regarding Mr. Stapley, he was shot four times; shot twice in the head. And again, the recommended cause of death was multiple gunshot wounds.

"Videotapes were introduced into evidence. Brenda O'Connor is told if she doesn't cooperate, that she's going to be killed. It's obvious from the tape that she's not there voluntarily, criminal acts are being perpetrated against her on the tape. And the discovery and the condition of the bodies of Mr. Bond and Mr. Stapley are important concerning Brenda O'Connor and Lonnie Bond, Jr., since mention is made of Mr. Stapley and Mr. Bond on the tape. And it indicates that the persons speaking on the tape know the circumstances of the death of both of these other victims."

One by one the prosecutor wove the links that bound the victims to Charlie Ng.

Martin shifted his notes, paused, and looked up again. "Kathy Allen went to Calaveras County because she was concerned, but her state of mind was that she believed Mike Carroll was missing. She was not intending to voluntarily disappear, but left to come to Calaveras County out of concern for Mike Carroll.

"Mike Carroll's house key was found in a trench in the property. His ID was found buried on the property. And these are items of identification that are commonly possessed on the person. His car is then sold. He takes no part in selling the car. It is again reasonable for the Court to infer that his death was caused by a criminal agency.

"Having established this corpus delecti, the statement of Leonard Lake made on the tape in the presence of Charles Ng becomes relevant and admissible. Kathy Allen is told that she would be taken out and buried in the same area that 'we buried Mike.'

"Paul Cosner disappeared under mysterious circumstances. Concerning his last known whereabouts, he was meeting to show a car on November the 2nd, 1984. After showing the car he intended to have a date with his girlfriend. Instead of showing up for the date with his girlfriend, his sister is filling out a Missing Persons report. The car is also missing.

"When we catch up again with the vehicle, it's learned that there is a bullet hole in the headliner on the passenger's side. There's a bullet hole in the passenger door panel, there are blood stains found about the front seat of the car.

"In Wilseyville we find items of Mr. Cosner's identification that have been buried. These are items that are commonly associated with the person; the driver's license, the other items of identification. It goes even further, his glasses are found with these items, certainly something that a person would continue to possess were they still alive.

"All of this evidence strongly suggests that Mr. Cosner is the victim of foul play. There's every reason to infer that he was killed and that his death was by a human criminal agency.

"The Dubs family. The victims in Counts XV, XVI, and XVII. All three, an entire family, mysteriously disappeared. Mrs. Dubs is on the phone the last time anyone hears from her, that includes her friends, George and Karen Tuck, and her neighbors. The front door of the Dubs' residence is open several days later. The key to that door is in the lock. And this is located there after a stranger walks from the house and there is property missing.

"There is a phone call to the office of Stan Pedrov, Mr. Dubs' employer, trying to make it appear as though the disappearance of the Dubs family is voluntary."

Martin raised his voice. "There is every reason to believe that this phone call is just not the truth, because Mr. Pedrov said it was very unlike Harvey Dubs to leave work, not show up without any word.

"We have a man, Mr. Dubs, who has a wife and a small child. He didn't even ask for his last paycheck for the dates between July 5 and July 25, 1984. All the facts and circumstances surrounding the disappearance of the entire Dubs family indicate that it's not a voluntary disappearance.

"We have a link to Wilseyville. The Dubs family's personal property is found there. The cassette recorder with the serial number, the video duplicator, which was a very unique piece of personal property, as well as a video receipt made out to Harvey Dubs.

"Count VII, Clifford Peranteau. Again, we have a person simply disappearing off the face of the earth. He's dropped off at midnight by his friend. He doesn't show up for work the following day, never shows up for work again.

"Again, property is missing from the victim's residence. The property is found in Wilseyville. We have a letter claiming that Cliff has voluntarily disappeared. The letter is sent to his employer, and it links this disappearance to Wilseyville because the typewriter in which the letter was typed was found at the Wilseyville property. Also at the property is the piece of paper found in the hidden cell in the bunker that says, 'Cliff, P.O. Box 349.'

"Mr. Peranteau's motorcycle is missing. Mr. Peranteau is not involved in any negotiations to sell the motorcycle. In fact, it's sold by Leonard Lake at Wilseyville.

"And lastly, as to corpus delecti, we have Count IX, Jeffrey Gerald. He disappears February 4, 1985. And his state of mind at that point is important. He intends to go to a moving job and return that evening. He never shows up for work again. His roommate never sees him again, and his mother would have expected to hear from him, and she hasn't.

"Same ties to Wilseyville. His camera is found in the trench. It's identified as his by the film. A guitar that looks like one that he owned is found in the residence. A turntable similar to one he owned is found in the Wilseyville residence. Personal property turns up missing from his apartment. His social security card is found in the trench.

"The Court can infer that there's death by a criminal agency.

"The second part of the people's analysis is the probable cause to believe that this Defendant is guilty of these murders. It is the People's theory the murders were committed pursuant to an overall conspiracy and common plan and scheme as to how these murders would be conducted and how the conspiracy would be conducted. It's a conspiracy between Charles Ng and Leonard Lake to murder people and to obtain each victim's personal property. And it is the obtaining of this personal property that is one of the common threads that links the Defendant to each and every one of the alleged homicides.

"The common plan involves a number of things: One is the receipt of the property, and also the sorting of the property. The evidence has shown that some of the property of the victims has been maintained by Charles Ng and Leonard Lake for their immediate use or conversion.

"Other property has been buried in protective containers that protects the items from the elements for possible retrieval and use at a later time.

"There is also the destruction and concealing of human remains that is a common element of these crimes. The common plan also involves attempts to misdirect friends and employers of the victims as to the cause of their disappearance. And also common to this plan is its home base, Wilseyville, California.

"Charles Ng was involved in a common conspiracy plan and scheme that necessarily has the sufficient premeditation and deliberation and express intent to kill that's necessary for a first-degree murder. This Defendant's specific intent to kill is demonstrated on the videotape.

"Kathy Allen is first depicted on that videotape with Leonard Lake and with Charles Ng, and with no one else, other than those two. The Defendant is personally present when Leonard Lake tells Kathy Allen, 'We'll put a round in your head. We will bury you where we buried Mike.'

"The scene with Kathy Allen depicts the residence in Wilseyville, but also the time and place is important to link the Defendant, because we have phone calls going from that Wilseyville property on April the 14th and April the 15th, 1985, at a time when Kathy Allen is there. Calls going from the property to Charles Ng's employer, and Charles Ng did not work during that period of time.

"So how do we know that this conspiracy goes beyond the two crimes concerning Kathy Allen and Mike Carroll? How do we know that there is a common thread? Because almost the exact same pattern is seen on the videotape with Brenda O'Connor. She is given a choice very similar to the choice Kathy Allen is given. And again, the plural is used by Leonard Lake, 'We've closed you down, we've took you away. We've took Scott away.'

"And again it's the same two, Leonard Lake and Charles Ng, engaged in a pattern of conduct with Kathy Allen, that is similar to that for other victims. There is reference made in the Brenda O'Connor portion of the tape back to the Kathy Allen portion. Leonard Lake says to Charles Ng, 'Now tell me, isn't she a little better than Kathy?' Charles Ng responds, 'Sort of, maybe a little, basically the same.'

"Concerning the conspiracy and common plan, Brenda O'Connor asks of Leonard Lake and Charles Ng, 'Is that why you invited us over here for dinner?' Leonard Lake says, 'Uh-huh.' Charles Ng answers, 'It's part of the game.'

"The Court will recall what action this Defendant is taking with Brenda O'Connor when she says, 'Don't cut my bra off.' His response to that is, 'You can cry and stuff like the rest of them.'

"Concerning her baby, this Defendant also had something to say. He says, 'Just don't ask, or it will be history.' This is an express statement by this Defendant tying him to the baby, Lonnie Bond, Jr. It indicates that he and Leonard Lake have it. It indicates to the People that this child has been murdered just like his mother and father.

Genealogy of Wayward Justice: The Tree of Prosecutors, Defense Attorneys, and Judges in the Ng Case

Original Prosecutors, 1985

District Attorney Arlo Smith and Assistant District Attorney Paul
Cummins, San Francisco
John E. Martin, Calaveras County

Original Public Defenders, 1985–1986

Garrick S. Lew, San Francisco   Michael N. Burt, San Francisco
Ephraim Margolin, representing Lew and Burt

❑ Plea bargain from defense rejected by California Attorney General's office, 1988.
❑ Attorney General Dan Lungren elected, 1990; assigns Deputy Attorney General Sharlene A. Honnaka as coprosecutor, removing San Francisco from the case.

Original Judge

Municipal Court Judge Douglas V. Mewhinney, Calaveras County

❑ Mewhinney rejects Lew and Burt, appoints Thomas M. Marvich and James William Webster, of Sonora, Tuolomne County, as public defenders.
❑ Ephraim Margolin argues Harris motion to Supreme Court, that "indigent's right to counsel of choice is abuse of judicial discretion": denied by 4–3 vote.

Second Judge

Orrin K. Airola, Superior Court, reappoints Marovich and Webster after preliminary hearing; sets trial date of January 12, 1993.

Third Judge

Claud D. Perasso, San Francisco, comes out of retirement to take over case after Airola is challenged for cause by Marovich and Webster and disqualified by a Merced judge.

Sixth Defense Attorney

Eric Multhaup appointed by Judge Perasso to assist Margolin.

Fourth Judge

Judicial Council appoints Donald McCartin, retired from Orange County, to succeed Perasso after prosecution successfully challenges Perasso on a technicality, December 1993; McCartin dismisses defense attorneys Marovich and Lew on a plea from Margolin.

Fifth Judge

James Kleaver, retired Siskiyou County judge, is tapped to choose a new venue for the trial; in April 1994, he chooses Orange County, and the public defender there immediately makes a peremptory challenge of McCartin, even though the State Supreme Court rejects defense charges against McCartin for "double cross" on trial venue.

Seventh and Eighth Defense Attorneys

William Kelley and Allyn Jaffrey assigned as public defenders for Ng in Santa Ana, October 1994.

Sixth Judge

Judicial Council assigns Judge Robert R. Fitzgerald of Orange County to replace McCartin, and in July 1995 trial date of September 6, 1996 is set.

Ninth and Tenth Defense Attorneys

On a motion by Ng on August 2, 1996, Judge Fitzgerald dismisses Kelley and Jaffrey and appoints Gary Poulson and George Peters to defend Ng.

Eleventh Defense Attorney

Richard Schwartzberg is appointed appellate attorney to represent Ng when the latter, one week after Kelley is dismised, changes his mind and petitions for a writ of mandate to reinstate Kelley as his counsel.

Seventh Judge

Superior Court rules that Judge Fitzgerald wrongly granted Ng's request for new counsel, then wrongly refused to have them reinstated; Fitzgerald is removed by the court for cause and John J. Ryan of Orange County is appointed to the case, announcing a September 1, 1998 trial date as "non-negotiable."

Twelfth Defense Attorney

James Merwin is added to the defense team; Ng again tries to have the team dismissed and to represent himself; his appellate attorney asks for and receives a psychiatric examination, but Ng is ruled fit to stand trial; Burt turns down offer to represent Ng.

❑ Trial date is postponed to September 14 by Judge Ryan because of difficulty by jury commissioner in providing enough jury prospects; selection begins.

"Leonard Lake and Charles Ng go down to the apartment that had been occupied by Scott Stapley and meet with Tori Doolin. There's an attempt made by Leonard Lake, and Charles Ng waiting outside to clean out the personal property of Scott Stapley. And again, we have this attempt at misdirection.

"Leonard Lake, a co-conspirator, in furtherance of his conspiracy with Charles Ng, says that the people at the house next door are all dead, but he's attempting to mislead Tori Doolin concerning the cause of death. He tells her further that all their identification was gone and their weapons just weren't found there.

"We have Lonnie Bond's First Interstate Bank card located at the Defendant's residence. It indicates that he took the personal property of yet another victim that he has killed. Mr. Robin Scott Stapley's Ricoh camera is found with the Defendant in Canada; when he fled from the United States, he took some of the victim's property with him.

"Let's go back chronologically to the first homicides that are alleged in this case, and that, of course, is the Dubs family. How do we know at this early stage chronologically of the People's case that this defendant is involved? Deborah Dubs finishes the phone call, which is the last time anyone has heard from her, and what is seen? This defendant is seen leaving the Dubs' house at approximately that time.

"Katherine McAuliffe sees a second person who is acting in conjunction with Charles Ng. And ultimately, the personal property from the house ends up in Wilseyville, California, and ends up in this Defendant's apartment.

"The crime against the Dubs has the same earmarks as the latter portion of the conspiracy, which has absolutely been established, because the Defendant has benefited personally in the Dubs case, just like with Mr. Stapley's camera, just like with Lonnie Bond's credit card. We have equipment consistent with equipment that the Dubs family owned, the same model, same make is seized at the defendant's Lennox Street residence. The Defendant has videotapes that is matched to those owned by Mr. Dubs, not only in description, title wise, but in handwriting.

"And back up to the Wilseyville property, we have the Captain Video receipt in the trench behind the bunker made out to Mr. Dubs, and it's in with other items that had been addressed or have the name of Charles Ng on them.

"Just like in the case of Kathy Allen, where there was an attempt to misdirect her employer concerning her disappearance. We have an attempt to make Harvey Dubs' employer believe that his disappearance, and that of his family, is a voluntary disappearance. And this attempt is made and the family is, in reality, dead.

"The last citation I'm going to make in my argument, the case of *People v. Miller*, a 1990 case, 50 Cal. 3d 954, and at 985, the following language is set forth:

'The likelihood of a particular group of geographically proximate crimes being unrelated diminishes as those crimes are found to share more and more common characteristics.'

"All of the following share common characteristics and a geographical proximity to the Defendant: Kathy Allen, Brenda O'Connor, Michael Carroll, Lonnie Bond, Robin Stapley, Paul Cosner, Clifford Peranteau, Jefferey Gerald, Lonnie Bond, Jr., Sean Dubs, Deborah Dubs, and Harvey Dubs."

Prosecutor Martin finished with, "The People believe that the Defendant should be held to answer on all counts. Thank you, Your Honor."

Chapter 17

The Defense

**Thursday, November 12, 1992, San Andreas,
Calaveras County Court House**

Judge Mewhinney nodded to the defendant's counsel. "Go ahead, Mr. Marovich."

"The Prosecution evidence relative to the Cosner count indicated that Mr. Cosner disappeared on November the 2nd, 1984.

"Mr. Cosner indicated to his girlfriend that he had a prospective purchaser for his car; he would be back shortly for dinner with her. He went out to show the car to someone and did not return. The evidence indicates that in June of 1985, some seven to eight months later, this car was found in South San Francisco, associated at that time with Mr. Lake.

"The inferences that can be drawn from the evidence found in the vehicle would indicate that Mr. Cosner was shot in the vehicle.

"I'm not disputing the District Attorney's argument relative to corpus delecti, as far as this sudden unexplained disappearance. But I am strongly disputing the District Attorney's version and interpretation of any connection or evidence pointing to a connection between Mr. Ng and the disappearance of Mr. Cosner.

"Mr. Cosner lived in San Francisco, Filbert Street. He was due back shortly to have dinner with his girlfriend. The inference is obvious, that he was going to show this car to someone in San Francisco. The inference, I believe, is clear that the blood that was detected in the vehicle as per, I believe, police officer Irene Brunn's testimony, the existence of those slugs,

.22 slugs in the vehicle, indicate that Mr. Cosner was shot in his car. And the further inference is that he was shot in his car in San Francisco.

"In terms of any connection of this car with Mr. Ng or Mr. Lake as far as the evidence presented in this case, the first inference of such a connection would be in April of 1985, some five to six months after Mr. Cosner's disappearance.

"Relative to Kathy Allen, there is evidence that Kathy Allen was picked up in a similar looking car at the Safeway in Milpitas. So in terms of the whereabouts, location of this particular vehicle, of the vehicle, the Honda Prelude, that Mr. Cosner went out to sell, or went out to show someone, there is no evidence for November, December, January, February, March, no evidence on this record of where that vehicle might have been during those five or plus months.

"After the search commenced at the Wilseyville property," Marovich continued, "properties in the general area of the County were searched, some Tupperware containers, one of which contained Mr. Cosner's ID, glasses, and several other documents with his name on the paperwork were found.

"The videotapes. Obviously, that's a graphic piece of evidence that has an impact. And it's understandable that the District Attorney would want to emphasize that as being evidence of this so-called conspiracy, common plan that he is espousing that existed between Mr. Lake and Mr. Ng.

"It has to be remembered, though, that all the evidence indicates that the events depicted on the videotape are at the earliest taking place in mid-April of 1985. The fact that a competent agreement, overall conspiracy might exist in April of '85 is certainly not indicative of such an agreement existing seven, eight, or ten months earlier.

"It would indicate that, perhaps, in April such . . . there's evidence of such an agreement, and, perhaps, subsequent to that, but working backwards, such as the District Attorney is doing, by emphasizing the tape that was in April of '85, reveals, I believe, a weakness or lack of evidence, substantial evidence, of the existence of that so-called conspiracy in the mid part, for example, of 1984.

"Relative to the Heale property and the burying in Tupperware containers of Paul Cosner's ID and other personal papers, and the gun that's been referred to, what is the purpose of burying these types of items, particularly an ID? A logical inference to have such a thing handy if a person wanted to assume somebody else's name or identification. And obviously, in this case, Mr. Lake is Caucasian. Mr. Cosner was Caucasian. Mr. Ng, of course, is Chinese, and would have no real purpose for burying for future use to assume somebody's identity, that of a Caucasian person, such as Paul Cosner.

"In addition, it's clearly established Mr. Ng lived in San Francisco. The Wilseyville property was owned by Lake's ex-wife's family. I think the inference would be that if Mr. Ng was burying things, it would be logical that he would be burying things where they were readily accessible to him.

"With respect to this so-called conspiracy and overall agreement, Mr. Martin refers to certain elements that accompany or followed certain persons' disappearance, and he emphasized, in that respect, misdirection to where, if someone disappeared, there would be a misdirection used to, as far as friends or family to, apparently, cover up anyone's disappearance or to delay this being discovered.

"Obviously in the Cosner situation, there's no evidence here of any such tactics by anyone involved with Cosner. That such 'misdirection,' quote, unquote, was not reported by anyone.

"It's our position that the evidence is simply insufficient to establish probable cause in this case that Mr. Ng was connected with Mr. Cosner's disappearance and/or alleged homicide.

"I want to bring up another point, a distinct point relative to the Cosner disappearance, because it's important. It appears that even assuming, for purposes of argument, that probable cause might exist, the statutes in the California Penal Code, dealing with territorial jurisdiction over criminal offenses, would be such that a Calaveras County Court simply, based on the evidence presented here, would not have jurisdiction over the offense involving the disappearance and the alleged murder of Paul Cosner.

"On the issue of territorial jurisdiction . . . that the car, the Honda Prelude, based on the evidence in this record, the earliest it could be placed in the County with any certainty, would be based on Kathy Allen being picked up in a similar looking car at Safeway, and only then because Kathy Allen, as per the "M. Lady's" tape, is shown, and it's pinned down in April being in Calaveras County.

"It is particularly important, Your Honor, in that there's the issue of vicinage. That a person charged with a crime is entitled to be tried by a cross-section of the citizens of that particular County or district, as it were. That's a right included in the Sixth Amendment of the Constitution of the United States, made applicable by the State's Fourteenth Amendment."

Defense attorney Marovich was claiming that it was impossible to impanel an impartial jury in Calaveras County.

Marovich turned, signaled his co-counsel, and said to the judge, "Mr. Webster will continue the argument."

The judge said, "Mr. Webster. You may proceed."

Webster said, "As far as the District Attorney's argument regarding the showing of a conspiracy, an overall conspiracy between Mr. Lake and Mr. Ng to murder and obtain personal property, as Mr. Marovich indicated, there is evidence to show that Mr. Lake was involved in the disappearance and murder of at least Mr. Charles Gunnar, and possibly someone by the name of Donald Lake, Mr. Lake's brother, during a time when Mr. Ng was not even in the State and was, in fact, incarcerated at Fort Leavenworth, Kansas.

"Not only was there evidence to show that Mr. Lake killed one Mr. Gunnar, there's also evidence that he used Mr. Gunnar's personal property and his ID. In fact, he was going by the name of Charles Gunnar for quite some time before there's any showing of any connection between Mr. Lake and Mr. Ng.

"There is obviously evidence to show that Mr. Lake and Mr. Ng were acquainted. But the first showing that Mr. Ng was ever connected with the Wilseyville property, is sometime in mid-April of 1985. The property and identification, which was found buried in certain areas of the Wilseyville property, and another piece of property in Calaveras County are connected with Mr. Lake, certainly, but not connected with Mr. Ng.

"Mr. Lake is the one who was a fugitive from justice. Mr. Lake is the one who was living under an assumed name or names, while Mr. Ng was living and working in San Francisco under his own name.

"Mr. Ng was involved in a traffic accident in late April of 1985 in Bakerfield, California, driving a vehicle belonging to one of the alleged victims. Mr. Ng waited around for twenty minutes to a half-hour for an officer of the Highway Patrol to show up. When one did, Mr. Ng gave him his real name, his real address, his real phone number, rather than leaving the scene of the accident. I think all of this goes to show that Mr. Ng was not involved in any conspiracy with Mr. Lake until at the earliest, mid April of 1985.

"Mr. Martin referred to a statement by Mr. Lake evidently in the presence of Mr. Ng that, 'We have taken care of you—' 'we,' meaning 'the star route gang.' And I would submit that there is no proof whatsoever that there is any such gang or that Mr. Ng was a member.

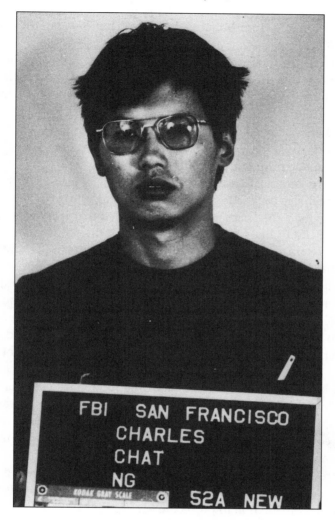

Charles Chitat Ng was booked by Daly City police for shoplifting in 1984, after finishing his sentence at Leavenworth. (AP/Wide World.)

"There are numerous phone calls that have been shown, phone calls to phone numbers belonging to Dennis Goza, the employer of Mr. Ng, to the employer of Kathy Allen, and to numerous other people that Mr. Martin indicates shows an intent to misdirect certain of these witnesses and/or—well, certainly these witnesses. I would submit that there is no proof whatsoever that any of the phone calls to anyone was ever shown to have been made from Mr. Ng's residence, but only from the Wilsey-ville residence.

"As far as the motorcycle of Clifford Peranteau was concerned, there was testimony that the ad in the newspaper to sell that motorcycle listed a phone number in South San Francisco. It was the phone number not of Mr. Ng, but of Claralyn Balazs and her father.

"As there has been no conspiracy whatsoever shown until the, the very earliest, April 7th, 1985, I would ask the Court not to consider any statements made prior to mid April of 1985.

"Clifford Peranteau disappeared approximately January 19th of 1985. The only evidence connecting Mr. Ng to Mr. Peranteau is the fact that they worked together. The District Attorney indicated that there was evidence that Mr. Ng didn't like Mr. Peranteau. I submit the only evidence is that they had two arguments, and at one time, Mr. Salcedo, in his affidavit, indicated that he dropped Mr. Peranteau off at his apartment in the early morning hours of January 19th. Mr. Ng worked the morning of January 19th at Dennis Moving Company. It would have been quite difficult, if not impossible, for Mr. Ng, who had no vehicle, and there's no evidence of any vehicle, to have gone and taken Mr. Peranteau to Wilseyville and then returned in time to go back to work the following morning at eight or nine o'clock.

"Mr. Ng, then, worked throughout the following week for Dennis Moving Company. He was working at any time that Mr. Peranteau's possessions apparently became missing from his apartment. Along with this, again, no connection and no probable cause to connect Mr. Ng to the death of Mr. Peranteau.

"There's also the fact that there is no evidence, whatsoever, to suggest that this Court once again has territorial jurisdiction, or that this County has territorial jurisdiction to prosecute Mr. Ng for Mr. Peranteau's death, even assuming that the Court decides there's probable cause to believe that the crime was committed and that Mr. Ng was involved.

"The motorcycle of Mr. Peranteau's, which was missing, and was just discovered within the last month or so in Oregon, was missing from Mr. Peranteau's residence some days after he disappeared when Mr. Ng would have been at work. The motorcycle was sold by Leonard Lake and taken out of a truck, which resembled the truck belonging to Leonard Lake's father-in-law, or ex-father-in-law, one Louis Balazs. Mr. Ng was not around. There is no evidence at all that he was around when this motorcycle was sold.

"And once again, as far as the conspiracy is concerned, the Gunnar remains show, and other evidence shows, that Mr. Lake was involved in all the factors of this possible conspiracy prior to Mr. Ng even becoming involved at all with Mr. Lake or acquainted with him, for that matter.

"Mr. Jeffrey Gerald disappeared on or about February 24th of 1985. The record will reflect that both Charles Ng and Mr. Gerald worked on February 22nd of 1985, that no one employed by Dennis Moving Company worked on Saturday, February 23rd, that no one worked for Dennis Moving Company on Sunday, February 24th, and then Mr. Ng returned to work, along with everyone else, on Monday, February 25th.

"There is nothing to indicate that Mr. Gerald went anywhere with Mr. Ng, only that he left his apartment on February 24th, as any statements of Ms. Kailer or Ms. Rosen that were contained in their affidavits were not introduced for the proof of the matter asserted, but rather for some reason maintained to be a hearsay exception regarding the corpus delecti exception to the hearsay rule, an exception to the hearsay rule which I have never heard of. And in reviewing the Evidence Book written by one Barnard Whitkin, evidently, he has never heard of it either."

This was an example of how obtuse the defense lawyers had become. The stupefying detail of quoting a textbook to a judge was an insult.

"Also in this count, once again there is involved the fact that there is no proof whatsoever of territorial jurisdiction as to Mr. Gerald. There is nothing, no evidence to suggest any kind of conspiracy, as we've indicated earlier, until sometime in mid-April of 1985, nor is there any evidence at all to place Mr. Ng at the Wilseyville property prior to mid April of 1985.

"There was no property which allegedly belonged to Mr. Gerald found at the Lennox apartment, which was evidently, well, there's been a showing that that was resided in by Mr. Ng.

"The only items of Mr. Gerald's property that were found were found at the Wilseyville property."

The defense team rebuttal continued. It was long and detailed, addressing every point made by the prosecution.

The defense's arguments continued on either judicial territorial grounds or that occurrences prior to April, 1985 should be excluded. The things that happened after April, 1985 were defended in a different way.

A spectator summed it up in one sentence: "Ng was duped; Lake did everything."

Webster finished with, "We submit."

The judge asked, "Mr. Martin, Ms. Honnaka, any rebuttal?"

Mr. Martin answered, "The People submit, Your Honor."

The judge said, "The Court will make the following finding: The issue before the court is whether or not pursuant to Penal Code Section 871 or 872 there is not or is sufficient evidence for a holding order as to the crimes charged in the Complaints consolidated or any other crimes shown by the evidence.

"The standard is whether a reasonable person would entertain a strong suspicion that the offenses have, in fact, been committed, and whether Mr. Ng is guilty thereof.

"As to Case Number C-851094, as to Count I, a violation of Section 187 of the California Penal Code, a felony, alleging that between January 1, 1985 and June 4, 1985, Mr. Charles Chitat Ng did willfully and unlawfully kill a human being, to wit, Kathy Allen, with malice, aforethought, premeditation, and deliberation, a violation of Section 187 of the California Penal Code, a felony, it does appear that that offense has, in fact, been committed. There is sufficient cause to believe that Charles Chitat Ng committed that offense in this County and State."

Over and over the judge repeated his decision, for Cosner; the Dubses; for Bond, his wife Brenda, and his child; for Carroll; Stapley; Peranteau; and Gerald.

Again and again the judge repeated, "It does appear that the offense has, in fact, been committed."

There was a palpable rush of breath in the crowded room as each count was read and pronounced valid. The relatives of the victims reached out to each other. Some were crying.

At last it was over. The spectators rose to empty out into the sunshine. But not before Judge Douglas Mewhinney rang down the gavel for the last time he would ever be officially involved in this case.

Charles Ng was to be bound over for trial.

The date was set for January 12, 1993.

Chapter 18

Third and Last Call

9:20 a.m., January 12, 1993, San Andreas, California

"The defendant complains of undiscovered discovery," Judge Claud Perasso told the court as he sifted through a sheaf of papers, "and inability to file 995 motion, change of venue motion, inability to have his forensic examinations completed." Peering over his glasses at John Martin of the Attorney General's office in Sacramento, he asked, "Any response?"

Martin said he had nothing to add to the papers he had already filed. Charles Ng's attorneys shot back with a quick rebuttal: they had only received the papers at 5:00 p.m. on Friday, and here it was Tuesday morning, but even so "it's not difficult to respond" because "the defense never agreed to the trial date of January 13," tomorrow. That date was set on December 2 by Judge Airola, who had replaced Judge Mewhinney, who had concluded the Preliminary Hearing, indicting Mr. Ng on 12 murder counts and indicated a trial date of January 12.

Attorney Webster now began a lengthy argument, continuing on for about forty-five minutes, that not only should the trial date be *postponed*—in legal terms *continued*—but that the next court event should be a "trial readiness conference," that is, just to talk about when the trial should occur, and the trial readiness conference should not begin until three months hence.

This is how nearly six years of delay began.

Webster recalled how he and attorney Marovich had successfully called for the disqualification of Judge Airola. It seems as if Airola was just passing through, since his only act was to confirm the trial date of January 12 that Mewhinney had set at the end of the preliminary hearing. During this transfer of powers, was Charles Ng even arraigned? No, said Webster. "The judge did not have jurisdiction" to arraign Ng. Not only that, but a defendant cannot be arraigned without an attorney present. And even though Webster and Marovich were physically on the scene on that December day, they were not Ng's attorneys that day because they were temporarily appointed only and he had fired them in one of the last days of the Peliminary Hearing!

Webster proceeded to recite the following objections and citations and cavils that only a law clerk could love:

- People v. Howard: the continuance in this case was denied, but it was a continuance in the *penalty* phase of a capital case, not the same as here.
- People v. Ware: the continuance was denied because the defendant gave virtually no reason for it.
- The People in this case have indicated "we only need four months to prepare for trial" but we need six months just to read the discovery, "not to do any investigation."
- Penal Code 1054.1 states the People must provide names and addresses of persons the prosecution intends to call as witnesses, but "there are some 600 witness names which have been turned over to us" and even if we could "narrow that down to about 300" how can we investigate them all?
- The same penal code calls for the People "to supply to us the existence of any felony convictions" of any of these witnesses. "We have received, I think, maybe two or three rap sheets at this point."
- The prosecution's experts have not given us any of their notes for our experts to check, just their conclusions. "According to the People's response, we should just be satisfied with that. There's nothing our experts need to do, because their experts are so good. . . ."
- And there was Proposition 115, one of many that have made California famous for upsetting the Sacramento state house. The essential thrust of that proposition was to speed the trial process by loosening the rules of evidence in preliminary hearings. Webster argued that he was being deprived of discovery prior to the preliminary hearing on the basis of this proposition. He cited the evidence the prosecution had obtained from a forensic odontologist—evidence about the teeth of the victims. This evidence was received in January 1992 "and not turned over to us until almost a year later."

- Charles Gunnar was Lake's best man at his wedding. He was also the identity Lake assumed after disposing of him in Wilseyville. Gunnar was the subject of a forensic anthropologist's report to the prosecution. "We did not receive that report, and it was not until we requested [it] that the prosecution discovered they didn't even have it."
- The 995 Motion on the above issues has to be filed, Webster argued, by February 18. How could they work on the case if they have to work on that motion? "Obviously, we cannot. . . ." And if that motion is lost, then "we will need to be spending most of our time in the filing of a writ" to appeal it. And the list of motions and writs would overwhelm a large legal office: "suppression motions, Kelly–Frye motions, discovery motions . . ."
- Finally, change of venue: "due to the widespread publicity in this case, which is statewide and, in fact, nationwide and throughout the world, once a venue is picked, then another public opinion survey would have to be done just in that venue to see if the defendant could receive a fair trial there."

The case was now spilling out of all corners. There was too much to do, too many loose ends to follow up.

"The People have had seven years or more to review and finalize this evidence, and we're still receiving evidence from them," Webster argued. "We are now cut down to four days—four six-hour days of visits with the defendant to try to review things with him and have him help us prepare, and the prison is two hours from our homes."

Again, Folsom Prison, built in the Gold Rush days, two hours down the road on Highway 49 to Sonora, had become the villain, just as it had been painted earlier for serving cold food to the prisoner.

Judge Perasso tried to put his well-known heavy foot on the pedal. As Webster wore on about handwriting exemplars "four inches thick" and "hundreds, if not thousands, of tiny pieces of bone fragments, tooth fragments" in the pathologist's offices in San Francisco, not to mention ballistics, the Judge averred, "Um hum."

"Under 987.50, a defense counsel is entitled to a continuance, and the minutes should reflect that just on the forensic evidence factor this matter can't be ready for several months." Turning to the prosecution, Perasso added, "What about the witness list?"

". . . . Probably by the end of this month." But Sharlene Honnaka countered, "The forensic evidence is basically a red herring. . . . there *were* thousands of bone fragments . . . but the reason these remains are not identifiable is they were burnt or smashed beyond recognition. . . . when they review this evidence. . . . they're not going to find anything exculpatory. . . . maybe they're more creative than we are and may think of a way to make that forensic evidence more important.

"If, of course, after their review tomorrow and the day after their forensic folk come up with some incredible new theory, of course, they can renew their motion to continue for a longer period of time. But it's the People's position that we're very concerned that that not be used as an excuse to really give a long delay to these already old proceedings."

But Webster would not relent. Age-dating of the bones *did* have a meaning for the defense. ". . . . Mr. Ng was incarcerated at Fort Leavenworth for two years during the time frame when Mr. Lake, his alleged coconspirator, was out doing who knows what. And if we can show that certain of those remains were disposed of while Mr. Ng was incarcerated. . . ." Webster's thought trailed off. "We've obviously shown *that* as to the body that was discovered two or three months ago."

The case was one that kept opening up, like a badly sutured wound. Yes, it had happened. Between the close of the preliminary hearing and the alleged trial date, another body had been unearthed on the Wilseyville property. Another body seized on as another cause for delay for the defense?

Arraignments and trials and sentencing and executions, as it often turns out, are about dates. Judge Perasso tried to put a circle on the calendar. "Let's assume that the arraignment was today, when would the 60 days have run? Today being the 12th."

Mr. Webster: March 12th or so.

The Court: That would be the 82nd day. It looks like the 23rd. Today is the 12th, right?

Mr. Webster: Right.

The Court: It's the 82nd day of the year, the 23rd, that's 60 days from today.

Ms. Honnaka: Your Honor—

Mr. Webster: It would be the 72nd.

The Court: Well, 72nd, all right.

Mr. Marovich: March 17th.

The Court: Well, I was an accounting major before I turned to the law.

Mr. Marovich: Judge, March 13th, I think, would be the 60th day from today.

THE COURT: Yeah, that's a Saturday, so it would fall on the 15th. Right. 72nd day. Right.

This exchange of testimony, at the modest rate of two dollars per page of transcripts, would sell to the reporters of *The Sacramento Bee, The San Francisco Chronicle,* and *The Los Angeles Times* for a profit of $6 for the court reporter. It was business as usual for Linda James, no matter how far from reality the words she was recording flew. She got them right, every word.

THE COURT: . . . . But at any rate, for our purposes, and because of the Court's position, under showing of 987.50, I think all of that other stuff is moot.

The bartering over dates went on.

"I think under the totality of the circumstances, considering the time required in the 995 statutes, the date suggested by the people seems appropriate, and that would be a trial date of May 13th, with a readiness conference on April 30th."

THE CLERK: We start on Wednesdays.
THE COURT: All right, we'll make that the 12th.

But it was not that easy. The argument wandered from what constituted an arraignment to whether or not Charles Ng, the defendant, had waived time. Then Webster and Marovich returned to the issue of their dismissal by the defendant. If they had been dismissed, then Ng was not represented by an attorney when he was arraigned, and that was a no-no.

But there were other motions as well.

MR. WEBSTER: The Notice of Motion and Motion for appointment of counsel for purposes of the Harris Motion, Your Honor, was not served on the People, as they don't have standing in it, as far as appointment of counsel.
THE COURT: OK.
MR. WEBSTER: The other one, Motion for Reconsideration, was certainly served on them this morning, just prior to the Court.

Next, Judge Perasso entertained arguments for a speedy trial from the State, or "The People." As the hearing wore on, and even the few newspaper reporters left, "The People" began to take on a hollow ring.

Then something finally happened.

The prosecution politely asked if Mr. Ng's civil lawsuit against the defense attorneys would "interfere with their effective representation."

Claud Perasso pressed attorney Marovich to divulge what he thought about representing a client who was suing him. After many asides, the defense attorney blurted it out: "Mr. Ng has had a longstanding relationship with Mr. Burt, and I think that's reflected in his desire to make a Harris Motion. If the Harris Motion is granted, I would be quite willing to step aside for Mr. Burt."

Marovich warmed to the defense. "All I can do is tell the Court that I would do my best if I stayed on this case."

Perasso replied laconically, "Well, that comes under the heading of 'anything is possible including but not limited to the world in ten minutes.'"

But the issue of Ng's lawsuit against his attorneys could not so easily be swept into the dustbin. A Superior Court Judge had taken up Ng's lawsuit against his attorneys. The judge had said on the record that the suit was not altogether frivolous. That dictum was beginning to bother the Sonora attorneys.

Judge Perasso and the public defenders debated this predicament into the early afternoon. The words "frivolicy" and "nonfrivolicy" entered the English language, and the court reporter supplied the spelling of these new words with the admonition "[sic]" behind both. In the end, Judge Perasso conceded that Ng's lawsuit against his attorneys simply "bordered" on the frivolous.

Finally, the real issue resurfaced: What is the trial date? Had Charles Ng waived the time issue back on December 2? Sharlene Honnaka again took the bull by the horns, quoting from the transcript of the December 2 hearing:

THE COURT: Well . . . . do you want your trial within 60 days, Mr. Ng?

DEFENDANT NG: I don't even have counsel right now, Your Honor, I don't know.

THE COURT: Well, I've appointed temporary counsel for you—but it's your choice.

DEFENDANT NG: I object to the Judge's appointment of Mr. Marovich and Mr. Webster as even temporary counsel.

THE COURT: All right. Do you want your trial set within 60 days?

MR. MAROVICH: Well, Your Honor, I think 987—

THE COURT: Now wait a minute, you have a right to a trial within 60 days of November 20th. . . . You have a right to increase that amount of time by waiving your right to have the trial within 60 days.

Ms. Honnaka summed up the impasse: "The point is that [the waiver of time] was requested personally of Mr. Ng on several occasions. And he clearly was disinclined to waive time. . . ."

Judge Perasso honed the issue down further, asking Ng directly if the May 12 trial date was acceptable, as his waiver indicated. The answer was yes. Perasso replied, "I believe that to be a knowing and intelligent time waiver."

MR. WEBSTER: . . . . to set aside Mr. Ng's plea? . . . . the Court is denying that, I take it?

THE COURT: Yes. . . . . If I were to . . . rearraign, it would just entail the clerk reading him the same document. And I think that would reduce the situation to absurdity. . . . So that's denied.

Yet Judge Perasso was far from out of the woods. Now both the defense and the prosecution saw thickets in the fact, as Marovich put it, "of being faced with the idea of going through Marsden Motions and making a 995" and "ineffective counsel." Martin was even more to the point: ". . . . Mr. Webster and Mr. Marovich would be very hard put to be arguing their own incompetence in the Justice Court level." Martin leaned toward "an abundance of caution."

The door now opened for an independent counsel to argue those motions, and it fell to Ephraim Margolin. Again the issue of the cage was raised, and dropped. And the issue of the gag order, and reaffirmed. At last Judge Perasso, noting he had to "start a murder case tomorrow" in Lake County, asked, "Anything further? Going once, twice, third, and last call."

The issue of the cage came back. The defense again called it barbaric. The prosecution answered, "Why not? If it was good enough in the Preliminary Hearing, why not now?" The Court listened again to the arguments that were brought in the Preliminary Hearing. The defense decided to let it go. "If we're finished on that topic. . . ." And now it was only the question of who might preside over the case.

". . . . If it's going to be tried, for example, in Los Angeles County, they might as well appoint somebody who lives there," Webster reasoned.

Judge Perasso concurred. ". . . They will assign one of the local retired judges of which there are 23,432, okay, or thereabouts."

It was common practice to bring back retired judges to sit on special cases that would likely last a long time.

Claud Perasso's comfortable but driving wit had moved the case toward the next level. As a retired judge himself, he knew the freedom to cut through detail that this position conferred on him. Unfortunately, he was unaware of what the prosecution meant by an "abundance of caution." Three weeks later, on learning that the Judge had failed to note on his perfunctory information sheet for this case that he had been convicted of a DUI (driving under the influence of alcohol) some years earlier, the prosecution saw a problem. What if the defense used that misstep to ask to throw out Perasso's rulings as being biased? Or simply clouded? Martin and Honakka voted for caution.

At the request of the state, Judge Claud Perasso removed himself from the case.

Chapter 19

Nine-Minute Agony

November 5, 1993, The Hague

The forty-ninth session of the Human Rights Committee of the United Nations finally issued their "Views" on *"Chitat Ng v. Canada,* Communication No. 469/1991," a forum customarily thought of as a place for wrestling with genocide in Cambodia or the extinction of Tibet. The com-plaint this time, however, was about the niceties of extradition. And one would have to read the Committee's report very thoroughly to see whom it came down on the hardest—Ng or Canada.

The United States had begun extradition efforts in November, 1987, which resulted in a judge's order from The Province of Alberta, Canada, for Ng's extradition in November 1988. Ng applied for "habeas corpus" in February 1989, and was denied. He appealed to Canada's Supreme Court and was turned down on August 31, 1989. But the Minister of Justice, Douglas Lewis, still had to decide if he would seek, under the extradition treaty with the United States, assurances from the United States that Ng would not be subject to capital punishment if taken back to California. In October of 1989 Lewis decided not to seek those assurances. Ng now ap-pealed the Minister's decision to the Supreme Court of Canada, which took up the issue on June 8, 1990. On September 26, 1991, almost sixteen months later, the Court ruled that the United States had a reasonable case. Ng was on the plane to California, finally, the same day.

The lawyerly education of Charles Chitat Ng in the intricacies of de-lay had obviously come a long way. And now the delays that had begun at the local magistrate's level had moved to the Provincial Court, to the highest court in the land, and finally to the Human Rights Committee of the United Nations. Behind each move was a motion from Ng himself that emanated from the law library he had been building in his Edmonton cell.

* * *

It was well over six years after the Lake–Ng killing ground was discovered in Calaveras County that the Supreme Court of Canada had surrendered Charles Chitat Ng to the United States. Ng had served out his six-year sentence for aggravated assault upon his arrest in Calgary. But there had finally been jubilation among the victims' relatives when news of Ng's departure for Sacramento, California was announced. None of those relatives was aware of the ongoing deliberations of the United Nations—one might rightly say those deliberations were academic.

In its final report on *Ng v. Canada*—three years after he was in California—the United Nations' Human Rights Committee expressed a wide range of disparate views:

"On 21 April 1992, the Supreme Court of the United States denied an individual stay of execution by gas asphyxiation in California by a vote of 7:2. One of the dissenting justices, Justice John Paul Stevens, wrote: 'The barbaric use of cyanide gas in the Holocaust, the development of cyanide agents as chemical weapons, our contemporary understanding of execution by lethal gas, and the development of less cruel methods of execution all demonstrate that execution by cyanide gas is unnecessarily cruel'.... In my view, the above summarizes in a very convincing way why gas asphyxiation must be considered a cruel and unusual punishment that amounts to violation of Article 7."

A dissenting opinion on this issue by a member of the Committee focused on the fact that the United Nations has a test of "the least possible physical and mental suffering" to permit any execution. The writer quoted the majority reasoning that "execution by gas asphyxiation may cause prolonged suffering and agony and does not result in death as swiftly as possible, as asphyxiation by cyanide gas may take over 10 minutes."

After several further pages of argument over what constitutes a proper, painless execution, the author concludes, "the Committee should not go into details in respect of executions as to whether acute pain of limited duration or less pain of longer duration is preferable. . . ."

Another dissenter pointed out that in many countries the method of execution is "hanging, shooting, electrocution, or injection of certain ma-

Were the victims' agony nine minutes long? One minute? Days?

terials. . . . I am totally incapable of indicating any absolute criterion as to the scope of suffering permissible under Article 7. What I can say is that Article 7 prohibits any method of execution which is *intended* for prolonging suffering. . . ."

Ms. Christine Chanet, dissenting from this view, had the last word on suffering: "I consider the Committee engages in questionable discussion when . . . . it assesses the suffering caused by cyanide gas . . . . and deems it unacceptable when it lasts for over ten minutes. Should it be concluded, conversely, that the Committee would find no violation of Article 7 if the agony lasted *nine minutes?*" [Emphasis added]

"A strict interpretation . . . . would enable the Committee to avoid this intractable debate on the ways in which the death penalty is carried out. . . ."

In the end, the Committee had a split decision: Canada had acted properly in extraditing Ng, but had violated Article 7 of the Covenant on Political and Civil Rights. Canada should have foreseen, the Committee ruled, that "Mr. Ng, if sentenced to death, would be executed . . . by gas asphyxiation," which would constitute "cruel and inhumane treatment." As Committee member Ms. Chanet had argued, apparently a nine-minute agony would have been OK.

The report of the Charles *Chitat Ng v. Canada* decision by the Human Rights Committee of the United Nations consumed almost thirty pages, single spaced, and was reprinted, early in 1994, by the University of Minnesota and the Australian Human Rights Information Centre. Meanwhile, a headline in *The Orange County* (California) *Register* proclaimed, "Wheels of Justice Frozen in Ng Case." The two facts were not unrelated.

With Claud Perasso off the case because of an oversight in not disclosing a prior conviction, and Orrin Airola gone before him because he was a long-term resident of Calaveras County, a new judge would look carefully at the enormity of the case before signing on. A new venue had not yet been selected, but Orange County was a strong possibility despite the fact that it was the home of some of the victims' relatives. One of them told an Orange County reporter that, from his experience in Calaveras County, there was no doubt the trial couldn't be held in the Sierra foothills. "They even asked this little 80-year-old lady about him and she said, 'Give him a fair trial and then hang the SOB.'"

Despite pleas from the defense attorneys assigned to Ng's case, a reporter from *The Sacramento Bee* had been granted an interview, before the preliminary hearing, with Ng in the new security wing of Folsom Prison. That long conversation could now be seen as another attack stroke by the "Ninja Warrior." The seed was planted to support the theory that Ng was, after all, under the thumb of Leonard Lake, the mastermind of the Wilseyville massacres. If the trial venue were changed—and Ng certainly knew it would be—that theory might not be laughed out of town.

Through February and March of 1994, Ng's former defense attorneys in San Francisco submitted motions to the State's Attorney General to move the trial to San Francisco. It was an article of faith in legal circles that this "most liberal city in the country, notwithstanding Boston" would never hand down a death penalty. It was another twist that only a cynic could love—equal to the Calaveras County attorneys having to argue their own incompetence if they wanted to continue to represent Ng. Now the San Francisco attorneys had to point to "seven alleged murders" committed in San Francisco by their client in order to argue for San Francisco as a trial venue.

The suspense was broken in early April when the State of California announced the best place in the state for a fair trial for Charles Chitat Ng. There was only one problem: the county had recently fallen victim to a financial disaster as a result of speculative investments of the county's portfolio by its chief financial officer. The county was in the red. Who could afford the baggage of Mr. Ng? The question was not lost on the defendant.

Chapter 20

Six Tons of Evidence

May 10, 1994, 8:30 a.m., Sacramento, California

The mammoth Mayflower moving van pulled away from the Attorney General's offices on 14th Street, wheeled under Interstate 5, picked up State Highway 16, and headed east toward Slough House and Route 49. There it rumbled along the quaint route of the '49ers through Sutter Creek and Drytown and Amador City and Jackson and Mokelumne Hill.

Driver Ned Thorsten had his papers clipped to the visor but he knew the first leg of the trip by heart. Riding herd with him was a state trooper, in neatly pressed khakis and a wide-brim hat. It was after Thorsten left the San Andreas court house at almost noon that he realized he was not going to get much physical help from the trooper. The poor fellow had one job only—to make sure the contents of the van got where they had to go, under unbroken seal. On unfamiliar ground for the next long stretch of this strange journey, he had to look forward only to trying to stay awake.

Comfortably settled into his favorite rig, the driver felt otherwise, even felt a little lift: he was headed for Disneyland!

In his mind the driver checked off the manifest of 26 boxes, tons of documents, and two heavy wooden crates: destination Orange County court house. From San Andreas the big rig rolled down 49 to Angel's Camp and Columbia, then into the prettified old town of Sonora. At the offices of two attorneys, Thorsten presented his papers and pulled out two hand carts: this would be a major packing job. Two and a half hours later he signed off on the checklist.

Thorsten's rig headed west this time, on Route 120 to Oakdale, Escalon, Manteca, and Tracy, where Interstate 5 cut south down the Central Valley. Five hours later, without so much as a pit stop, fearful of taking a break because of the traffic looming in the suburbs of Los Angeles at quitting time, the driver pushed on through the San Fernando Valley, past Alhambra and Downey. Finally he pulled into the vast parking lot in Anaheim.

Here he could catch a good night's sleep before delivering his legal cargo to Santa Ana in the morning. The state trooper agreed: their per diem easily covered the cost of a motel room; the good citizens of the state were not being robbed. The driver and the trooper were on salary and had no reason to prolong their trip.

May 11, 1994, John Wayne Airport, Orange County

Two stout marshals escorted a timid Charles Chitat Ng across the tarmac to a van idling near the terminal. The prisoner wore gray dungarees. For passengers waiting for connections to LAX it was not an unfamiliar sight. There were always VIPs passing through here with bodyguards, all of them trying to look inconspicuous.

It was difficult to see that the prisoner's folded hands were actually handcuffed.

May 11, 1994, Orange County Jail

As recently as last month, the reporter bragged to the secretaries gathered outside the admitting room that this case could have gone to Sacramento. The Judicial Council, that strange California legal entity that most people never hear about, had picked two potential sites—ignoring San Francisco. This had enraged the defense, the reporter explained. They—that is, San Francisco's Margolin and Sonora's Webster and Marovich—thought they had a deal with the state that they could present an argument for a trial in the city. Now there was no argument, just a coin flip between Sacramento or Santa Ana. *The Sacramento Bee* hadn't been exactly a wallflower over this case—they had printed the exclusive Ng interview. The wire services checked the *Bee* first for facts about the story. The *Bee's* photographers had grabbed the best shots of the Wilseyville cabin, the secret cell, the crematorium. So guess which city, the reporter asked, might have a more difficult time selecting an impartial jury?

When the Mayflower van pulled into the jail parking lot at 11 a.m., the secretaries had gone back to their desks and the reporter was joined by a ring of journalists familiar from the days of the Preliminary Hearing almost two years before. Yes, they all agreed, it was difficult to fathom where two years had gone. One blamed Perasso: when he gave Margolin the green light to file a Marsden Motion, and then rubbed salt in the wound by approving another expensive attorney, Eric Multhaup, to assist him, he should have known the prosecution would be angered. And that's the real reason, the young woman argued, why the state dug up dirt on Perasso and forced him to back off the case. Possible conflict of interest: disrespectful of a previous conviction. There went at least six months, she said. Everyone nodded.

The state trooper supervised the handling of each carton as it moved by cart and dolly into the hall of justice or the county jail. Two wooden crates required a forklift; they were marked "Folsom MaxS," presumably containing Ng's books and computer from the maximum security prison northeast of Sacramento. The driver acknowledged he had picked up the crates in Folsom on his first stop. The state trooper continued checking off the consignment, ignoring reporters' questions.

May 12, 1994, Orange County Court House, Santa Ana

Judge Donald McCartin held an impromptu press conference in his temporary office to explain to visiting reporters how he and Orange County wound up with the Ng case. With bankruptcy looming, one reporter asked, how could the county pretend to want to take on this case? He cited the County of Siskiyou, already running up $1.2 million in lawyers' bills for a single case. He noted that the legislature had just passed a bill, SB 1322, Chapter 437, to assist "the county of Calaveras" in paying for its "estimated $6 million" in the Charles Chitat Ng case.

"What genius wanted an Ng case in Orange County?" a reporter asked.

McCartin explained that he just happened to be a resident of Orange County when he was tapped, in January of that year, to succeed Perasso. His first act was to grant Margolin's motion, under Marsden, to dismiss Marovich and Webster. Then he negotiated a deal with Margolin and Calaveras prosecutor Martin to open up the change of venue process. This he said, was exactly what Perasso was intent on doing.

Then what happened to his promise to Margolin to allow the defense to present arguments about venues to the Judicial Council? There was no promise, McCartin insisted. He removed himself from the site selection process, he said. A retired Siskiyou County judge, James Kleaver, was assigned by the Judicial Council to make the venue selection. That was that. And Judge Kleaver happened to choose the County of Orange. Let's face it, he said: the trial's going to be here.

August 15, 1994, San Andreas, Calaveras County

For eight months, attorneys Marovich and Webster had been excused from the Ng case. Their files were now in Orange County, along with everything of Ng's from Folsom and everything the state could spare from Sacramento. Ng's computer and his books had long since been unloaded and put at his disposal in the Orange County jail. But the McCartin issue rankled. Margolin had pulled a fast one, they reasoned: perhaps they were also stung by their dismissal from the case under Marsden. But now they also had claimed fraud against McCartin for allowing the Judicial Council to appoint a judge to choose a venue without hearing arguments from the defense.

The Marovich–Webster case against the Margolin writ went to the State Supreme Court. The ruling came down quickly: the Court would not review the issue. The two Sonora attorneys were now officially out of the loop.

September 11, 1994, Santa Ana

Now temporarily representing Charles Chitat Ng, the Public Defender's Office of Orange County made its first move. Judge McCartin, as a resident of Orange County, should be removed from the case. The logic was not clear, but its effect was: as a peremptory challenge it was the defense's call. On the case just long enough to upset the defense by not consulting with them on a new venue, McCartin went back into retirement in Orange County.

The Public Defender's Office wasn't going to stop there. Before a new Judge was assigned to the case, a challenge was thrown up. It would take at least two years, the lawyers contended, to study the three tons of records that had been peremptorily dumped on their doorstep by a moving van four months before. The problem was not with the movers—they had done their job. The problem was not with the physical evidence—that was safely stored in San Francisco. The problem was how the files had been stored.

"Previous defense documents are illegible, five hundred pages of police reports are missing, hundreds of photographs are unlabeled, and thirteen boxes marked 'shred' contain important documents." The accusation went back from the Mayflower van to the offices of the attorneys in Sonora. The state trooper had watched everything between Sonora and Santa Ana. No one along the way had scribbled "shred" on thirteen boxes.

With another set of defense attorneys, still nameless, came one consistent refrain: "two years to study the case." But now, after years of handling documents, another issue confronted attorneys trying to make sense of the case: the evidence was becoming dog-eared.

Chapter 21

Delta Special Revenue

July 15, 1995, Santa Ana, California

"It looked as if someone had shuffled it, thrown it up in the air, jumped up and down on it, and then stuffed the documents into produce boxes." This was the assessment by the Public Defenders Office of Orange County on looking further into the files and materials turned over to them by the defense attorneys from Calaveras County. "Hundreds of pages were pasted up with Post-It notes, with undecipherable jottings on them, hundreds of photos were dumped into boxes without any captions on them, negatives were separated by trash of all kinds," they told a writer for the legal journal, *The Daily Record*. Deputy Public Defender William Kelley and his co-counsels, James Merwin and Allyn Jaffrey, now officially the heirs of the work of Marovich and Webster, had also to look forward to a new trial judge, Robert Fitzgerald. They were not pleased with this prospect.

It seemed to be time for some assertiveness on the bench, and Fitzgerald was known for that. He immediately vowed to "speed things up." Talking freely with reporters, he assured them he could be fair to both sides. In fact, if he were still practicing law, he felt sure he could "take either side of the case." Not counting the sitting judge who had inherited Ng when he was extradited, there had now been five judges who had taken a crack at being impartial toward the accused serial killer: Mewhinney, Airola, Perasso, McCartin, and now Fitzgerald. A reporter cracked that it was now a "serial judge" case.

Nevertheless, Judge Fitzgerald stepped up to the plate with a trial date. There would be no waffling, he averred: September 6, 1996 would be the day.

The inventory of the moving-van shipment from Folsom, Sacramento, San Andreas, and Sonora to Santa Ana was now complete. Ominously, among the items were forty boxes of "personal effects of Charles Chitat Ng" and several containers of videotapes—one hundred and fifty of them in all.

October 27, 1995, Washington, D.C.

The U.S. Department of Justice received a letter from William Kelley, Esq., Deputy Public Defender of Orange County, California, requesting all government files relative to Charles Chitat Ng, including those relating to the extradition negotiations with Canada from 1985 through 1991. Kelley cited the Freedom of Information Act.

One month later, a second request arrived at the Justice Department from Kelley, noting that his first correspondence hadn't even been acknowledged.

After another thirty days, a letter was sent to the Orange County Public Defender advising him that a search for the documents would begin.

April 16, 1996, Sacramento, California

For the second time, Deputy Public Defender Kelley submitted a writ to the Appellate Court asking for the removal of Judge Fitzgerald from the case. "He was steamed, and rightly so," said co-counsel Merwin. "There we were in open court, trying to explain to the Judge why we were far away from being ready to set a trial date. We were overwhelmed with problems of obtaining the evidence and the interviews we needed. And the Judge makes a wisecrack."

According to *The Daily Record,* the exchange went something like this: "Your Honor, two of my investigators have had heart attacks, one fatal. One of my attorneys had to be taken off the case for medical reasons. The computer that's crunching our files breaks down every day."

"Everybody is dying but Mr. Ng," the Judge shot back. He chuckled. "That's a little gallows humor."

Kelley cited the Judge's response, verbatim, as evidence that Fitzgerald was prejudicial to the defense of Charles Ng and should be removed.

Meanwhile, within blocks of the Appellate Court offices, the State Treasurer was issuing another monthly check to Orange County to help pay for the investigators, legal staff, and computers that were falling under the weight of the van-load of data. The previous year, noting the bankruptcy of Orange County, the Assembly had passed, without debate, a special appropriation to cover costs of the trial through 1996–1997. Based on budgets submitted from Orange County, the cost to the taxpayers would be $2,195,406 in 1996 and $2,393,059 in 1997. There was no budget for 1998, because, the arguments went, Judge Fitzgerald was on the case and at last there was an end to the nonsensical delays that had made a mockery of justice in the case "for more than a decade."

There was little likelihood that taxpayers would feel the bite of the Ng case. Even if one burrowed assiduously through the proceedings of the Assembly for 1995, one was unlikely to find the appropriation. It was earmarked under the label of "Delta Special Revenue."

The San Francisco Examiner had begun to keep tabs on Ng with a series of editorials during the O. J. Simpson case—itself a model of excess. Even before Simpson had gone to trial, on August 21, 1994, the *Examiner* headlined its Sunday editorial page "O.J. and Charles Ng" and cut straight to the heart of the matter:

> Further delay in Ng's case contributes to public cynicism over our legal system, it wastes tax dollars, and it tears at the hearts of the murder victims' families. We all deserve speedier justice.

The editorial was not lost on Sharon Cosner Sellitto, two thousand miles away in Ohio. "Believe me," she wrote in answer to the editorial, and to the people of California, "O.J. Simpson isn't the only one buying a multi-million-dollar defense—so are you."

July 9, 1996, Washington, D.C.

The Justice Department advised William Kelley that their investigation of his request had turned up an 800-page file on the Ng extradition case and other federal investigation into the murders in Wilseyville. It would be available for a fee of $70.

Kelley wrote back with a check for $70. More than a month later, he waxed philosophical: It had been ten months since his original request, and besides he still had plenty to read from the van load. So it didn't matter too much, now, if he hadn't received the 800-page file.

Ten months after his original request, he hadn't.

August 2, 1996, Santa Ana, California

Judge Fitzgerald, twice stung by the rebuke from Public Defender Kelley, and acting on a letter from Charles Chitat Ng, decided to take the bull by the horns and remove Kelley and his team from the case. He announced in the same breath that new attorneys for the defendant would be Gary Poulson and George Peters. The same reporter who had declared this a "serial judge case" now dubbed it a "serial public-defender case." One had to keep a score card: First there was Burt and Lew, then Webster and Marovich, then Kelley and Merwin, with Margolin and others always in the background, and now Poulson and Peters.

Reporters had become accustomed to the snail's pace of judicial progress in this ongoing battle. Their newspapers were writing editorials with the subtext "Justice delayed is justice denied." Relatives of the twenty or more known victims in this case were bolstering their pleas by getting out letters to various editorial columns. Although the O.J. Simpson case had long ago gone to trial and had a verdict returned during the time Fitzgerald had presided over this phase of *People v. Ng*, the Public Defender's office was nonplused. "I understand that the prosecution has had this case for ten years and they're geared up and ready to go. But I've only had it for about two years," Kelley told *The Daily Record*. "It takes two years to bring a normal homicide to trial."

The mathematics was now becoming clear to the public, as it had been to Ng for some time. Two years times five teams of defense attorneys equals ten years.

Kelley and team took their dismissal with the equanimity of a stockholder who has just seen his holdings plunge: we're in it for the long term. "We are organizing the case in a way that will help us if we stay on it. If the new lawyers get the case, we will show them where we've been and where they need to go. We've done a lot of stuff in this case, believe me. The case file is way better than when we first got it."

September 27, 1996, Santa Ana, California

The newly appointed defense counsel for Charles Chitat Ng said in court today that his team would set a trial date "in the near future." His previous expectation that a trial date could be set so soon was clouded by a new appeal from Ng. He acknowledged that the trial date set by Judge Fitzgerald, September 6, had come and gone, but that much had happened in the meantime to make this point moot.

What was the new appeal from Ng? Richard Schwartzberg, an appellate-court specialist living in Southern California, received a phone call in early September from the Fourth District Court of Appeals. There was a letter here, he was told, from Mr. Ng, which demanded that his Santa Ana attorneys be returned to defend him. Schwartzberg acknowledged that he had heard about the case, but was distant enough from it to be interested, without prejudice. Another hired gun was on the scene.

The writ of mandate from Schwartzberg followed in a few days. It was all too easy, he admitted. "I don't think you see too many cases where a defendant asks for a new lawyer, his request is granted, and then he says, 'Hey, I wasn't too bright'. Judge Fitzgerald didn't inquire of Mr. Ng what his complaints were before he ruled. The judge basically listened to him say he wanted a new lawyer and gave him one." The question lingered in the air: why?

In *The Orange County Register* it was stated that Ng told the judge, "I can't say for sure, but I lost the trust and confidence that I think I need to, to, uh, to have, to have him as my counsel."

Columnist Debra J. Saunders, of *The San Francisco Chronicle,* had followed the case for several years, with biting commentary on the antics of the judiciary in a case that was costing the taxpayers $100 an hour or more for every lawyer involved. Her take on it: If the defendant didn't "like" his attorney, that was all it took for Fitzgerald, uncharacteristically, to cave in.

The assault on Fitzgerald was escalated by an affidavit filed with the California Supreme Court from Kelley's co-counsel, James Merwin. Although the affidavit called for the removal of the Judge, the intensity of the issue wasn't evident until the particulars were read.

A separate letter to Supreme Court Justice Ronald George accompanied the complaint. In biting terms, Merwin asked why the mandate of a Marsden Motion—that a full hearing be held if a counsel were to be removed from a case—was never carried out. He insisted the Public

Where Did the Money Go?
Those Involved in the Ng Case from Law Enforcement

Federal Bureau of Investigation

Psychological profile on Ng
Military records and background on Ng
Federal fugitive warrant
Coordinated and supervised international search for Ng
Offered successful interrogation methods for interviewing Ng
Obtained federal search warrants for Postal Service
Provided clerical assistance and methods of record keeping
Conducted interviews of twenty-one women identified in photos
Performed ballistics tests
Conducted out-of-state and international interviews
Provided subsurface interface Radar Unit

California Department of Justice

Criminalistics laboratory
Forensics photography
Latent prints
Homicide Analysis Unit
Bureau of Investigations
Missing Persons Unit
Questioned Documents Unit
Public Information Officer
Personnel provided
Facilities for processing evidence
Infrared viewer
Chronology, map, and evidence identification
Printing services

Office of Emergency Services

Mobile van with five completely equipped work stations
California Rescue Dogs Association

California Conservation Corps

Labor for evidence retrieval

California Department of Forestry

Inmate labor
Tools and equipment
Records of burning permits and reports of smoke for Wilseyville area

Law Enforcement Agencies Involved

Alameda County District Attorney's Office
Alameda County Sheriff's Office
Bureau of Alcohol, Tobacco, and Firearms (ATF)
Calaveras County District Attorney s Office
Calaveras County Sheriff's Department
Calgary Police Department
California Highway Patrol
Capitola Police Department
Chicago Police Department
Cook County Sheriff's Office
Daly City Police Department
El Dorado Sheriff's Office
Fresno Police Department
Hollister Police Department
Humboldt Police Department
IBM Security Division, San Francisco
Los Angeles Police Department
Los Angeles Sheriff's Office
Mendocino County Sheriff's Office
Merced Police Department
Milpitas Police Department
Morgan Hill Police Department
Office of the Attorney General, Alberta, Canada
Pacific Bell Security Division, San Francisco
Palo Alto Police Department
Placer County Sheriff's Department
Royal Canadian Mounted Police
Sacramento Sheriff's Office
San Diego Police Department
San Diego Sheriff's Department
San Francisco Chief Coroner/Medical Examiner
San Francisco District Attorney's Office
San Francisco Police Department
San Jose Police Department
San Louis Obispo Police Department
Skokie Police Department
South Lake Tahoe Police Department
South San Francisco Police Department
Stockton Police Department
Sunnyvale Police Department
U.S. Attorney's Office, Chicago and Washington, D.C.
U.S. Postal Inspection
Ventura Police Department
Washoe County Sheriff's Office
Watsonville Police Department

Defender's office, of which he was a part, had done a "diligent" job in defending his client. But when it came to characterizing the judge, Merwin's choice of terms was unsparing:

> Had the court conducted even a cursory hearing into the petitioner's ill-considered claims, it would have discovered that they were meritless. . . .

Kelley had tried at several times to have Fitzgerald taken off the case. Merwin argued that this was the motivation for the Judge's removal of the Public Defender. "The transcript alone," he argued, "will show Judge Fitzgerald's intense dislike for deputy Kelley that colored his evaluation of the information adduced at this hearing."

Charles Ng had now achieved a level of confusion among the judiciary that even he might not have believed possible, ten years ago, in his jail cell in Canada where he honed his legal skills. He had set the wheels of interminable appeals in motion, and now he could now count on all the players to keep rolling.

November 12, 1996, Santa Ana, California

Charles Ng's designated appellate attorney had told reporters three months ago that "it is inconceivable that the state Attorney General's office would allow the dismissal of the present defense attorneys and face another two-years' hiatus" in bringing the Ng case to trial. As of this date, however, the new attorneys were not only in the saddle but were starting their own 'two-year study.'"

All of this could have been avoided, Schwartzberg argued, if the Attorney General's office itself took some initiative. "If Dan Lungren said the Court of Appeal should hear this on its merits," the attorney suggested, "a hearing would have been granted in a minute." But the Fourth District Court of Appeal declined to hear it. That meant the Orange County team took it to the California Supreme Court. Though it was turned down at the highest state court, it was a victory for the defense. They had time playing on their side.

Something I Fantasize

September 16, 1996, Santa Ana, California

Less than a month after Judge Fitzgerald had given his blessing to Charles Ng's request to dismiss his attorneys, the defendant had changed his mind. Fitzgerald, under attack by the defense motion to the California Supreme Court to rehire the attorneys and dismiss the judge, now ordered a psychiatric examination of Ng to determine why he had vacillated once more. And he denied Ng's motion to rehire Kelley and his defense team.

To certain critics of the system—everyone from the victims' relatives to newspaper columnist Debra Saunders, of *The San Francisco Chronicle*, to constitutional lawyer Ephraim Margolin—it was as plain as day why Ng was able to try.

"Nobody cares," said Sharon Sellitto, Paul Cosner's sister, implying that Ng was simply taking a call out of the defense's playbook. Sellitto went on to voice her opinion. "They're all billing by the hour. Before this thing is over and they can say it will never happen again, some people need to be made to take responsibility."

Saunders headlined a column, "Good Time Charlie," and catalogued the delaying tactics masterminded by the supposedly misunderstood defendant: he hadn't overlooked the United Nations Commission on Human Rights when he was in Canada, and he hadn't overlooked the possibility of a federal civil rights lawsuit "protesting his confinement in Folsom Prison."

Ng's special attorney for constitutional issues "had an even harsher opinion of the prosecution's tactics," reported *The California Lawyer*: The cost and delay in the case is "a paradigm of government stupidity," said Ephraim Margolin, abetted by judges who "adhered to technicalities at the expense of justice."

Yet a psychiatrist was indeed called in by Judge Fitzgerald to determine why Ng changed his mind. Dr. Gary Dylewski talked with the defendant and presented to the Court an explanatory picture of the man's mind. "Ng realized he had misplaced his frustration upon those persons who were making their best efforts to prepare his defense."

But there were few observers of the case, other than Dr. Dylewski, who thought Charles Ng "frustrated." Others felt Ng was clearly running things, as he had for the last six years of courtroom preparation in California.

Judge Fitzgerald was put on hold while the State Supreme Court deliberated what to do with the writ filed by Ng's "dismissed" defense attorneys. At long last, when they were expected to hand down their ruling, they passed the issue off to a lower court.

February 2, 1997, Sacramento, California

Charles Chitat Ng's new defense attorneys sent their last invoice to the State. It was ruled, by the Fourth Circuit Court of Appeal, that they had been "wrongly appointed." Unlike the Supreme Court, the Appellate Court quickly decided also that Judge Fitzgerald had wrongly granted the defendant a favorable decision in his Marsden Motion and had again wrongly denied Ng's appeal to change his mind! Not only would Kelley, et al, be reinstated, but the Judge himself "should be disqualified in the interest of justice." The court implied that Fitzgerald had also given the impression of moving too fast on the case, with too much eagerness to plow ahead regardless of legal reverberations. Too fast? The words seemed unbelievable to anyone who had followed the convolutions of the last five years since the Preliminary Hearing.

It had now indeed become a "serial judge" case. The Judicial Council took another look into its bin of possible judges, and found Superior Court Judge John J. Ryan, of Orange County, as the seventh judge to preside over the case.

With new determination, Judge Ryan hauled the reinstated defense team before him and hammered out a "firm" trial date of September 1, 1998. It was a Tuesday—admittedly, a year and a half away, but a firm date.

February 18, 1997, Las Vegas, Nevada

The idea that there was now some possibility of closure to the legal nightmare brought new accounts of the case—and of Charles Ng—into public attention. There had been lurid stories before of Ng's obsessions, his propensity for cruelty, his sexual fantasies. Former prison-mates from Leavenworth and Canadian institutions had recounted his detailed sadistic drawings, his bragging about surviving no matter what. One of these men submitted an affidavit, under oath, about Ng's prison confessions.

The account of the survivalist instincts of this self-proclaimed Ninja warrior came from an unusual source: a witness to Ng's first experience as a United States Marine.

Brad Chapline had been a Marine stationed in Hawaii when Charles Ng was charged with breaking in and stealing weapons from a Navy base on the island. Chapline was assigned to guard Ng in the Navy brig and to accompany him to the mainland when and if Ng were convicted by a court martial. He overheard Ng say to a fellow prisoner, "If I can't be famous, I'll be notorious."

As Chapline told the story, Ng soon made a move toward notoriety. As the day approached when his orders to stand trial were to be delivered, he deliberately got his leg entangled in an industrial machine in the prison workshop. In the infirmary, he was diagnosed with a broken tibia. The next morning he slipped out of the hospital and caught a flight to San Francisco. The FBI tracked Ng down two months later at the Philo farmhouse of Leonard Lake and "Cricket" Balazs, who had befriended him. This time, it was Lake who skipped bail while Ng was quickly charged and sentenced to Leavenworth. Chapline was brought from Hawaii to accompany Ng to the federal prison.

Chapline said, "Ng was no dummy. Intelligent, well-spoken, very well educated."

Ng was a master of martial arts and willing to take out anything in his path that barred his personal freedom. The prison guards at Folsom responsible for Ng during his stay at the San Andreas Court House, seven years later, made the same assessment. They designed Ng's infamous cage.

March, 1997, the Internet

A new magazine called "Sprak!" introduced a "Serial Killers" video, clearly made by someone else, to the list of pornographic materials it offered for sale. The video was illustrated with a sadistic drawing interspersed with insets of the faces of Leonard Lake and Charles Ng. The promotional material that accompanied the illustration implied that these were the infamous sketches made by Ng in Leavenworth prison. The caption over the distorted body of a bound woman was the plaintive refrain of one of the victims shown in the Lake–Ng videos: "So tell me where my baby is."

The exploitation of the infamous Lake–Ng videos by others was just beginning.

May 29, 1997, San Francisco, California

ABC-TV, which had run several stories about the Lake–Ng case over the last few years, now became a forum for the defense. Deputy Public Defender William G. Kelley, arguing that the "gag rule" imposed during the Preliminary Hearing was no longer operative—at least for the Orange County defense team—approached the San Francisco ABC affiliate with a proposition. If the station would give him a prime-time spot, he would provide a "sensational" videotape made by Leonard Lake.

This was the last piece in the puzzle, Kelley argued. It would show the motivation behind the mass killings in Calaveras County. And San Francisco television would be the perfect venue for this new disclosure—for it was a San Francisco police investigation that broke the case in 1985, and a San Francisco newspaper that proclaimed in a banner headline on Saturday, June 8, 1985, "Mystery Graves Uncovered," "Skeletons Could Be 4 Who Disappeared in S.F." The San Francisco District Attorney at the time, Arlo Smith, had offered an assistant DA, who was experienced in the case, to the state during the period when Ng was in a Canadian jail. But by the time Ng was extradited to California, Smith had lost the 1990 election for California's Attorney General to Dan Lungren. It was only then that the State decided to take over the prosecution. "They wanted the show to themselves," Smith said in a statement to *The Sacramento Daily Register*.

True, the trial was supposedly set to start in fifteen months, but the jury pool in Orange County would hardly be polluted by a TV broadcast four hundred and fifty miles away. Besides, the intent of showing the video was not to hamper the defense of the accused, but to "set things straight." It would not create any grounds for appeal if Ng were convicted.

The ABC-TV special-projects team in San Francisco agreed to bring at least two experts on camera to comment on the video. One would be a psychologist experienced in cults and personality-domination; another would be San Francisco's Public Defender, Jeff Brown. The O.J. Simpson case had come and gone, but not the expert witnesses. Kelley would introduce the video; well-known anchors from the KGO-TV newsroom would set the stage.

Leonard Lake's homemade video had finally reached prime time. He could not have imagined, when he set his camera up in his cabin hideout, and focused it on himself sometime in 1984, to spill out his demonic plan, that he would achieve the notoriety Ng had bragged about. He was now acting out the central character in the novel, *The Collector*, by John Fowles. He would find his "Miranda," the lovely captive in that novel, and then. . . .

"What I want is an off-the-shelf sex partner. I want to be able to use a woman whenever and however I want . . . . and when I am tired or bored or satiated. . . . I simply want to put her away."

His woman captive would take care of all the chores, and then would go back to her "little cell." Like Fowles' protagonist, Lake was hesitant, but when the moment would come he would take the risk. "Whether I do this or not will remain to be seen. Obviously, I've never done such a thing before, and it may not work out. However, I want to try. It's something that I fantasize."

The ABC-TV experts summoned for the viewing didn't mention that among the items found at Lake's mountain retreat were a diary that explained this obsession and a copy of *The Collector*.

Instead, they focused on what the video said about the relationship between Lake and Ng. "It's clear," said the psychologist, "that Lake was the leader and Ng was a follower." Did the television show in San Francisco strengthen Kelley's case in Santa Ana? If it affected any potential jurors, it was a violation of the system.

To the victims' relatives, who had been interviewed previously by ABC-TV in a sympathetic story about the pain caused by the many delays in the case, there was a clear answer. They felt it was a perversion. It was an invasion of privacy, for sheer sensationalism. "If the TV stations have learned anything from the Simpson case," said one of the victims' relatives after watching the Lake tape, "they don't show it. This is shameless exploitation."

On a radio talk show in San Francisco the next day, a caller identified herself as a potential victim of Charles Ng thirteen years earlier. "I'm coming forward to dispute the idea that Ng was a dupe of Leonard Lake. I'm not going to give my name. I'm afraid of that guy." She described how Ng had followed her home from a bus stop, and peered at her through her bay window. He stalked her again a few days later. "He had eyes I will never forget," she said. "Like a shark going after its prey. I found out three months later he was the fugitive who was caught in Canada. I could have wound up in that mountain cabin."

A friend of the Dubs family—Harvey, Debbie, and Sean—all of whom had disappeared from their home on the quiet street in San Francisco in 1985—called *The San Francisco Chronicle* columnist Debra Saunders to add her complaint. The witnesses to that disappearance identified two men resembling Lake and Ng who left the Dubses' apartment that fateful day. "I don't see how he can get away with it," Nancy Moss said. Saunders replied, "Never underestimate what slime can do with bales of tax money, no scruples and lawyers who choose not to defend, but to obstruct and delay."

October 5, 1997, San Francisco

The San Francisco Police Department responded to a query from the prosecution in the Ng case, admitting that they had lost the complete file of the twelve murders for which Charles Ng was indicted in his Preliminary Hearing. "We were doing our regular house-cleaning," a deputy at the Hall of Justice told *The San Francisco Chronicle*, "and some boxes were mislabeled."

Would this loss have any effect on the trial scheduled for September of 1998? No, said State prosecutors in Sacramento: we have enough evidence to convict Mr. Ng. But a prediction made by the defendant five years earlier was coming true: witnesses would die and evidence would be lost.

Within a month, the man who had identified Ng as the killer of a cab driver in San Francisco—the only eyewitness to alleged killings by Ng—died of natural causes in a prison in Canada.

January 20, 1998, New York City

Barbara Walters introduced a segment of her "20/20" ABC-TV show with the comment, "This is the most hideous murder case I have ever heard of." For the next twenty minutes, graphic details from the network's files laid the background of the Lake–Ng killing ground. Commander

Diarmuid Philpott, recently retired from the San Francisco Police Department and the officer in charge of Missing Persons when the crimes were uncovered, confirmed Barbara Walters' opinion. "It was horrendous."

Criminologists and legal experts dissected the legal maneuverings. Summation: the delays were unconscionable, but no one person could be fingered. Something had to be seriously wrong with the judicial system—at least in California.

May 10, 1998, Santa Ana, California

For two weeks Ng had argued in the Court of Judge John J. Ryan that "I can't put my life in their hands." He was referring to his reinstated counsel, William Kelley and James Merwin. For their part, Kelly and Merwin were arguing before the same Judge that this kind of behavior by Ng proved that he had an "irrational obsession" and therefore he couldn't stand trial. What appeared to many as a three-ring circus was completed when Ng asked for his old friend from his first run-in with the law in California, Michael Burt, to come south from San Francisco and defend him.

Deputy Public Defender Burt legally represented Ng on the murder charges in San Francisco—the case in which both the files had been mistakenly thrown out and the eye witness in Canada was no longer of help, because he was dead.

Judge Ryan allowed Ng to press his claims in open court. No longer wearing the orange jumpsuit that made him stand out as a prisoner in Calaveras County, Ng exuded the businessman's air that had done much to bolster Simpson's image at the defense table: khaki trousers, gray shirt with button-down collar. He bantered with Judge Ryan with an air of confidence.

Judge Ryan lectured Ng that if he persisted in acting as his own lawyer—*pro per* or *pro se*—he wouldn't be entitled to having investigators work for him or to an expense account for office work. The Judge had gone overboard, and Ng knew it. With the equanimity of a seasoned veteran of the criminal courts, Ng quietly disagreed.

"Based on my experience and knowledge," Ng argued, "anyone facing the death penalty has *ipso facto* a greater claim to legal assistance than someone facing a lesser penalty."

The judge's reply sent shivers through the relatives of the victims who were following the case. "You may know more than I do," Judge Ryan replied weakly.

But Ng wasn't yet done with this new judge. He had read the report of the psychiatrist who had examined him to see if he was competent to carry out his own defense. Kaushal K. Sharma, of Huntington Beach, based his evaluation on a comparison with others he had studied for similar reasons. "He was able to describe in minute details [sic] the sequence of events, the legal representations, even the case law, better than 99 percent of the criminal defendants I examine."

Under these circumstances, it was not surprising that Judge Ryan held out the hope that Public Defender Burt might finally be the person to represent Ng. The judge called Burt several times to discuss this final concession. And it was quite a concession, since Ephraim Margolin had been arguing for years, right up to the Supreme Court of California, to have Burt and his partner take over the defense.

Surprise: Burt announced that, among other things, *he* couldn't be ready for the September 1, 1998 trial date. For Ryan, this was the last straw. "I suppose if we had straightened that out, it would have been something else," Ryan conceded. "It appears to this court that Mr. Burt really doesn't want to represent Mr. Ng." The judge gave Ng another few days to make up his mind. "I need some time to get clear . . . on this thing," Ng said. The Judge replied that he would rule on the matter in 30 days.

One month later, in the Orange County Courtroom where Charles Ng was to go on trial, it was a warm Spring day: a soft rain has fallen throughout the state. The airwaves were filled with the sounds of Frank Sinatra, whose quiet death the country was mourning. On this mid-May day, after a few weeks of consideration, the presiding Judge has made up his mind. Mr. Ng's request was granted. He would be allowed to have the representation he had requested.

Himself.

August 15, 1998, Santa Ana, California

Charles Chitat Ng suddenly lost the nonchalance he had exhibited to his court-appointed psychiatrists and Judge Ryan. In his first presentation of elements of his case in court, he searched for words and called on the defense attorneys nearby to quote some legal phrases to him. The judge was not amused. If jury selection was to begin on September 1, it was obvious to him that Ng would never handle the legal process on his own.

The judge decided the process would continue because he was reappointing Kelley and Merwin—the defendant would be properly represented by legal help.

Judge Ryan insisted the date of September 1 was final. Kelley and Merwin, never far from the courtroom door, were called back to the defense table. The process would continue. Jury selection would begin.

August 24, 1998, Santa Ana, California

Judge John J. Ryan announced, according to the Associated Press, that jury selection will be delayed in the long-awaited trial of Charles Chitat Ng because it was becoming difficult to select a pool of one thousand people from Orange County who would be eligible. It was felt that this large pool was necessary in view of the number of people who were already familiar with the case through extensive newspaper and television coverage.

"This is the worst of all fantasies," one of the victims' relatives said to reporters at the courthouse, "that even with all this time the court hasn't been able to calculate what kind of time it might take to put together a jury. This is not the end of the nonsense."

The victim's relative was right: There were still many twists and turns in Ng's defense.

But first, in Part III, we discuss the greater societal ramifications that would become evident at the end of the trial. The final chapter, "The Trial and Verdict," shows why the Ng case epitomizes those issues.

Part III

Justice

If a capital case cannot be decided in three or four years, society is cheated and every theory of justice is subverted.

—Judge Robert G. M. Keating, New York City

Chapter **23**

Society

What kind of a message does the delay in the Ng case send to society?

Is it about lawyers and their ability to manipulate the courts in a capital case? Is it a signal that the judicial system is seriously flawed? Or is it worse: that nobody cares?

There may be a "death of outrage," as William Bennett recently put it—referring to public attitudes in general.

As a society we are inundated with stories of injustice, so much so that the Charles Ng case has barely reached national media attention despite thirteen years of reporting on the case by the Associated Press and TV networks, including ABC among others.

In the plethora of murder cases that now receive national attention, only a few have the special twist to excite us any more. The O.J. Simpson case spawned a hornets' nest of attorneys stinging each other on national talk shows, and, just when that case was leaving the front page, red meat for their fare was fortuitously provided by the Kenneth Starr investigation of shenanigans at the White House. The result has been a continuous drone of confrontation at the highest levels of politics that has drowned out discussion of lesser distortions of justice.

The public may still care about cases such as the Ng fiasco, but it has lost the focus of the case as it has dragged on for almost a decade and a half. The response that is finally coming—not just from victims and victims' relatives, but from people who read newspapers and write letters to the editor—is that those entrusted to bring criminals to justice have simply botched the job.

And who are these people? The list in the Ng case begins at the Attorney General's office.

"The One Guy Who Could Have Moved This Along. . . ."

District Attorney Terrence Hallinan of San Francisco was known in his youth—and in his young career in the law—as "Kayo" Hallinan. The pugilistic escapades of those days have remained part of his character over the years. He is a man who doesn't pull punches, and the authors found that out in his assessment of this case. Frustration and even angst over the Charles Ng debacle still haunts the prosecutor's office at the Hall of Justice in the City.

As befits a man whose family name has long lingered in San Francisco, Terry Hallinan's office on the third floor, west end of the hall is classier than its surroundings. When the old, rococo Hall of Justice on Portsmouth Square, which had survived the great earthquake and fire of 1906, was given over to the wrecker's ball in the 1960s, it begat two architectural disasters: the Holiday Inn that took over its location and the new Hall that was obviously designed by someone in the motel business. The cheapness of municipal governance of this era was not kind to its citizenry, nor, indeed, to justice, if the ugly utilitarianism of the courtrooms sandwiched in the lower floors is any guide. In times past, courthouses inspired citizens with their look of permanence and dignity.

Yet District Attorney Terrence Hallinan brought with him to the hall a photographic gallery of his days on the Board of Supervisors and his experiences growing up in the shadow of his fabled father, Vincent. A glance around the room speaks volumes about the years when Vincent Hallinan wore justice on his shirtsleeves like a badge of honor. Justice. One has the feeling, entering the son's austerely decorated, denlike office, of walking into a history that this housing-development building has tried to deny him.

Kayo's lined face seems weary, even at 11 in the morning, but it quickly ignites into smiles and expressions of surprise as the conversation moves into specifics.

"Tell me again why Claud was moved off the case." He was referring to Judge Claud Perasso, who took over as the trial judge in San Andreas on the supposed trial date of January 12, 1993. "He was one guy who could have moved this thing along."

When told that the prosecution called a technical matter into question—he hadn't disclosed a DUI on the papers he filed for the assignment—Hallinan was incredulous. "Claud, a DUI?" As if to say "Then it can happen to anyone," he sighed and almost inaudibly continued, "Why in hell did the prosecution ask him to step down?"

When told that the state argued that this showed a bias against law enforcement, he answered, "Ridiculous."

It was pointed out to him that the real reason was hinted at in an article in a California law journal. The people from the Attorney General's office didn't like the fact that Perasso had OK'd Ephraim Margolin to represent Ng in a motion to the Supreme Court.

He was still unconvinced. "I don't believe it," he said.

Hallinan was then informed that the prosecution even objected to having Margolin provided with an assistant to research the case.

He replied, "Then I think I can see what's wrong. Where was the Attorney General when this was going down? Was he overseeing these jokers? Was he calling them in once a month and asking for a report on what they were doing? Any blame for stalling this case should be laid at the AG's [Attorney General's] office."

"I Didn't Know Them. . . ."

About one month before the interview with Hallinan, the case was discussed with one of the highest paid attorneys in Boston, a man who a few years before had been an "AG" for the State of Massachusetts—and also its Lieutenant Governor. Francis Xavier Belotti—Frank to anyone who knows him—has a physical affinity to Kayo in one respect only: pugnacity. Where Kayo has a gangly frame, Frank is compact and intense. He works out, sometimes in his office, to keep himself years ahead of the reaper. As a result, he looks a dozen years younger than his seventy-one.

Frank likes to tell stories, even with himself as the butt of the joke. He doesn't like to drive, and can laugh disingenuously about a fender-bender and the cascading consequences to someone like him who would rather accept any settlement that would avoid lawyers than miss a get-together in a North End restaurant among tables of his friends.

Like Kayo, Frank Belotti has an intense feeling about why things go wrong in cases such as that of Charles Ng, and again it has to do, not with the law, but with the people who are charged to carry it out. If Hallinan feels that the cities are being let down by the state, Belotti feels that the state is being let down by the feds. "Let down" is saying it politely.

In the witness-protection program—the darling of federal prosecutors—plea bargains for those who give state's evidence are so common, Belotti believes, that a new criminal class has been given a virtual pass.

He is reminded of a case featured on the popular TV program "60 Minutes." A former Mafia don and hit man complained to the interviewer that because of a judge's ruling he had lost the early parole he was promised by the feds, in exchange for "ratting" on his colleagues. The interviewer replied, "But you killed twenty-two people." The don's answer: "But I didn't know them. . . ." Belotti recounted his own horror stories about "casual murderers" who think they can always count on "the feds" to save them in the end.

Like the problem in California, where state prosecutors seem to be unsupervised, the problem in Massachusetts has been a federal program that is not being addressed with sufficient oversight. As Belotti says, "The feds are a law unto themselves. They give justice a bad name. They add to delays in the courts because they create legal nightmares for us. Anything we have accomplished in bringing justice to the people has been done over the bodies of the feds."

"It's Over. . . ."

The frivolousness of some civil lawsuits that judges excoriate, and often punish with fines, is no stranger to criminal courts. In criminal courts, however, the interests of society, not simply individuals of society, are at stake.

This fact is the linchpin of the case against those who have prosecuted Charles Ng. Society has suffered when the federal system and the state system have failed to move the case forward expeditiously. As Frank Belotti and Terrence Hallinan have said, it is not the laws that are responsible for the failures of these systems, but the people who administer them. The people who have a duty to prosecute must be held to a standard that avoids frivolous behavior.

The arbitrary call for the dismissal of a judge by the state prosecutors—in the instance of Claud Perasso—was frivolous. The prosecution al-

leged a single irregularity in the forms that judges routinely and perfunc-
torily fill out when taking a case. The prosecution did not argue why this
oversight was determinitive of the judge's partiality to the defense. They
simply cited the oversight and asked for the judge's dismissal.

As a result of that action alone, the Ng trial was delayed by about two
years. Those two years cost the citizens of the state some $4 million. Worse,
those two years were years of continuing grief for the relatives of the victims in this case. Finally, those two years seemed to make a statement that
society did not care.

The Chief of Police in San Francisco during the Lake–Ng investigation
was Con Murphy. A soft-spoken man, now long retired, Chief Murphy
pointed out that the division of duties is a potential flaw in how justice is
achieved.

Murphy's role was essentially done when his investigators from
Missing Persons followed their leads to the Wilseyville mountain cabin.
Lake was in a coma, soon to die; Ng was on his way to Canada; and San
Francisco investigators had already obtained a legal wiretap on Ng's sister
in Calgary, giving them advance knowledge that this is where he was
headed. This was good, even extraordinary police work. And when Ng
was wrestled to the floor of a Hudson store in Calgary, and his gun taken
away from him, the police work of the Canadians was over.

Derry Philpott, then in charge of Missing Persons, also experienced
this feeling of "it's over." Appearing on an ABC-TV special of Barbara
Walter's 20/20 in 1998, Commander Philpott, now retired, recalled clearly
the feeling of relief that they had "got their man." "It was the most despicable crime I have ever seen," he said.

Then law becomes order—the criminal apprehended becomes the
criminal prosecuted. And in this gulf between law and order, both Philpott
and Murphy believe strange things happen. There is seldom a seamless
connection. The accused now has the right to an attorney, and the attorney
has the right to "damage control." Now the plea bargaining can begin. The
television series "Law & Order" gives a rather accurate picture of what can
go on between the defense and the prosecution. The question is, Does it
add up to justice in the eyes of society?

Neither Murphy nor Philpott knock the system. Both stated, in different words: the division between law and order generally works. Why it
didn't in this case, they don't know. But they have a good idea it's the
sheer size of the case.

Why should the sheer size of a case leave the public empty-handed? Were those who were running the case out to lunch on this one?

If there was ever a broken window, left unrepaired, the Ng case is it. The glass, caked with blood, is all over the street.

- The Attorney General's office in Sacramento could have been more aggressive in supervising the state's prosecution team.
- There is no state or federal authority, other than the Attorney General's office, that could have monitored and held accountable the actions of the State prosecutors in their tactics in this case.
- Redress for grievances from victims and their relatives has largely been left to the media; in short, the authorities have allowed the victims to carry the water.
- The Attorney General's office has become less a prosecutorial than an administrative one—primarily engaged in dealing with appeals; it should do a better job or go out of the business of conducting criminal trials.
- The state-appointed defense attorneys have ignored the concerns of the public, and have even attempted to try the case on television. Prosecutors in Terrence Hallinan's office said, "After all the sweat put into this case by our office, it was despicable to see the defense showing Leonard Lake's self-made video on television. That pandered to the worst in public opinion."
- Orange County further insulted the intelligence of the public by delaying the trial two more weeks because finding one thousand potential jurors "was difficult." The public may be inured to delays in this case, but it is not credible that such a problem wasn't foreseen months or years ago.

"Tough on Crime"

Despite the fact that the evidence in the Ng case was studied and restudied by both defense and prosecution for years before the trial began, the judge predicted to the press at the start that the trial might last as long as the end of the millennium. Such a statement leans on the accepted wisdom of capital cases. But both defense and prosecution have ignored the judgment of Ephraim Margolin, who argued successfully to Judge Perasso that this case should not be treated as an ordinary case.

The lessons that can be learned from this case, as far as society is concerned, are the following:

- ❑ Justice is at least the duty of the Attorney General's office.
- ❑ If the Attorney General's office remains unresponsive, the system must be reformed.
- ❑ Defense attorneys, state-appointed or not, must be held accountable to concerns of the public, and this fact should limit their defense tactics.
- ❑ The decay of the judicial system should be just as much a concern of society as urban decay—and decay is obvious in the Ng case.

Society makes its decisions based on its perceptions of how things are going. Is crime really down? Is violent crime up? Has crime penetrated lower age levels in society? Are more children carrying guns to school, and why?

These are not issues of capital punishment, or of gun control, or of "tough on crime" politics. These are issues of accountability to society. It's time to ask the "system" to tell us how it has let us down, and what it can do to re-instill trust in its guardians.

Chapter 24

Performance

We gave them an incentive they could understand—money.

—KATHERINE LAPP

Just as there are honorable, hard-working people at the top of every profession, and at the lower end goof-offs, the reverse is also true. But some rules of behavior are different across the board in the judicial system. Few professions other than that of judge grant their members the license to choose their own working hours, at the expense of everyone else who depends on them, and use that privilege regularly.

Lawyers know this, most judges will admit this, and most citizens called to jury duty soon suspect this. In the case announced to potential jurors as "People v. Ng, Charles, Chitat, #94ZF0195," in Orange County, it soon became obvious that somebody—and who else could it be but judges?—considered their time to be infinitely more valuable than that of the jurors—or anyone else's. Consider what went on between the judge in this case and the potential jurors.

Starting on September 15—until five hundred people could be selected for possible duty—some three thousand ordinary citizens went through a process that could be characterized as nothing less than thoughtless. Their names were culled from the lists of registered voters. They were sent a fourteen-page questionnaire that read like an SAT exam. Sample: "8. Have you or someone you know had special training or education in the following fields: law/legal, criminal justice, psychiatry, medicine, psychology, science?" Two lines are then given for the answer, if you have placed a check mark next to any of the above.

The last six pages of the questionnaire were devoted to the death penalty. Sample: "Do you believe in the adage 'an eye for an eye'? If yes, what is this belief based upon?" And, next, "How strong is your belief in 'an eye for an eye'?"

There was no mention in the questionnaire of the juror's financial or emotional ability to undertake sitting on a jury for six months to a year. All newspaper accounts of the pending trial reported nine months to a year as the estimate of the judge. And in the schedule printed on the walls of the Orange County Courthouse was a simple reminder: trial likely to last until June of 1999. And this was only September, 1998.

Jurors assembled in the first floor of the cavernous Orange County Court House as if they were in line for tickets to the Superbowl. The line was light at 8:00 a.m. but soon stretched down the hallways in a tightly packed formation toward the central office. Having received their badges, the jury prospects proceeded to the eleventh floor, where they again queued up, this time in front of the door of Department 45. Many simply milled around, talking, gazing out at the county jail across the street and the City of Santa Ana and beyond, trying to put a good face on an excruciatingly meaningless exercise. Jury duty is often like this anywhere, but here the problem was the method of jury selection. No chairs were to be found anywhere, even for the elderly. Worse, there was little information about the process they were caught up in, or about when they would be able to go back to their jobs or homes.

Finally, a clerk of the court would emerge from this mysterious "department"—a courtroom with the appearance of a high school classroom—and announce that the ten o'clock group would be entering at eleven o'clock, because of delays, and anyone who was scheduled for eleven o'clock should not enter at this time, but later. "Later" was not defined.

Some two hundred people thereupon filed into the courtroom, some of them ushered into the jury box itself to save space. There were very few seats at the back of the room to accommodate reporters. But by this time—four days into the jury-selection process—the media had gotten the picture. It would be another exercise in numbing judicial delay.

"Never mind!" the system seemed to say. Everything will become clear at the proper time. The Judge will preside and make sense of everything.

After the potential jurors had found seats, the play was about to begin. What they saw was a table just beyond the railing that separated them from the area of the bench. At this table, facing the judge's commanding desk, were five people with their backs to the audience. At left were a man and a woman, the two prosecutors from the State of California, the same lawyers who had carried the preliminary hearing to completion in Calaveras County. At right were two men in business suits flanking a heavyset Chinese man in a sports shirt. All five could be seen flipping sheets of yellow pads again and again, as if studying the role they were about to perform.

"Thank You—You Are All Dismissed"

But there was a surprise that surely struck home to anyone who had followed the case. Security was minimal—in stark contrast to the fortresslike atmosphere of the preliminary hearings. Two bailiffs stood beside the clerk's desk. Another shuttled back and forth from the doorway to the railing, making sure that everyone had "checked in." Charles Ng was utterly defenseless against anyone who felt outraged enough to walk up to the low railing and take out his or her anger on the hunched back of the defendant.

This possibility was not an idle speculation: the aging father of one of the victims was quoted in a California newspaper only days earlier that he would like to serve justice on Mr. Ng, and in person. Several newspapers had sent reporters to Michigan and Ohio to interview families of two of the victims. The stories of outrage they reported from grieving and despairing relatives of the victims were heart rending.

In contrast to the courthouses in Sacramento and San Francisco or even little San Andreas, there were no metal detectors at the entrances to the building. An assistant prosecutor who was hurrying his displays to another courtroom was asked why this was so. He knew immediately what to answer. "Money," he said, as he rubbed his right thumb and forefinger together. "This county is broke."

The interviewer pressed on, "But surely you could put a metal detector at Department 45. Who will be responsible if someone takes out the justice of the Old West on this guy?"

He shrugged.

When asked about the ludicrous parading of potential jurors through the courtroom, he said, "It's the system. They have to winnow the first group down to about five hundred people before they can seriously begin questions and answers of the remainder in open court."

In four days, the clerk of the court said they had run one thousand six hundred people through Department 45, and netted about sixty for that first "winnowing." The original estimate was that it might take one thousand potentials to produce the first group of real prospects. Now it looked as if three thousand potentials might not get the prospects much beyond one hundred.

So it went for the rest of the day, and the next, and the next. The citizens had performed their civic duty, had filled out a massive questionnaire, had taken a day off work or other duties, had seen nothing but a static courtroom, and had heard nothing but the words from the Judge: "You are all dismissed."

Why wasn't it possible for these potential jurors to mail the questionnaires to the court? What state law or rule of the court required two highly paid attorneys from each side to sit all morning in Department 45 without saying a word? To the public there is little meaning in this apparent bureaucratic waste, even though it may be legally necessary. With even the reporters gone, who had an incentive to call anyone to account to change this apparently mindless system?

Was there another way?

"I'm Dark Today"

The problem of judicial efficiency was reviewed with several former attorneys general—names supplied by Frank Belotti, who some years ago had formed an organization of former attorneys general. Mr. Belotti's recommendation carried a great deal of weight. Strong opinions were delivered in these interviews, from states across the country, about where the judicial train had gone off the track.

It's virtually impossible to question a judge—even from the attorney general's office—about how he decides to spend his time. The phrase that kept coming up in conversation was "I'm dark today." The phrase meant, simply, my office lights are out. Nine times out of ten, when the lights were out they were out on Fridays.

Yes, judges have to have time to catch up on their work. They have to dictate letters, study cases, write opinions. But perhaps their time could also *include* time to consider the time of lawyers, court workers, and even potential jurors.

One of the country's most qualified experts on courtroom efficiency, Katherine Lapp, is a special assistant to Governor George Pataki, overseeing the justice system for New York State. She usually spends the first three days of the week in Albany and Thursdays and Fridays in New York City. Her job is to translate the governor's judicial policies into action in the courts and often in the prisons. Prior to this awesome assignment, she worked with Judge Robert Keating for the mayor's office of New York City, pushing reforms to unclog the courts in the five boroughs.

The amount of delay they discovered on a preliminary inspection of the courtrooms of the City, Ms. Lapp said, was "abominable." Judges had been "turned into clerks," following old, thoughtless routines whereby the word "adjourn" was the ruling dictate. If an attorney suggested that his witness might take a half hour to testify, and it was twenty minutes before noon, down would come the adjournment gavel—for lunch. The courtroom would fill up again at about one o'clock, but the judge would not make his reappearance until one-thirty or so. It was not unusual for a morning adjournment to end the day's work entirely. And if this came on a Thursday, the case might not resume until the following Monday.

Judge Keating and Ms. Lapp restructured the system by beginning in King's County Supreme Court with a case-processing reform. Judges were hand-picked here for certain cases. The order came down from the top: judges were to understand from now on that "We control our courtroom" rather than quarreling lawyers or missing witnesses or the vagaries of long lunches, conflicts of schedules, or the prospect of a long weekend.

The ultimate incentive, Ms. Lapp felt, was very simple: extra money. When cases were finished expeditiously and the calendar began to meet its deadlines, judges and their support staff were paid more. When told it seemed surprising that this could be done, Ms. Lapp confirmed that was the ultimate carrot, and well worth it.

Murderers List

The same question was put to Frank Belotti in Boston. He concurred, and with a broad laugh. When he was attorney general, the jury selection process was reduced to five questions—quite unlike the fourteen pages handed out to prospective jurors in the Ng case. "We had to treat lawyers and sometimes even judges like children. One of our best judges decided to lock the courtroom doors at eight in the morning, and if you weren't in the room you had to wait until one-thirty in the afternoon to find out what happened. Finally, attorneys and witnesses began showing up on time."

When asked about other incentives—such as money—he replied, "You mean paying them more? That might have worked too. But we began speeding things up by separating the cases. The public defender's staff handled the garden variety cases. Then we got hourly guys for the capital cases. We called it the 'murderers list.'"

Mr. Belotti was apprised that in California defense attorneys were being paid $100 an hour or more to defend Charles Ng. These were local attorneys in Calaveras or Orange County, some of whom did not charge nearly that amount in previous cases. He assured us that would be considered excessive in Massachusetts. "Probably $65 an hour is about right. And that's for lawyers who get three, four hundred in their own practice."

When asked how fast a murder case proceeds now, he responded, "In Massachusetts, eighteen months is plenty. But we don't have the death penalty. Without a doubt that's the problem you have in that serial murder case in California."

Chapter 25

Politics

The terrible mix of prosecution and politics. . . .

—SCOTT THUROW, on the Rolando Cruz case

Politicians have seized upon the issue of violent crime with the same intensity with which they wrapped themselves in the American flag in the Cold War years. To be soft on crime is a serious charge, worse perhaps than to be soft on Communism. The worst fear of a politician is to discover, as Michael Dukakis did, a Willie Horton blamed on one's executive decision.

A politician doesn't have to claim a broad background in the criminal justice system to announce how "tough on crime" he is. The district attorney of Orange County, technically in charge of bringing Charles Ng to justice, is the experienced Mike Capisi. He lost the primary in 1998 for the office of Attorney General, vacated by Dan Lungren. In California, as elsewhere, recent elections have shown that a person with no courtroom experience, but great name value, can run for chief prosecutor, and win.

This might be called the "negative effect" of politics on justice: the idea that winning office by an election qualifies a person to do a job. As a former Assistant District Attorney of Alameda County, California, Bill Sharon, said, "the negative effect of politics on the judicial system is accelerating wherever term limits come into play. Politicians play musical chairs when their terms are up, and they run to the closest chair, whether it fits their qualifications or not."

Bill Sharon has been in private practice for more than forty years, and is now on the boards of several international corporations. But the genial Bay Area attorney considers his years in the courtroom—sandwiched between Navy service in the Philippines in World War II and starting his own firm—as a highlight of his life. And the Sharon family has had many exciting moments—from those who built the Palace Hotel in the 1870s to his father, who flew in the Lafayette Esquadrille. "Public service means being in the public eye, but it should also be considered an honor. I see the latter part diminishing—and a case like the Ng affair, with dozens of attorneys and judges taking a crack at it unsuccessfully, further diminishes the confidence of the public in their elected officials."

When asked what could be done to bring honor back into the politics of justice, Mr. Sharon's answer was typically direct: "Assign a judge to the case to see it through from beginning to end. Make it a matter of honor for him or her to perform well."

"And the same applies to the prosecution?"

"Exactly. Look, a DA is like the director of a movie, in which he is also the leading man and the camera man and even the script writer. When he goes into that little chamber between the rail and the bench and the jury box, he creates a scenario and plays it to everybody in the room. What he says has to be believable to the entire audience—even to the defense."

"How is that different from what happened here?"

"The unconscionable delay from the indictment to the trial. It's become a stale, warmed-over movie."

"But how do you answer the defenders of the status quo who say this case is different because of the tons of evidence?"

"That's just my point. The prosecutor can't let the tons of file cabinets tell him how to direct his movie. He has to absorb and then shape the evidence—not the other way around."

"And if he doesn't?"

"Unfortunately, voters have short memories, and there's really no judicial review—except for gross professional misconduct."

"Then it seems hopeless. The present system can't cope with serial killers."

"Except for one thing. A grand jury. . . . Unfortunately, what the public knows about grand juries has been clouded by recent events in Washington."

Who Guards the Guards?

In the Ng case, the State of California decided to bring an indictment by means of a preliminary hearing rather than a grand jury. A jury is "grand" only in the old English sense of "large." It is a panel of citizens, chosen through interviews and appointments, that generally "oversees" the operations of all parts of the government, from cities to counties to states to the highest legislative and executive authority in the country.

The public has learned much about how grand juries function from the public record of the Special Prosecutor appointed to investigate President Bill Clinton. The public learned from transcripts of interrogation of witnesses that the names of the grand jury are not revealed to anyone, including the witnesses called to testify. No witness can be represented by an attorney. No rules of evidence apply. The grand jury is a mirror image of the "star chamber" proceedings of the Middle Ages.

How did grand juries get this powerful authority, and why do we still have them?

Bill Sharon was asked if a grand jury could have saved the Ng case.

"No lawyer likes a grand jury, unless he has a weak case. Remember how Perry Mason usually got the criminal to break down on the witness stand and 'fess up? That doesn't happen in the real world. Except in the grand jury."

"So the prosecutors felt the evidence was so strong they didn't need a grand jury?"

"I'm not saying that was a bad decision, but grand juries also serve a special purpose, and this may have been it. It's a corrective tool, many times." Mr. Sharon gave the example of the Rolando Cruz murder case in Naperville, Illinois in 1983. Scott Thurow pursued this case in his dual capacity as author and attorney. It was election time, and in Dupage County the conviction of Mr. Cruz for a murder he supposedly had confessed to was sought, in Mr. Sharon's words, by a district attorney in need of votes. The conviction was twice thrown out, but even after convincing DNA evidence there was a third trial. Finally, after serving ten years for a crime he didn't commit, Mr. Cruz was acquitted and freed. The odor of the case was so bad that a grand jury took it upon themselves to indict the prosecutors."

"Obviously, this was a time for someone to prosecute the prosecutors. It was Socrates, I think, who asked 'In a just society, who guards the guards?'"

One Day, One Jury

Law Professor John Coons, who has taught at Boalt Hall, at the University of California, Berkeley, for most of his career, expressed concern about how difficult it is to change the direction of the law. He said that politicians try to take the pulse of society and base their platforms on that pulse, rather than change the pulse. His example: the public generally believes that death is the end of everything—even though this is supposedly a religious nation. Therefore, the idea that death is the ultimate punishment pervades all political thinking. Not even Mario Cuomo, one of the nation's most successful politicians, could overcome that perception, and his stand against the death penalty no doubt cost him many votes in his loss to George Pataki.

"You have these large societal forces," Professor Coons said, "including the desire of politicians to avoid term limits, and no amount of statesmanship is likely to turn back that tide."

In small ways, the growing perception of the public that something is amiss in the judicial system seems to be creating a tide that is positive. In contrast to the "negative effect" of politics on justice, as cited above by Bill Sharon, this might be called the "positive effect." In September of 1998, Governor Pete Wilson of California signed the so-called "One day–one trial" bill. Clearly, the state legislature had taken the pulse of the public and discovered that jury duty that requires people to be kept on hold for two weeks until they are either called or dismissed is not liked very much. As an editorial in *The San Francisco Examiner* phrased it, this requirement has made "a hash of work and family schedules." Under the old system a juror who served a day or a trial of a few days still had to make himself or herself available to be called back during the remainder of the two weeks. With the new bill, anyone who is called for jury duty has merely to serve one day or for one trial, and then be dismissed.

This small step forward would not have saved the four thousand or more potential jurors in the Ng case the loss of that first day when they were called to Department 45, as described in a previous chapter. But if popular, it may convince politicians that they have a lot more to do in reforming an archaic system. Instead of thinking of the effects of term limits in their case, they might think of the effect of *no terms at all* for judges in cases that are highly visible to the public. In other words, they might think of taking politics out of criminal justice.

These Are the Rules. . . .

When interviewed in his office in the Brooklyn Courthouse building, Judge Robert Keating had returned to private practice with a nationwide company that operates, among other things, methadone centers for drug abusers. He is still very much involved in what he terms "the dual criminal justice track." Violent crimes and drug-related crimes are these two main themes, and life problems form what might be called a related undercurrent (spousal abuse, sexual abuse).

Judge Keating was appointed by Mayor Ed Koch, along with Katherine Lapp, as mentioned previously, to form a plan to help move the prosecution of cases in the five boroughs. Since there were at the time some five hundred assistant district attorneys in the system, with a budget of about $3 billion, this was a formidable task. The Drug Courts and Domestic Courts were especially bogged down. Judge Keating echoed what attorney Bill Sharon said about getting these two tracks to "stay on track." It was a problem of each judge individually. The problem was to get each one of them to announce in court, at the beginning of each case, "These are the rules," and then to stick to them.

Judge Keating gave the famous "Son of Sam" case as an example of judicial efficiency. "This was a classic case," he said, "a multiple murder, vast public attention because of the rising tension in the City, good public defenders."

In the end, Assistant District Attorney Al Peischman wrapped up the case in very acceptable time by keeping everyone in the courtroom to the rules.

When Judge Keating was asked specifically if judges work better when they don't have to look over their shoulders at the voters. "Perhaps," he answered. "There is a real tension there. But I've found that most judges have a sense of personal accountability to the public, even if they're appointed for life terms, and that's not a bad thing."

But when the question is phrased in terms of high-profile, violent cases, the answer is easier. "Yes," Judge Keating agreed, "using retired judges in long-term capital cases would keep the pressure of an election year out of the issues."

In Massachusetts, where judges are appointed for life at the Superior Court level, Frank Belotti confirmed that everything is speeded up by the absence of politics. "Especially at sentencing, there are fewer lingering delays."

Katherine Lapp added to this debate the fact that the public is primarily concerned about crime in general: is the trend up or down? Her measure is the proportion between violent and nonviolent crime. "In New York State, we have finally reached the welcome stage where we can say the proportion has now been reversed from previous years. Violent crime is now less than half of all crime. That's good."

Unfortunately, there are no statistics yet about violent criminals becoming more adept at defending themselves in court.

The debate in years past was over such vague measures as whether there was a crime wave or not. In *Thinking About Crime* (Basic Books, 1975), James Q. Wilson had to deal with this perception and how it affected politics. Politicians were split between conservatives and liberals over whether crime was raging or under control. "By 1970," he wrote dryly, "enough members of the liberal audience had had their typewriters stolen to make it difficult to deny the existence of a crime wave."

The politics of crime has now turned to what to do about (a) drugs and (b) leniency of the courts. By most measures, crime is down, but the perception of a lack of safety in the streets is up. The equation, therefore, remains: greater sense of danger among the public equals greater caution among politicians equals longer delays in bringing violent criminals to trial. As long as many prosecutors and judges in criminal cases have to answer to the public at election time, they cannot afford to jeopardize a case by moving too swiftly. They would rather err on the side of delay than risk a rushed jury decision, as happened in the Simpson case, or a reversal on appeal.

Excessive caution throughout the judicial process equals the delay of justice. It is an unfortunate equation, especially for the victims.

Chapter **26**

Closure

What other thing do you do but make them thieves and then punish them?
—Sir Thomas More

When the father or mother of a murdered son or daughter sits through more than seventy hearings without an end to the ordeal, who has been hurt most? The complaint of Sir Thomas More four centuries ago about the penal system of his day might be rewritten today about victims and relatives of victims in our judicial system: What other thing do you do but make them victims and then punish them?

The chief aim of the Victims' Rights Amendment sponsored by Senators Diane Feinstein and Jon Kyl is to provide closure—in the form of information, restitution, protection, and speedy justice. At first blush, this characterization may seem simplistic. But a quick look at the amendment makes this point.

When the National Governors Association released its policy statement on victims' rights in 1997, the intent was defined in five briefly stated points, and those were essentially repeated in the proposed constitutional amendment that was voted unanimously out of the Senate Judiciary Committee in 1998. These points have to do with the right of the victims (or their relatives) to have information, to appear and speak at hearings, to receive restitution, and to enjoy reasonable protection.

The final Senate version of the proposed amendment adds the *right,* on the part of victims, *to a speedy trial* of the defendant. This crucial change reflects the growing concern, just in this short time, that criminals are becoming more adept in delaying justice.

245

Diane Feinstein herself is surely aware of the Charles Ng case, and perhaps in some measure based the new wording of the amendment on it—especially concerning protracted legal delays. She was the Mayor of San Francisco who issued the reward for the capture of those responsible for the missing persons in San Francisco in 1985. Several months after that reward was posted, law enforcement agents apprehended Lake and Ng and solved the case.

The governor's statement emphasized the statistics on crime as "a plague": more than forty million victims, eleven million of them victims of violence, with about $20 billion in financial loss from swindles, scams, property damage, injuries, lives cut short. As we have just seen, the statistics on crime can be argued several ways. The amendment may seem most appealing because of the perception that society is in greater danger, and this amendment will reduce dangers from criminals on their release. But doesn't this amendment also allow victims to recover from their loss, to end the pain, to come to grips with a diminished view of their lives, and to go on?

This is closure.

"This Is a Greek Tragedy"

Paul Cummins is everybody's vision of what a prosecutor should be—except a criminal's. In his third-floor office at the Hall of Justice in San Francisco, his husky frame outlined against a view of the grittier regions south of Market, Assistant DA Cummins projects determination and patience. Soft, measured statements. What's off the record. The people on this case he admires. What a trauma the victims have been through. His bald head for such a young man completes the picture: he has nothing to hide and cares little for false appearances.

"This is a Greek tragedy," he says. "There are lots of feelings around here about this case." In 1985, when the case went down, Cummins was the man the District Attorney picked to take it through prosecution. He probably knows more about what actually happened than anybody else.

How do you get closure on a Greek tragedy?

Cummins answered that you let the victims know that there are good people working for them in the system. People such as the Canadian Mounty, Raymond Munroe, whom Cummins met in Canada after Ng was captured there. Mounty Munroe doggedly pursued the Charles Ng case from day one in Calgary until Ng was finally sent back to California six years later.

"There was a feeling throughout Canada that this was becoming a safe haven for murderers," Cummins explained. "A fellow named Kindler had escaped from a Philadelphia prison, headed straight across the border, and was captured, but even though he was charged with some very bad murders he put up a successful extradition defense. Then there was another American named Ng, out of Seattle, who fled to Vancouver after a murder charge against him. There were debates going on furiously on TV and talk radio about 'American murderers' when I was up there. Everybody thinks Ng just went to jail and everybody went to sleep on this one. Not so. The mounty kept after him. His investigation of the evidence and his presentation to the various magistrates was classic."

Why is it so hard to move things along in a case that appears so obvious? Cummins suggested it's part of our Anglo heritage: "Juries want to be absolutely sure. In English courts, in fact, the simple question to the jury put by the judge is 'Are you sure?' Jury instructions here are more complicated, but the tradition remains."

If closure is so important to victims, why isn't more attention paid to victims in making judicial decisions that slow things down? Why don't we hear more about good police work, good prosecutorial work?

These and other questions were put by the authors to former Mayor of New York Ed Koch. In many ways, Koch reminded the authors of Cummins—even though years apart, they share the hint of dialect of their native cities and the bluntness of their language. The former mayor was upbeat about the crime statistics, and noted that many of the good things going on in the city are never reported: "We're not imposing jail on the small fry," he said. About the victims' rights amendment proposed by Feinstein and Kyl, and lambasted in *The New York Times* as a matter best left to state and local government, he volunteered, "The *Times* has its head screwed on wrong about a lot of things."

What encouragement can politicians and public servants give to the victims of crime? Koch thought for just a moment. "Well, we're giving them truth in sentencing."

"You mean less leeway for the parole board?"

"When the judge says ten years, it doesn't mean five. The new law in New York is in the right direction."

"Dead Man Walking"

The movie and the book of the same name had a surprising undercurrent of philosophy about closure for relatives of victims. As the questionnaire for the jury pool in Orange County put it, "Do you believe in an eye for an eye?" Ed Koch echoed the sentiments of many when he told us, "I believe in the death penalty—if you take a life, you forfeit your right to life." The surprising thing about a theme of *Dead Man Walking* is that it contradicts these apparently obvious conclusions.

The theme in point is that forgiveness, rather than vengeance, has a healing effect on the relatives of victims. It is a theme that seems to have worked in practice for the protagonist of the book and of the subsequent film. The theme seems to verge on the extreme idea that no person is basically evil, or, to put the matter another way, that no evil act cannot be explained by some causative factor beyond the control of the perpetrator. Yet, in retrospect, this theme is not about the mind and soul of the criminal, but about the mind and soul of the victim: How can the victim or the victim's relatives overcome the anguish of being violated by another human being?

Between diametrically opposed views on how evil happens is a wide spectrum of opinion, with many subtleties. But neither of these extreme views takes the victim into account.

The first of these views is that of George Will, the syndicated columnist and Sunday morning television guru, who consistently upholds the conservative banner: whether the issue is recreational vehicles (highway safety) or campaign financing (freedom of speech). The touchstone for Will's recent comments on criminal justice was the Kaczynski case, entitled "Death Penalty Must Be Imposed on Kaczynski." Retribution is Will's theme here, and he engagingly assigns human qualities to society. Society's "desire for vengeance against the vicious" is "wholesome." Society should have "serenity" in expressing its "retributive anger."

The other extreme is that of Dorothy Otnow Lewis, a psychiatrist and professor at New York University, who has made a special effort to study prisoners on death row and how they got there. In her recent book, *Guilty by Reason of Insanity,* she reports that she tried and failed to find an example of a remorseless killer deserving of capital punishment. She ascribes every example of murderous behavior that she was able to examine to either childhood abuse, or multiple-personality disorders, or outright mental derangement. In her own words, "retribution" so beloved by George

Will is simply additional criminal behavior. The death penalty is never justified, and on these grounds alone.

Between these extremes are the views of many other observers of society that what drives the death penalty is the mistaken idea that the relatives of victims, not some personalized "Society," demand it. Thus the power of practical argument in *Dead Man Walking*.

The deterrent value of the death penalty is somewhat related to the idea of relief to the victims. The ultimate deterrent to a killer ever taking out vengeance on those who put him in jail is his own death. The killer who is executed will not kill again—a rather strong argument in "lifer" prisons, such as Pelican Bay, California, where guards might feel their lives excessively at risk with no deterrent at all. Inherent in the victims' rights amendment proposal is the idea that safety for the victims' relatives is a prime consideration. A criminal who escapes prison, or whose term is inexplicably commuted by a thoughtless governor, might well want to take out his own retribution on those who testified against him at trial.

Various police officers who tracked down Charles Ng gave startling opinions on this subject. Captain James Connolly of the San Francisco Police Department, a religious man, had formed a group of like-minded individuals on the police force called Cops for Christ. Captain Connolly was struck by the theme of forgiveness in *Dead Man Walking*. He told us he believed it to be true, and read that the deterrent value of the death penalty was not statistically demonstrated. At the same time, he told the authors how he once went face to face with a trapped man with a gun, who confessed later he dropped the gun and surrendered because "I didn't want to die."

"Some Prisons Are Not Better Than Death."

Ed Koch is characteristically outspoken about the idea that the death penalty is sometimes not as strong a deterrent as living out a life in certain bleak prisons. "If that's so," he says, "why do they fight so hard to avoid the death penalty in court, then also on death row?"

Personal decisions about life and death—to be or not to be—may vary with the day and the hour and even with the last bad meal. The extreme example of state cruelty in imposing death was that of Robert Alton Harris, in the mid-1990s. Investigator Joe Long, who is known throughout California for his work for the prosecution in several jurisdictions, described the pitiful condition of Harris on death row. His lawyers had made the usual appeals up to the evening of the impending execution at San Quentin. "In his case at that time, the method of death was by cyanide capsule. In the execution room, facing the final moment as he surveyed the onlookers through a thick window, he heard the pill drop. Then the telephone rang. All hell broke loose. He was wrestled out of his chair. The Ninth Circuit Appellate Court had granted him a stay."

The pill finally dropped for good a few hours later. Whether one favors the death penalty or not, few would agree to this kind of psychological torment.

Caryl Chessman is a name almost forgotten in the national consciousness, but in the 1960s he established the current pattern of legal appeals against executions. Movie stars carried placards outside San Quentin; priests maintained midnight vigils. What is significant here as in the cases of Harris or Kaczynski is this: Was anything being done to aid the victims or their relatives in these executions? Or were the executions being rationalized as the only way to bring closure to the relatives of the victims?

Defense attorney Ephraim Margolin mentioned that in the case of at least one of his clients, a Mafia don whose appeal he lost, the prison in which he was finally confined for life "was not better than death." The families of the victims of Ted Kaczynski may not feel quite the same about the federal prison in Colorado where the Unabomber is now confined. The relatives may never know whether the conditions in this prison truly constitute punishment for the crime the man committed. The question remains: if they knew more, would they feel a greater sense of closure? This is the kind of issue that is missing from debates about the death penalty.

Suppressing the Records

The old-fashioned Suffolk County Courthouse in Boston is as different from the motel-style Orange County Courthouse in Santa Ana as two cultures can be. True, the Suffolk County locale is hidden behind the "Crescent," a phalanx of civic offices that curve along what is known as "Government Center." But once one passes through the arches of the Crescent, and ascends the steps of the older structure, one can see the comfortable architecture of a more leisurely era. Only the metal detector at the entrance reminds one of the newer realities of crime.

At the end of a long hall to the right is a high-ceilinged room dedicated to the press—in this case, one could call it *The Boston Globe Room.*"

Battered desks that now mainly serve the purpose of holding computers are spread throughout the boxy room. Two men are on phones in a far corner. Behind a desk strewn with galley pages, tearsheets, and a cascade of memos is the man who has watched the violent crimes of Greater Boston played out in the courtroom for the past nine years.

John Ellement clears a desk and quickly acknowledges he hasn't heard of the Ng case in California, but the news is spread fairly thin when a case goes on for thirteen years. Compartmentalized though it may seem, his job is clearly a serious matter to him. In his early forties, tall and athletic, Mr. Ellement still exudes enthusiasm about the changes in the judicial process. This, after all, is New England, whose institutions of higher learning and judicial forebears link the United States to its roots in England. Upon hearing about the case, he is fascinated about the delay of justice—the extradition arguments, the tons of evidence, the cost to the taxpayers.

It comes as a surprise to Ellement, as it did to others interviewed outside California, that Mr. Ng was able to command attorneys and staff working at a combined rate, from time to time, of several hundred dollars an hour. He clears up a key point at once: there is a greater sense of closure in a federal plea-bargain for life without parole—Elwop, as it is known in California—because of federal law. A life sentence in a federal prison *means* life. There is no possibility of parole hearings, or commuted sentences by a governor. This is the "certainty of sentence" that many victims' families can appreciate.

The possibility of rehabilitation is logically a safety benefit to victims, in that rehabilitation should at least reduce vengeance by criminals against their accusers. Is this "first line of defense" realistic? Prisons are well known as colleges of crime. Why not diminish, rather than increase, the propensity of the criminal to fall back into a pattern of vengeance, a life of crime?

Reporter Ellement considered this reasonable enough in theory, but counter to centuries of the practice of penology. Society seems afraid to ask if the penologists may be wrong.

Recidivism has a bad name, and is in fact a poor word. The tendency of a criminal to steal again, drive drunk again, kill again is "recidivistic behavior." The repeat offender has perhaps been best described in the "three strikes" laws that are now widespread. Katherine Lapp said that repeat offenders are about as common now as at any time she studied them. James Q. Wilson reacted to the suggestion that rehabilitation might be possible by saying "there are no studies that show violent criminals can be changed." Recidivism is apparently going to be with us forever.

An important part of victims' rights, Mr. Ellement explained, has been in rape cases. Rape crisis clinics are now common—places where victims can go to report the attacks on them, whether or not they go to the police first. The issue now has become the privacy of the reports that victims give when they first come to the clinics. Wendy Murphy, an organizer of legal protection for clinics in Boston, was largely responsible for achieving the right of clinics to "suppress the records" of these rape-case reports. By doing so, the clinics can defend themselves from automatic subpoenas from defense attorneys, who are looking for damaging information that victims may have given the clinics under the stress of reporting attacks on themselves. In this case, victims are far from passive participants.

It seems clear from this one instance that a victims' rights amendment can be justified on grounds that go well beyond the goals the Senate Judiciary Committee has stated: restitution, information, protection, all of which add to the closure that results from a speedy trial. The ability of victims to lawfully "suppress evidence" is a step toward broadening the scope of the amendment and its support.

Psychology or Physiology?

Perhaps no other aspect of the judicial system enrages victims' relatives as much as psychiatric evaluations of defendants. In the Superior Court opinion that ousted Judge Robert R. Fitzgerald from the Ng case, the Public Defender of Orange County, Ronald Y. Butler, joined by Assistant Public Defender Carl C. Holmes and Deputy Public Defenders William G. Kelley and James G. Merwin, and represented by attorneys Richard Schwartzberg, Gary M. Poulson, and George Peters—an impressive array indeed—cited the analysis of a Dr. Gary Dylewski, a psychiatrist, that Ng had tried to fire his attorneys, Kelley and Merwin, because of a "mental state."

The battle between psychiatrists and physiologists over what constitutes a "mental state" has been going on for decades. The dispute is often framed in terms of Freudians versus those scientists who study the chemical constitution of the brain. It was Linus Pauling who co-founded (with Dr. Richard Kunin, a San Francisco psychiatrist) a field known as Orthomolecular Psychiatry to study and promote awareness of such "imbalances in the brain." The latter phrase is often ridiculed by old-line psychiatrists as new-age vapors. They seem oblivious to the increasing sophistication of MRI and PET scans. The study of the brain and its connections through the central nervous system via hormones and neurotransmitters is science. Psychiatry without MRI and PET scans remains at best an imaginative art.

Thus the common-sense outrage over what the prisoner's "mental state" might be, in the absence of any actual tests.

Would it be some sort of closure for victims' relatives to know that their loved ones were murdered not out of conscious evil, but because of physiological damage to the brains of the perpetrators? Brain damage, after all, has been well identified in the case of fetal alcohol syndrome, acute alcoholism, and even nutritional and sensory deprivation. The brain atrophies, like any muscle, when it is not used. Several studies have shown it atrophies much of the time during imprisonment. Would it make sense to study the brains of criminals before, during, and after incarceration to see if this is why recidivism is difficult to overcome? Would it not be very cost effective to rehabilitate prisoners in general by watching the brain during imprisonment, and taking steps to allow prisoners' brains to grow instead of to atrophy?

In short, by neglecting rehabilitation as a matter of policy isn't society ensuring high levels of recidivism—and isn't recidivism a major danger to society? The question can reasonably be asked: are victims and the families of victims more likely to achieve closure knowing that a violent act was essentially an accident rather than the result of malevolence?

Dr. James W. Bergland, President of the Patmos Foundation, a prison-visitation organization in New York, believes a large proportion of prisoners come to jail brain-damaged and can easily become worse in present conditions of confinement. Asked about the problem of victims' rights, he noted that his foundation deals ostensibly with criminals rather than victims. Patmos facilitates the visitation of some eighteen thousand relatives of criminals each weekend, by assisting the logistics of moving these people, mainly from New York City, to the seventy prisons throughout the state. He sees the role of the foundation as to provide one leg of the triad for rehabilitation of criminals: family structure. The other two are a job skill and a high-school level of education.

But despite the emphasis on helping the prisoner, the foundation realizes that the lives and interests of criminals and victims are intertwined. Studies show that most victims come from the same culture as the criminals who have taken advantage of them. Without doubt, the safety of victims cannot be assured by a policy of information alone.

Dr. Bergland, who began his career at Harvard Divinity School, where he studied under Paul Tillich and Reinhold Niebuhr, started up Patmos in 1984 after an analysis he did of the roots of recidivism. He believes now, from the records of what Patmos has achieved, that sixty percent of inmates have "measurable brain damage."

Not "mental states," but "brain damage."

Michael Burt, Charles Ng's first defense attorney in the Calaveras killings, agrees that MRI and PET scans should be considered in capital cases. "Many of these people have gross brain damage."

When reporter John Ellement, of *The Boston Globe,* was asked what he thought of this assessment from his practical experience in covering the Suffolk County Courthouse, he said, "From what I can see from behavior in court, I would guess it is at least that."

Mr. Ellement referred to several recent books that have dealt with this subject. In *Whores of the Court,* by Margaret A. Hagen, Ph.D., the reference in the title is clear: "Psychological testimony is a total fraud," she writes. *With Justice for Some,* by George P. Fletcher, broadens the discussion of victims' rights in criminal trials. *Justice Overruled,* by Judge Burton S. Katz, takes on the criminal justice system from top to bottom. For the most part, however, these critiques of the system do not do justice to the roots of the problem: the criminals themselves.

When a System Fails. . . .

There can be no doubt, as Senators Feinstein and Kyl have argued, that basic change is needed to restore the balance between the rights of defendants and the rights of victims.

Because of the obvious abuses of psychiatric testimony in court, because of the confusing parry and thrust of lawyers and prosecutors, because of seemingly endless appeals, and finally because of a breakdown in the concept of a speedy trial, victims and their families are frustrated by the judicial system. The Charles Ng case is only one example—but an egregious one. On balance, it seems clear that the only real hope for reform that will bring a sense of closure to the open wound of neglect of victims is a strong national initiative.

That initiative could well be the Victims' Rights Amendment to the Constitution. It is long overdue.

Chapter 27

The Trial and Verdict

October 24, 1998, Santa Ana

Two days before his trial was scheduled to start, Charles Ng decided to speak out. This was the second time he had tried this tactic. After the interview he had given at Folsom Prison before the preliminary hearing, his attorneys had put a virtual gag on him. But now, again, he was desperate.

He was interviewed by Tony Saavedra, reporter for *The Orange County Register*.

Ng claimed he was an innocent man being railroaded by a judicial system more interested in popular opinion than truth. "I'm just like everybody. I have feelings. I need to eat, sleep. I need to have friends and I want to vindicate myself when I am falsely accused."

The reporter asked Ng about stating, "No pain, no gain. No kill, no thrill."

Ng answered, "In the Marine Corps, you say those things, locker-room-type talk. Probably it was took as some macho joke, but after [the killings] occurred with this thing, they try and exaggerate.

"I don't like to blame people for certain things when they have no chance to defend themselves. But this is the evidence. They have Lake's diary, but they want me as the scapegoat.

"They put me in Orange County, where they know this is prosecution heaven.

"All I really want to do is go to trial as soon as possible with a competent lawyer I trust. The person who is supposed to defend me has no attorney–client relationship with me. He's not my lawyer."

Ng was no longer the lean Ninja warrior. Now he was pudgy, face bloated.

He said, "All the media reports are always blaming me . . . as some kind of manipulator. But everything is out of my hands. It's in my lawyers'. They chose the strategies."

October 26, 1998, Santa Ana

After a decade and a half of delays, the trial of Charles Ng finally began. The jurors sat in the jury box as Judge John J. Ryan entered and took over the high bench. Sharlene Honnaka, the state's prosecuting lead, stood. She began with a simple summation, "Leonard Lake and Charles Ng turned Blue Mountain Road into a mass graveyard, a killing field."

Honnaka signaled a bailiff. A video was inserted into a VCR. Ng fidgeted in his seat. Two feet in front of him stood a small TV that flickered to life with the color image of the movie taken fifteen years before.

Two large monitors faced the jury. The eighteen people seated in the box, twelve jurors and six alternatives, leaned forward.

In a few moments, victims in the spectator seats began sobbing.

Two videos involving Kathy Allen and Brenda O'Connor were shown. Honnaka said, "Twelve people disappeared off the face of the earth. Leonard Lake and Charles Ng planned and committed the murders charged in this case."

Honnaka concluded her opening statement forty-five minutes later.

The defense lead, William Kelley, began his presentation with, "The defense is pretty simple. I am not going to say that Charles Ng is an angel, because he's not. That's pretty evident. But he is charged with murder, not cutting off people's clothes, as offensive as that may be."

Fifty minutes later Kelley finished his opening statements.

At the first recess, Sharon Sellitto, sister to Paul Cosner, told the press about Ng and Lake on the video, "It was like they weren't even talking to a human being. I was stunned. I had no idea that they were that cruel."

Lola Stapley, mother of Robin, said, "I want to throw up."

That night, in Coldwater, Michigan, Brenda O'Connor's parents turned on the TV for the eleven o'clock news. Without warning the video showing their daughter appeared.

The father told the media, "We were shocked. Not seeing your daughter all those years and then seeing her and then Ng is cutting the blouse off my daughter."

The couple directed their anger at the prosecution. Mr. O'Connor stated, "They could have shown a little decency in telling us that there's going to be something on the eleven o'clock news."

The San Francisco Chronicle interviewed Peter Arenella, a criminal law professor at the University of California at Los Angeles, about the prosecution's insensitivity. "To me this is being done for purely shock value and the appeal to people's prurient interest. It's unhealthy and adds to this trend that we now have in using criminal trials as entertainment."

A *TV Guide* column by J. Max Robins reported that news directors of the various stations that aired the film generally defended their choices, arguing that the coverage was accurate and thorough and that the decision to air the video was handled responsibly.

Jeff Wald, news director of KTLA in Los Angeles, said, "We warned our viewers before we showed it and we used a very short excerpt. We're not in the censorship business. By showing what we did, we were indicating how horrific this case really is."

"We're about putting out good, accurate, truthful information. Sometimes, that isn't always terrible pleasant information. It's the definition of news."

The San Francisco Chronicle interviewed scholars and attorneys on the First Amendment rights argument.

The associate director of the University of Southern California's School of Journalism, Joe Saltzman, said, "As a journalist, I don't like anyone telling me what I can and can't see. Why blame the media? Blame this horrible killer-rapist."

The chief attorney in the San Francisco public defender's office, Peter Keane, said, "You're seeing someone in that kind of distress with a total sense of hopelessness, terror, and anxiety. And you combine it with his anxiety for her baby—it was gut-wrenching. To show that is to exploit the most poignant aspect of human terror."

October 27, 1999, Santa Ana

On the second day of the trial, Sharlene Honnaka once again played the two videotapes in court.

Kathy Allen's sister, Dian, wept openly. She said afterward, "I felt like it was me. I could tell she wasn't going to say anything because she was scared. She was trying to save her life."

* * *

As the trial continued, two jurors were dismissed during the week of opening statements: one for illness, the other for the death of a near relative. Judge Ryan expressed worry about having enough jurors to last the rest of the trial.

At the end of November, a month later, after meticulously chronicling the events that happened in 1985 and carefully presenting the physical evidence, the prosecution rested its case.

The defense then took up its case under the umbrella Kelley mentioned in his opening statement, "The other guy did it."

January 18, 1999, Santa Ana

The defense suddenly electrified the courtroom with the surprise announcement that their case would conclude with Ng taking the stand. At the same time they innocently asked that Ng *not* be cross-examined on certain subjects—like statements made on the videotapes.

When Judge Ryan ruled that he had every intention of allowing the prosecution full reign on their inquiries, the defense recanted. Ng would not take the stand.

January 25, 1999, Santa Ana

Ng had attorney Lewis Clapp read a letter. In it, Ng once again made a familiar maneuver: he insisted his attorneys be fired.

With an air of disbelief, Judge Ryan studied the document for a moment, then denied the motion.

The next day the prosecution began its closing arguments. The videotapes were played for a third time. Honnaka said, "This defendant and Leonard Lake were both involved in killing these twelve victims. They are equally guilty, no matter who pulled the trigger."

California law explicitly states that any participant in planning and executing a homicide is considered equally responsible for the crime.

Step by step Honnaka reviewed what had happened from the capture of Lake for shoplifting at the South San Francisco lumberyard to the capture of Ng in Canada. She reminded the jury of evidence piled on evidence incriminating Lake and Ng. Evidence unearthed by law enforcement, evidence analysis by pathologists, an anthropologist, forensic experts.

Honnaka pointed empathetically to the boast the two men made, on video, that they had already killed two men.

She said, "They had the kind of relationship where they trusted and bonded with one another. They had the kind of relationship where they would allow themselves to be videotaped with a victim admitting to another murder.

"If Charles Ng and Leonard Lake together intended these twelve victims to die, if they each performed acts to further that goal, then they are equally guilty under the eyes of the law.

January 27, 1999, Santa Ana

The following day, Ng's defense team stood before the bench for its final arguments.

Ng, once again, asked for the dismissal of counsel.

The judge denied the request, again.

Ng handed the bailiff a note. The deputy sheriff gave it to Judge Ryan. The judge asked Ng to confer with him in chambers.

Judge Ryan returned to the bench. He granted a surprise last-second request. Charles Ng *was* to be allowed to testify.

William Kelley, who had counseled vigorously against just such a ploy, said, "He has a constitutional right to testify, whether we want him to or not.

January 28, 1999, Santa Ana

Having bought one more day of delay, Ng took the stand. Guided by defense attorney Lewis Clapp, he reiterated that he had nothing to do with the killings. He said, "There is a line I won't cross. Just basically, something like killing somebody—something serious—I won't do.

"Since the time I was arrested, the media and pretty much everybody else has had that attitude . . . the guy is guilty.

"Lake came to me one day and basically asked me to help him with some jobs."

Ng explained further. The first job: remove two bags full of items from the Dubses' apartment.

The second job: help bury the bodies of Lonnie Bond, Lake's neighbor, and Robin Stapley. Lake had claimed that there was a methamphetamine lab next door. Ng stated, "He was worried about them drawing heat in terms of bringing the sheriff up there.

"Lonnie Bond's body was hidden under the porch. Lake told me to put on handcuffs, a gag, and a sleeping bag.

"He wanted them to appear to be killed by drug dealers, bike-type people."

Defense lawyer Clapp asked, "Did you know he was burying things up there?"

"That's part of the survivalization philosophy. He figured if it was buried, it was safe."

Clapp showed the jury pictures of the concrete bunker, then to Ng. "Were you aware that he was making that a sex-slave cell?"

"No. Just to protect him and his valuables from fallout and things like that."

"Did you know women prisoners were kept inside?"

"I think he said there was a secret chamber, but that was his domain. His privacy area. He didn't want me to go inside."

When the defense finished with its questions, prosecutor Sharlene Honnaka stood up.

Ng removed his thick glasses and peered at them. He rubbed his hair a few times, picked at something on his glasses, then put them back on.

Honnaka began her cross. She was remorseless.

QUESTION: Was Ng there when Kathy Allen called from the Wilseyville cabin to tell her boss she was leaving her job at Safeway?
ANSWER: I don't remember.
QUESTION: When and where did Ng meet Lake on certain days?
ANSWER: I don't recall.
QUESTION: What did you do for the six hours it took Lake to go pick up Allen in San Jose?
ANSWER: Maybe watch some TV?

Carefully, yet relentlessly, Honnaka continued to expose a memory that *could* recall that Lake once left his toothbrush at Ng's apartment, but *couldn't* remember events involving the disappearance of people.

The judge called for an early recess.

January 29, 1999, Santa Ana

The courtroom was dark.

February 1, 1999, Santa Ana

Once again Honnaka presented the two videotapes. She carefully pointed out each moment where Ng taunted the two females.

Ng said, "I actually feel pretty regret about this. This is one point in my life I surrendered my independent judgment."

Honnaka reviewed Ng's testimony about helping Lake bury Lonnie Bond and Robin Stapley. Then again the prosecutor showed the video with Brenda O'Connor.

Pointing at photos of the bodies of Bond and Stapley, she asked, "You saw these two dead bodies and you don't think Lake's going to kill this woman and her baby?"

Ng answered, "At this time I don't know that this was her husband and her friend."

Again pointing at the image of Brenda, frozen on the video, Honnaka asked, "You never had sex with her?"

"I couldn't do it," Ng said. "Initially, I was thinking about doing it, but I felt sorry for her."

Ng fidgeted, squirmed, rubbed his hand through his hair, then said, "I was worried about what kind of mess I was getting into. I tell Lake this is getting too far. I don't think I want to be thrown into this thing."

"Then why," Honnaka asked, "were you still with Lake six weeks later shoplifting a seventy-five-dollar vise?"

Honnaka then presented cartoons drawn by Ng while in prison in Calgary. The first depicted Ng killing a baby in a microwave. The second showed Ng frying a baby in a wok. The inscription below Ng's figure read: "Daddy died, Momma cried, Baby fried." The third had Ng, waving a baby in a pillowcase, smashing the infant against a wall. Next to Ng's figure were the words "crash" and "smash."

Another cartoon was introduced that showed Lake drowning a baby wrapped in a pillowcase. The inscription read: "Lake Baby Dies School."

Meticulously, Honnaka introduced evidence from a handwriting expert that Ng was the author of the inscriptions.

Ng's explanation: just a satire based on the wild accusations in the charges against him.

Honnaka presented two more cartoons as evidence. The first depicted Lake brutalizing a naked and chained woman. The second showed Ng sodomizing a woman as he was choking her with pantyhose. The inscription read: "Master Ng—death grip."

A final cartoon placed into evidence showed a woman carrying a plate with a burned body of a baby on it. The inscription read: "Slant's Day Care."

Honnaka introduced evidence that Ng's nickname in the Calgary prison was "Slant."

Ng's explanation: "All the drawings, cartoons, depictions is essentially a satire of the fantasy, depicting the situation and the accusations about me at that time. It has nothing to do with reality."

Honnaka pressed on. Cartoon after cartoon was displayed until the tally reached one hundred and fifty. It was a long and increasingly grisly session.

Ng said, "I can explain away what the cartoons mean. The inmates in Calgary harassed me as a baby-killer because of news reports. But they're still just satires with no basis in reality."

Honnaka showed the videotape of Brenda O'Connor again. She paused the tape at the point where Ng said, "You can cry and stuff like the rest of them, but it won't do you any good."

Honnaka asked, "What do you mean by, 'the rest of them?' "

"There's no rest of them. I just try to protect that seriousness . . . so she wouldn't resist."

"Why did you cut away her bra and say, 'You're totally ours?"

"I don't want to act like a wimp, put it that way."

Honnaka stood directly in front of the defendant. In a terse voice she said, "You don't want to act like a wimp with a woman who's asking about her husband and her baby and her friend?"

"At that time I didn't know who those people were."

Sharlene Honnaka rested the case for the prosecution.

After the judge called it a day, Ng's attorney, Kelley, stated outside the courtroom, "Ng has a pretty macabre sense of satire."

February 2, 1999, Santa Ana

Once again Ng took the stand, answering a series of questions from his defense team. He was asked about his relationship with Leonard Lake. "He was the only person I could open up to. He didn't reciprocate, of course." Ng fidgeted in his seat, constantly rubbing his hand through his hair. He continued with, "I almost pleaded with Lake. I want to get away from this. I don't want any part of it."

Ng argued that he had no self-esteem, that he acted tough with Brenda O'Connor because he was trying to impress Lake, because Lake hated her.

Ng finally admitted to drawing one of the cartoons.

"Why did you draw—"

"I can explain this away." Laberge, a prisoner in Canada in the cell next to Ng, used to goad him into drawing. "The cartoon is a relief," Ng said. "Every time I sent Laberge a cartoon or we collaborated on a cartoon, he'd laugh."

When asked about his relationship with Leonard Lake and Claralyn Balazs, Ng stated, "They were more like a family than the parents I left behind in Hong Kong.

"My family loved me and tried to send me to the best schools. But there was very little in terms of closeness or emotional love. At least, they didn't know how to express it. I had a sense of belonging when I was with Claralyn and Leonard."

The defense asked to call two further witnesses: a jailhouse informant and Claralyn "Cricket" Balazs.

Judge Ryan said, "I'll make it easy for everybody. We're just going to go straight through."

Once again Sharlene Honnaka began the prosecution's closing summation. She said, "It's never Ng's fault. His testimony is always to blame someone else."

Then, for a final time, she played the videotapes. Honnaka pointed at the screen. "These actions speak louder than any words from the stand."

February 3, 1999, Santa Ana

Sharlene Honnaka finished her summation once again as she had done the first time. "The question is this: Is the defendant involved in these twelve murders? The evidence clearly shows that he is."

She held up the videotapes. "Listen to the plain words on these videotapes. Ng simply had no explanation for a lot of the plain language that was on them."

William Kelley rose to address the jury. "You can't like my client. It's impossible. But you have to set that aside. You have to think about whether he murdered or conspired to murder."

Kelley talked about the two videotapes. He said, "No matter how many times you see that tape, there's one thing that you don't see. Anybody's murder."

A huge board, about five-by-ten feet, was brought into the courtroom by the defense. In the center was a photograph of Leonard Lake. Clustered about him in a circle was almost three-and-a-half-dozen targets, each with a red dot in the center. Each of the targets had the name of a victim or a potential victim by it.

Kelley pointed at the photo and said, "Is there any doubt in anybody's mind that if there were a kingpin in this case, he's the man?"

Kelley explained the meaning of the forty-one dots. Twelve were the victims whom Ng was accused of murdering.

"These twenty-two," Kelley said, as he pointed to a specific area on the board, "represent people who were sexually abused, targeted for murder, or stole from by one man—Leonard Lake."

Rummaging in his briefcase, Kelley removed a few items and placed them on the table. He said, "This represents items that were directly connected to Ng. The grand profit. Why would you enter into a criminal enterprise if there is no reward?"

Kelley held up a book. It was John Fowles's work *The Collector*. He said, "Lake brought the fictional person in this book to life."

February 4, 1999, Santa Ana

Lewis Clapp, Kelley's cocounsel, took most of the day reviewing the case. He enumerated, point by point, much of what the lead defense attorney had covered. He was passionate in his plea for the jury to find Ng not guilty.

Clapp said, while holding up the two videotapes, "Things are not always what they appear. I beseech you not to be sucked in by your emotions."

February 5, 1999, Santa Ana

The courtroom was dark once again on a Friday.

February 8, 1999, Santa Ana

First Sharlene Honnaka gave her rebuttal statements.

For the defense, Lewis Clapp argued back that Ng should be guilty of only kidnapping and assault. He said, "He is not guilty of those crimes. Where is the evidence that he knew Lake intended to kill or that he actually helped Lake kill? It's just not there when you're talking about murder."

Judge Ryan took his time in giving his instructions to the jury. At 2:45 p.m. the case was turned over to the nine women and three men in the box.

February 10, 1999, Santa Ana

Bill Wallace, of *The San Francisco Chronicle*, wrote, in a story titled "Ng trial characterized by odd twists and turns," "Claralyn Balazs, Lake's exwife, took the stand as a much-anticipated witness, but neither side asked her a single question."

The writer quoted Michael Rustigan, a criminologist from San Francisco State University: "I think it's perhaps the strangest case in the annals of serial killers from the standpoint of the trial. In terms of legal process, I'd have to say it's one of the most bizarre, confusing, and outrageous cases I have ever seen."

February 24, 1999, Santa Ana

The jury returned a verdict of guilty on eleven of the twelve counts of murder in the first degree.

A New Direction

"This is all about a five letter word—delay."

—DWIGHT STAPLEY

The test case presented here as a denial of justice because of judicial inefficiency is overwhelming in detail and in horror. The question lingers: What have we learned so that this does not happen again, and so that justice can emerge, even now, from this nightmare?

In Part I, "Law," we saw the elements of the atrocities of the murderers and the hard but effective police work in responding. Of scores of officers involved in capturing Lake and Ng and developing the evidence against them, special mention should be made of Policewoman Irene Brunn and Officer Tom Eisenmann, who pulled together the pieces of a frightening pattern of missing persons. The crime scene they uncovered in Calaveras County was like that of a wartime atrocity. But this was hardly the end of the work: hundreds of witnesses had to be interviewed, and several hundred pounds of human remains and other evidence had to be identified and catalogued. These monumental tasks were completed with precision and dispatch, providing prosecutors with the tools they needed to bring indictments on twelve counts of murder against Charles Ng.

In Part II, "Order," the tortuous path of prosecution was traced from the courts of Canada to the State Department of the United States and finally to several jurisdictions in California. Although the possibility of Ng receiving the death penalty in California impeded his extradition from Canada for six years, this was not the major reason why "order" broke down in this case. As described here, both the prosecution and the defense continually tripped over themselves in the years Ng was in California. In all, seven judges were called to preside over the case. Three sets of public defenders and their aides, plus a team of attorneys representing those defenders, were employed at various times to wrangle over six tons of evidence. The defendant himself was allowed to act as his own attorney twice, with disastrous results. He sued his own attorneys twice and demanded the dismissal of several judges. In the last two years alone of pretrial preparations, the legislature of the State of California had to appropriate more than two million dollars each year to assist Orange County in handling the case. And the case still had not gone to trial. Was the defense totally to blame? One of the defense attorneys famously wrote to the California Supreme Court, "The prosecution in this case has never failed to miss an opportunity to miss an opportunity." Again and again, the hopes of the families of the victims for a speedy conclusion to this tragedy were dashed by failures of the courts to come to grips with the complexity of the case.

In Part III, "Justice," the implications of this landmark case were measured by opinions from "law and order" authorities across the country as well as from disinterested observers from politics, science, and academia. The authors found disbelief that such a case could be so badly mishandled—but they also discovered that judicial inefficiency was a problem everywhere. They found strong support for the victims' rights amendment to the U.S. Constitution, as proposed by Senators Diane Feinstein and Jon Kyl. One of the chief elements of that amendment bears directly on this case: the right of victims and their relatives to secure a speedy trial of those who victimized them. From this case alone it appears obvious that state and local governments do not have the tools or the will to face this issue squarely.

Conclusively, the system failed the victims and the victims' relatives in this case. In Part III, obvious implications for reform emerge from interviews the authors conducted. These reforms are presented below in essence, but greater detail would be beyond the scope of this book.

The authors reviewed the evidence of the case highlighted here with a cross-section of authorities from all areas of the country, in various professions and fields of expertise. Two types of recommendations emerged—both aimed at helping victims as well as society: immediate, obvious reforms, and long-range, more basic approaches.

To summarize these succinctly:

Immediate reforms

- Remove politics from the death penalty by allowing only retired jurists to hear these cases; give them the mandate to see them through from beginning to end.
- Further diminish the concept of parole, especially in cases of violence, by legislating that ninety percent of a sentence must be served; this provides for "truth in sentencing" while giving some flexibility to the prison population.
- Extend the concept of special, secure prisons, as exemplified in New York State, to make sure that "life without parole" becomes believable to the public.
- Rewrite the codes on legal representation to limit the waste of taxpayers' dollars and to establish some sort of national standard of what constitutes "public defense."
- Encourage the reduction of multiple murder cases to one or two counts to avoid the masses of evidence that have jammed the Ng case; write provisions that would ensure the possibility of subsequent trials on other counts to avoid the fear of reversals of the first counts on appeal; in general, do not "reward" mass killers because of the volume of evidence they have generated.

Long-range approaches

- Begin now a study of practical rehabilitation in the form of education, job training, and fostering family integrity—no matter how idealistic this may seem at present, for it is the only realistic answer to repeat offenders.
- Study the possibility of the use of scientific medicine, i.e., MRI and PET scans, to establish benchmarks for measuring the health of prisoners' brains during incarceration—again, no matter how idealistic this may seem at present, for it is at least a technology that offers some objectivity in making sure that prison sentences are based on just punishment.
- Analyze the possibility of closure for victims by providing more information to victims and their relatives, at time of sentencing, about the measurable physiological characteristics of the criminal: especially possible brain damage, such as that resulting from fetal alcohol syndrome.

*   *   *

This book has not been about the death penalty, but its specter hangs over it. No one on either side of the Ng case denies that much of the thirteen years of delay in bringing it to trial resulted from excessive caution about applying the so-called ultimate penalty.

If the debate over this penalty were framed not as a moral dilemma but as a practical choice, based on achieving speedier, less expensive trials, could the polarization over this issue finally be broken? Are we blinded by the natural desire for retribution? Or is retribution, as many argue, not only just, but also good for society and worth any price?

There are no easy answers to these questions, but perhaps the sheer extremity of the Ng case has at least, and at last, brought these issues into stark perspective.

Something that started with killings in 1984 and an arrest in 1985 took until February 24, 1999, for the criminal to be found guilty.

How much longer will it take to administer punishment?

No matter what the jury decides in the punishment phase—life without possibility of parole or the death penalty—this is an incredible appropriate example of Gladstone's remark: "Justice delayed is justice denied."

Glossary of Legal Terms

Appellant. The party who appeals a decision to a higher court

Continuance. The adjournment or postponement, to a specified subsequent date, of an action pending in court

Demurrer. A motion to dismiss for failure to state a claim upon which relief may be granted

Discovery. Procedure by which one party gains information held by the adverse party, concerning the case, such as in a deposition

In camera. In chambers: a judicial act while court is not in session

Magistrate. A public civil servant, invested with some part of the legislative, executive, or judicial power

Motion. An application to the court requesting an order in favor of the applicant

Quid pro quo. Something for something: a consideration

Recuse. Disqualify a judge, jury, or administrative officer for prejudice or interest in the subject matter

Summary judgment. An immediate disposition of a legal action on its merits without resort to a lengthy trial

Vicinage. A particular area where a crime was committed, where a trial is being held, or from which jurors are called

Writ. A legal order issued by the authority and in the name of the state to compel an action